The Trail of 1858
British Columbia's Gold Rush Past

The Trail of 1858
British Columbia's Gold Rush Past

Mark Forsythe and Greg Dickson

Harbour Publishing

CONTENTS

The Gold Regions of British Columbia

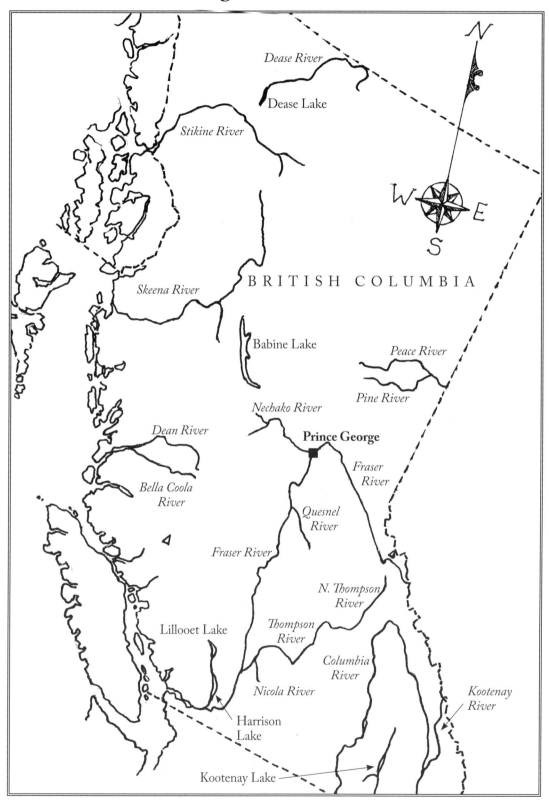

Foreword

2008 marks British Columbia's 150th anniversary as a modern political state. The declaration, which took place on November 19, 1858, in Fort Langley, was made by Governor James Douglas, who affirmed the formal creation of the Colony of British Columbia. The struggle to that moment had a great deal to do with the Fraser River gold rush and subsequent gold rushes of the era; it was populated with a veritable cast of thousands, who played various roles in the political development of what became today's thriving province.

We are indebted to Mark Forsythe and Greg Dickson and all their CBC listeners for this remarkable series of reflections on many aspects of the gold rush and its people, as well as its political, social and institutional impact on our lives today. Can we even imagine a flotilla of some 80 canoes carrying a thousand Haida, pulling into the Fraser estuary today, as they did then? Do we know the stories of those larger-than-life individuals from every racial background who populate our past and whose intelligence, experience and hard-nosed leadership forged a legacy of which we are the main beneficiaries?

There was Governor Douglas, who for a time wielded simultaneously the great powers of both the Hudson's Bay Company and our incipient province. We remember our first judge, Matthew Baillie Begbie, whom no one called the "hanging judge" until he was fifty years dead! There was Colonel Richard Moody, whose Royal Engineers laid out the fundamental infrastructure that survives today under layers of concrete and asphalt stretching across BC. There were strong women, too, some anonymous brides and others who were ignored by polite society. This land, now our province, has always been a place of contrasts, a place where there is sufficient space and goodwill to allow widely differing opinions to survive and even, on occasion, to thrive.

Surely at no other time or place in human history has such an assorted cast of characters come together to establish a "new state." Vast numbers of diverse First Nations lived and worked here, as well as some prairie Cree and Iroquois voyageurs. They were joined by Chinese, Hawaiian and US citizens—including many of African descent—along with Europeans from all corners of the Old World. All of these differing peoples came to this land—thousands at a time—in search of gold and a new and better life.

Together, they created a near-cataclysmic meeting of cultures, languages and traditions that miraculously became today's British Columbia. Perhaps it is time for our province, often characterized as "young," to incorporate the story of the human family who have lived here since time immemorial into those contained in this well-researched history. All the elements are here to create a precious founding tale of who we have become as a people. Could there be a better 150th birthday gift for all British Columbians, past, present and future?

I encourage all residents and visitors to read this well-documented story—a tragic, comic, dramatic and everlastingly stirring chronicle of the "beginnings" of our beloved British Columbia. Congratulations to all contributors! This is our story, too!

—Iona V. Campagnolo

INTRODUCTION

"Victoria is the way it is today because of the gold rushes. BC is the way it is because of the gold rush."

—*from a tour of Ross Bay Cemetery guided by Yvonne Van Ruskenveld, volunteer with the Old Cemeteries Society*

When many of us think of the gold rush, we think of the Klondike in 1898, or maybe, under the influence of American television, the California gold rush of 1849. But British Columbia had a spectacular gold rush of its own that had a profound effect on our corner of North America.

Gold fever started in the southwest corner of BC in 1858, and with the Fraser River as a fuse, it raced north into the central Interior, setting off major strikes like firecrackers at Hill's Bar south of Yale, and many other little sandbars along the river. The miners, many of them Americans, clambered on upriver, searching for greater riches in the Cariboo. It was the explosion that opened up a new province, the spark that created a justice system unique in the West, a representative government and a roadmap of streets and highways.

Looking back 150 years, we see that today's British Columbia could easily have become part of the expanding American empire, just another Alaska. How did those early leaders secure our ties to empire and the rest of Canada? And how did we develop a relationship with our First Nations, very different from the lawlessness and slaughter of the Wild West just south of the 49th parallel? That is part of the story we tell here. Along the way, we celebrate some of the people who were at the centre of it all: a mixed-race colonial governor called James Douglas; a British bachelor judge named Matthew Baillie Begbie; the peacemaking Chief Spintlum of the Nlaka'pamux (Thompson); Nam Sing, the first Chinese miner in the Cariboo; Nellie Cashman, the enterprising Irish woman whose good deeds earned her the title "the miner's angel;" the flamboyant prospector Billy Barker; Sophia Cameron, the young wife of a prospector; the newspaperman and reforming politician Amor de Cosmos; the Royal Engineers who built the roads; the many women who came to the new colony on the bride ships; the notorious American Ned McGowan; the Hawaiians and black Americans who flooded into BC with all the others; and the First Nations, whose ancestors had lived here for thousands of years, and who at first resisted the invasion and then reluctantly lived with it.

The painter William Hind was one of the Overlanders who came to BC in 1862, travelling overland from eastern North America. He went on to create one of the iconic paintings of the gold rush, a prospector with all his earthly belongings panning beside a wilderness stream. *British Columbia Archives PDP-02612*

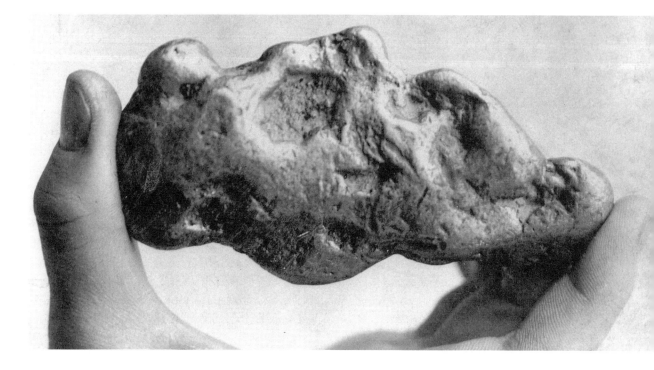

This was every miner's dream: a gold nugget the size of your fist. This one was found in the Cariboo.
British Columbia Archives A-05577

The gold rush transformed a lonely outpost of the Hudson's Bay Company. Roads carved the landscape east and north, and west again. Cattle ranches and farms pushed back the wilderness. Trees turned into towns, some of which survived. And it was a multicultural partnership even at the beginning. Native people found the first gold, did a lot of the mining and bred the horses that supplied the camps. black Americans fled slavery in the United States to serve as policemen, militia officers, barbers and merchants. Chinese immigrants worked the claims that others abandoned and then became farmers, merchants and railway workers. Hawaiians started out as Hudson's Bay labourers, then joined the gold rush and built roads—all at a time when British colonists and American miners were engaged in a struggle for supremacy. Hurdy-gurdy girls from Holland, journalists from London, merchants from the Jewish diaspora and miners from every corner of Europe and the New World joined the rush and became part of BC's history.

In 1857, the colonial population of BC hovered around 500 people, mostly Hudson's Bay Company employees working in co-operation and sometimes conflict with about 70,000 Aboriginal people. The northern reaches of this place were so remote that some called it the Siberia of North America, a long way from anywhere. Fort Victoria, the only community of any size, was a remote, sleepy trading post with very little excitement other than the occasional altercation with First Nations groups.

All of that changed overnight in the spring of 1858. As Lieutenant Richard Charles Mayne, a Royal Engineer, described it: "That most infectious of all maladies—a gold fever—had broken out, and had seized every man, woman and child... Everyone, whom a few weeks ago we had left engaged steadily in pursuits from which they were reaping a slow sure profit, seemed to have gone gold mad... The excitement in Victoria was indescribable... The value of land was raised immensely... Merchants' stores were rising in every direction. On the shore of the harbour, wharves were being planted... sailing ships, laden with every description of articles which a migratory population could, and in many cases could not, want, flowed into the harbour. Victoria appeared to have leapt at once from the site of a promising settlement into a full grown town." Thirty thousand miners came in that first year. It happened that fast.

Nine out of ten of those first fortune seekers were Americans. Many came from California, having been through one gold rush already. That rush was over and they were searching for a new Eldorado. Word of gold on the Fraser sent them scurrying north by ship and trail. They brought the culture of the pistol and the bowie knife and vigilante justice. They also brought with them the belief that the only good Indian was a dead Indian. And they were ready to fight Indians and whoever else stood in their way on "Fraser's River."

One man did stand in their way. James Douglas was the government in the British northwest, and he would improvise order out of chaos and put down any rebellion the Americans might dream up. "If the majority of immigrants be American," he wrote, "there will always be a hankering in their minds after annexation to the United States." Douglas had been around when Americans poured into the Oregon Territory, driving out the fur trade he loved and the British way of life he stood for. He wouldn't let that happen again north of the 49th parallel. If it meant war, Douglas would go to war. But first, he would try to control the country through craftiness and manoeuvre.

Before London could act, he would anticipate. He would issue proclamations imposing Hudson's Bay control over all commerce on the mainland, requiring mining licences for all immigrants and forbidding any permanent settlement. When colonial officials in London learned of his actions, they approved, objecting only when the Hudson's Bay Company's interest took precedence over their own. Even Douglas's critics knew that he was the only man for the job and gave him almost dictatorial powers over the affairs of both Vancouver Island and the mainland. And Douglas thrived on control.

The new country was not as hospitable to the new immigrants as California had been. Winters were harsh, floods threatened, local Natives were hostile and, after a few spectacular strikes, the gold seemed to run out. By the summer of 1858, some Americans were dismissing the Fraser as a humbug. They were impatient and homesick. But the rush was not over. It pushed north to the Cariboo and greater riches yet. Other booms erupted in the Boundary, Similkameen, Kootenay, Peace River and Omineca areas. The rushes were not an American affair, but a multicultural bonanza.

This is the story that emerged for us as we travelled the gold rush trail, rafted past the rich bars of the lower Fraser, drove the Cariboo Road and walked the streets of Barkerville. It's a thrilling story, not well known to many British Columbians and yet fundamental to an understanding of why we are the way we are. CBC listeners have helped us along the way, sharing their stories and their love of gold rush country. The stories they've told us are the lifeblood of this book. We hope you enjoy them as we have, and then get out and explore gold rush country yourself!

—*Mark Forsythe and Greg Dickson*

1

THE SECRET'S OUT
The Fraser River Gold Rush

I t was as though a giant crack had been pried open. Gold miners rushed in like a wild spring freshet, and in their wake, everything changed—for the fur colony, for First Nations and for a remote wilderness on the edge of empire. The year was 1858. Although parts of eastern Canada had been settled for some 250 years, British Columbia as we know it didn't exist on the maps.

The Hudson's Bay Company (HBC) had planted itself on the white sands of Camosun Harbour in 1843, not far from today's Empress Hotel in Victoria. Fort Camosun (renamed in 1852 for Queen Victoria) had a water supply, sheltered harbour, lands for farming, stands of oak, pine and spruce, and a position that could be defended. Wood smoke coiled from behind the palisades, home to HBC employees, their families and a few farmers. James Douglas ("Old Square Toes") was at the helm, wearing two hats: chief factor of the HBC and governor of Vancouver Island colony, which had been declared in 1849. In *British Columbia: A History*, Margaret Ormsby notes that the HBC carefully guarded its monopoly, relying on stable trade with First Nations: "To ward off competition, the [HBC ship] *Beaver* continued to make regular cruises along the seacoast long after the Haidas and other northern Indians had developed a preference for selling their furs at Fort Victoria, for them the great emporium. In the spring of 1858, when the gold-miners arrived, the old coastal vessel was absent on one of these missions."

Opposite: Fort Langley. *Harper's Weekly,* October 9 1858

The Hudson's Bay Company used the SS *Beaver*, the first steamship on the Pacific coast, first as a supply ship and later to establish British sovereignty over the colony of British Columbia. The ship was wrecked off Prospect Point in 1888. *British Columbia Archives A-00010*

Hints of gold were in the air as early as 1851, when a short-lived rush hit the Queen Charlotte Islands. The crew from the HBC vessel *Una* blasted for gold on the southern part of the islands, and struggled with the Haida over the spoils. On the return voyage to Vancouver Island, the *Una* grounded on a reef near Neah Bay. After a clash with the Haida, it sank—taking the gold to the bottom with it. Ten American vessels followed in 1852, and the Haida continued to interfere with prospecting and mining (including some hostage-taking). By the end of the year, this gold rush was over.

In 1856, another Aboriginal group near Fort Kamloops spooned gold from the Thompson River and traded it to the HBC. Then, in February 1857, the company shipped 22 kilograms of gold to the mint in San Francisco, and the secret was out. The California rush of '49 had peaked and faded, and lavish newspaper accounts of a new El Dorado created a frenzy; word arrived that T.H. Hill had discovered one of the richest river bars in the world in the Fraser Canyon, and the rush was on. At first most miners came from California, but others later arrived from Britain, China, Italy, Germany, Mexico, Hawaii and other places. Many of them deserted their jobs and businesses for that glittering possibility of striking it rich on the Fraser.

Mystery Woman

Apr 15, 1862—A presentable looking, middle-aged lady was observed on Esquimalt wharf wearing a complete suit of gentlemen's clothes—breeches and all! After the steamer *Oregon* had cast off, she quietly mounted a fine horse, in true gentleman style, and rode off briskly towards Victoria, leaving a large and curious crowd of spectators to wonder as to who she was, whence she came and whither she was bound. The lady did not seem in the least annoyed by the many quizzical glances directed toward her, and exhibited the utmost nonchalance throughout. Her appearance created quite a sensation among the usually staid and phlegmatic Esquimalters.

—from the British Colonist, *selected by Leona Taylor*

Fort Victoria, the only ocean port, was the gateway to the diggings. The *Commodore*, a sidewheel steamer from San Francisco whose 450 passengers were stacked aboard like firewood, was the first to land. "The townspeople were just leaving church to return to their whitewashed cottages," Ormsby writes, "when she entered Victoria harbour on Sunday morning, April 25, 1858...with surprise and fascination they watched her approach the landing-place, make fast, and then disembark a stream of men, most of them wearing red flannel shorts and carrying packs containing blankets, miners' washpans, spades and firearms." As they disembarked, Fort Victoria's population doubled. Within days there were 2,000 hopefuls waiting to reach the river in New Caledonia—not yet a British colony.

Fort Victoria, headquarters of the Hudson's Bay Company in the Pacific Northwest after 1843, turned into a boomtown with the arrival of California miners in 1858. For a while, the Fort rivalled San Francisco as the busiest port on the west coast. *British Columbia Archives A-04104*

Captain of the *Commodore*

Captain Jeremiah Nagle was instrumental in bringing people on the regular steamship run from San Francisco. Victoria and San Francisco were the two big centres on the coast, and most people in Victoria had relatives in San Francisco. The connection was north-south, not east-west. Of course there were no railways; there was no road. Vancouver wasn't even a town—few people settled there before the railway arrived in the 1880s.

Victoria was very much *it*. Many people among the first batch who arrived here rowed to the Fraser River on their own. There's a place on Mayne Island, one of the Gulf Islands, called Miners Bay because they would row that far, camp out and then row the rest of the way

The SS *Commodore* was a steam-powered sidewheeler that changed Victoria in an instant. On the fateful Sunday morning when the ship arrived, bringing the first contingent of miners from San Francisco, Victoria's population doubled. *British Columbia Archives B-02713*

15

to the mouth of the river on the mainland. Eventually, quite the steamship service was built up between Victoria and the river, and up to Yale, and then people could use another service farther up the Fraser, past the canyon, which was unnavigable.

Captain William Moore, who owned and operated paddlewheel steamboats on the river during the rush, then went on to pioneer steam technology in the North, is also buried here. He's the founder of Skagway, Alaska, because he foresaw the Klondike gold rush. He was one of the many folks who followed the gold rushes through and through.

—from a tour of Ross Bay Cemetery with Yvonne Van Ruskenveld. The cemetery opened for business in 1873, when the city of Victoria purchased land from Robert Burnaby (after whom Burnaby in the Lower Mainland was named). Ross Bay is the final resting place of numerous gold rush figures, including Governor James Douglas, Judge Matthew Baillie Begbie and Billy Barker.

A tent city mushroomed virtually overnight. Thousands more people soon followed, mostly men from California, carrying guns, bowie knives and their own sense of rough justice. Their countries of origin spanned the globe: China, France, Germany, Italy and the United States—including many black Americans hoping to escape persecution. Many of the newcomers had no idea where the Fraser River was, or that it flowed through British trading territory. D.W. Higgins prospected, mined, traded, became a newspaperman and later served as speaker of the provincial legislature; his book *The Mystic Spring* takes us to the centre of the rush, where he too chased the "Golden Butterfly": "All along the river, wherever there occurred a bench or bar, miners were encamped 'Waiting for the river to fall,' when they expected to scoop up the gold by the handful and live at ease forevermore. The result was a practical exemplification of the larks one hopes to catch when the skies fall."

Comings and Goings

Apr 25, 1859—About 80 canoes containing nearly 1,000 Indians arrived from Queen Charlotte's Is. They have pitched their lodges at the N end of the town. They have brought several very fine specimens of gold-bearing quartz, and some fine gold. They have also specimens of iron ore.

RNV/Apr 30, 1859—It is seldom we are called upon, in this Island, to notice the solemnity of a sailor's funeral processions, by the burial of Mr John Jeffries [Jeffrys], Paymaster of HMS *Pylades*. With all the pomp and circumstance of war, the coffin was brought to the HBC wharf, accompanied by several barges fully manned, where it was met by the Marines, who had marched from Esquimalt. It was then conveyed on a gun carriage, to the church, from thence, after the impressive burial service was read, consigned to the grave. The Pall, 'the Union Jack' was borne by 4 officers in full uniform; the train attendant was the tars of 'Old England' and the Capts of *Pylades* and *Tribune*. The usual naval salute on such occasions was fired when the coffin was lowered. Buried at Victoria.

—from the British Colonist, *selected by Leona Taylor*

The whole world was on the cusp of profound change: trade was expanding, the globe was shrinking. The first underwater telegraph cables were being laid, mass-produced newspapers spread word of current events, steamships moved more people more swiftly. Many city dwellers lived on very low wages—the time was ripe for adventure. Steamers pulled into Victoria virtually every day, some of them nothing more than dangerous junk buckets taken out of retirement. Twenty thousand people arrived before the gales of fall. Historians estimate that 30,000 miners came to the Fraser River region that year (mostly Americans, as word of the strike didn't get to eastern Canada until much later that spring). Some bypassed Victoria, moving along the Whatcom Trail, through Point Roberts or along trails into the Okanagan.

Party par excellence

We gave a ball to the ladies here; two of the men of war the "Satellite" & "Plumper"[British naval vessels stationed at Esquimalt] with ourselves, determined to join together & give a grand ball to the ladies of Vancouver Island... Every body came to the ball from the governor downwards nearly 200 in all & we kept the dancing up with great spirit till 1/2 past 3 in the morning. Every body was quite delighted with it & it goes by the name of 'the Party' par excellence; nobody says balls in this part of the world, it is always party. The ladies were very nicely dressed, & some of them danced very well, though they would look much better if they would only learn to wear their crinoline properly, it is most lamentable to see the objects they make of themselves, some of the hoops being quite oval, whilst others had only one hoop rather high up, the remainder of the dress hanging down perpendicularly."
— *Lieut. Charles W. Wilson, Victoria, March 15, 1859, from* British Columbia: A Centennial Anthology

Governor James Douglas was more than anxious about the sudden flood of miners, and had previously warned the London Colonial Office that a gold rush could have dire consequences for HBC trade. The miners, he declared in 1858, "are represented as being, with some exceptions, a specimen of the worst of the population of San Francisco; the very dregs, in fact, of society." Too many Americans could mean trouble with the Indians, and the all-important trade in furs, salmon and cranberries. In their book *British Columbia, Land of Promises*, Patricia E. Roy and John Herd Thompson consider Douglas's dilemma in another context: "As a fur trader, Douglas had witnessed the influx of American settlers into Oregon that had trumped Britain's claim to the area. He also knew that gold and the Americans together had turned a Mexican colony into the state of California." Manifest Destiny was never far from his mind. The phrase was first promoted in the US in 1845 by John L. O'Sullivan, a journalist and Democrat who believed the US was destined by God to "overspread" the continent. He pushed for annexation of the Republic of Texas and Oregon Territory, and he believed Canada would eventually ask to be absorbed into this "great experiment of liberty." A cautious Douglas appointed gold commissioners to assert British authority. He had two Royal Navy ships in his back pocket at nearby Esquimalt, one of which he stationed at the entrance to the Fraser River. The ship flew the British flag, and the gold commissioners aboard charged every miner a 10-shilling licence fee.

Yale

This Fraser Canyon post was named after the man in charge of Fort Langley, James Murray Yale.

The Gold Commissioner's Residence

In 1867, Peter O'Reilly bought the Point Ellice House in Victoria (now a provincial heritage site) from the builder. He was a former member of the Irish Constabulary and had been hired as a gold commissioner by James Douglas and was sent out to help keep the peace. Later, he served as magistrate in the Interior. His wife Caroline, a member of the Trutch family, was well connected in Victoria society. Her brother later became BC's first lieutenant-governor.

Peter was away much of the time, so he and Caroline wrote many letters discussing the daily life of the family and household. These and other family records and journals are kept in the BC Archives, giving British Columbians a comprehensive picture of family life in early Victoria and in the Yale area, where Peter O'Reilly carried out much of his work.

Three generations of O'Reillys lived in the house, and in 1975 one of Peter's grandsons sold it to the government of BC, complete with all furnishings and personal effects.

The province's Heritage Branch chose to feature the period 1890–1920 in their display of the many thousands of artifacts in the historic house museum at Point Ellice. The site is known for its authentic portrayal of daily life at the time, and the influence of the gold rush is seen in the many family journals.

—*Gail Simpson, Capital Mental Health Association, Point Ellice House, Victoria*

News of the Colony

May 16, 1859—That infamous character 'Tipperary Bill' who killed John Collins, in this colony last summer, and who was allowed to escape, has been tried and convicted of the murder of one Doak, in San Francisco, and has been sentenced to be hung.

Jun 11, 1859—On Sunday afternoon, the town was thrown into a high state of excitement by hearing volley after volley fired in the direction of the Indian villages. A large crowd rushed towards Victoria Bridge, and from there witnessed the fight between the Songish [Songhees] Indians, on the west side of the Harbour, and the Stickeens [Stikine] on the eastern side. After shooting for upwards of ½ hour, the Stickeens raised a white flag, and the fight ceased. One Stickeen was shot in the leg, and a woman in the side. One Songish Indian was struck by a ball, in the head.
— *from the* British Colonist, *selected by Leona Taylor*

Meanwhile, Victoria was in a state of chaos. In just six weeks, 225 buildings appeared around the fort, most of them stores laden with supplies for the miners. San Francisco-style saloons appeared, where, according to one account, "liquor was cheaper than water." Prostitution thrived in the dance halls and "houses of ill fame." That summer a gun duel was fought on the streets, and a near revolt erupted when a crowd of armed Americans called for a take-over. Their displeasure over the miner's fee had already been registered in a Washington State newspaper:

> Soon our banner will be streaming.
> Soon the eagle will be screaming,
> And the lion—see it cowers,
> Hurrah, boys, the river's ours,
> Then, hurrah, not wait for calling,
> For the Frazer's river's falling

In a letter dated July 14, 1858, George and Ann Deans, Hudson's Bay Company labourers, described a land boom taking Victoria by storm: "The houses is going up like magic. There is hundreds of rich gents just living in canvas tents. The rents for the houses is most awful high. We have bought another town lot and 200 acres just on spec. Geordie bought it at 1 pound and is seeking 10 pounds per acre."

The once quiet outpost had become a booming centre of commerce. The population grew tenfold by year's end to 5,000. BC's first hospital was under construction and its first bank opened for business in March 1859. Work started on government buildings at James Bay: unique log, brick and wooden pavilions that raised eyebrows: "The *Colonist* denounced the buildings as 'a burlesque on architecture,'" Donald Luxton wrote in *Building the West*, "and the *Gazette* ridiculed them as 'the latest fashion of Chinese-pagoda, Swiss-cottage and Italian-villa fancy bird cages.'" People enjoyed English diversions like cricket, and theatre (performed inside an old Hudson's Bay Company storehouse). Key public figures of the era made appearances passing through Victoria: the frontier judge Matthew Baillie Begbie; the newspaperman Amor de Cosmos (formerly Bill Smith of Nova Scotia), who later became

Victoria, shown here in the winter of 1862, was a favourite wintering place for miners. After a gruelling season in the goldfields, they sought the stimulation of bright lights, music and other diversions. *British Columbia Archives A-02999*

Fort Langley, the birthplace of British Columbia, was an early provisioning point for the gold rush. By 1862 the fur trade was over, and Fort Langley was a quieter place. *British Columbia Archives A-04313*

premier; Lieutenant Colonel Richard Moody (the colony's chief engineer and lieutenant-governor); and Chartres Brew, the Irishman who later led the province's police and served as chief gold commissioner. The village of Victoria incorporated as a city in 1862.

Fort Langley

This Hudson's Bay Company fur- and salmon-trading post was named after Thomas Langley, a director of the HBC. The fort supplied the first miners to arrive in 1858.

Fort Langley, Before and After

Fort Langley was built by the Hudson's Bay Company as a fur-trade post. The trade underwent several transformations over time, but none was as sudden or as devastating to the company, and especially to its Aboriginal trade partners, as the Fraser River gold rush. Not only did the rush bring 30,000 newcomers into the region, it led to the establishment of the Colony of British Columbia.

During the west coast fur-trade era, roughly the late 1700s until the gold rush, what is now British Columbia was referred to as New Caledonia, or the Columbia Department. The 200 or so employees of the Hudson's Bay Company married Aboriginal women and a peaceful trade was carried on: Aboriginal traders brought furs, salmon, berries and other products to the HBC posts and traded them for textiles, tools and luxury goods such as tobacco.

HBC managers had known about gold finds in the Fraser River since 1856, and tried to keep it secret. But when they had collected 800 ounces of gold at the fort, they sent it to the San Francisco mint to be refined, and word got out. A stampede of miners—30,000 of them—passed through the posts of Victoria and Langley during the spring and summer of 1858. Boatloads of people arrived from all over the world.

Prospectors journeyed to the goldfields via the Fraser River, and for the first months they had to change boats at Fort Langley. A tent village sprang up overnight, and there the prospectors camped out and waited until the next boat to the Fraser Canyon was available. During the spring of 1858, the store at Fort Langley sold $1,500 worth of food, clothing and mining supplies to the miners every day. That was a huge amount of money in those days, the equivalent of about $38,000 today.

With the arrival of so many people, confusion arose and many disputes broke out between the miners and the Aboriginal inhabitants. Also, most of the newcomers were Americans, and the British feared that they would try to take over the territory. Just 14 years before, James Polk had been elected president of the US after campaigning on the aggressive slogan "54-40 or fight!" which referred to his determination to control the land west of the Rockies all the way to the Alaska panhandle. Even though Vancouver Island and the mainland were British territories, few of the residents were loyal to Britain. Governor James Douglas asked the British government to accelerate their plans to set up a colony on the mainland. In the meantime, he didn't wait for the government to act. To protect the interests of the Hudson's Bay Company, the Aboriginal people and the colonists, he anchored a ship near the mouth of the Fraser and sold gold-prospecting licences, which were mandatory.

The British government passed the law creating the colony of British Columbia in August 1858. Queen Victoria chose the name, and she chose James Douglas as the first governor. He officially proclaimed the new colony at Fort Langley on November 19, 1858. A group of Royal Engineers was sent from England as law enforcers, surveyors and builders of roads and other community structures. Douglas invited many people to come and settle here, but ordered that reserves be set aside for Aboriginal people.

After the gold rush, the fur trade in southern BC was pretty much over. The Hudson's Bay Company in the area became a retail store and no longer needed Fort Langley, so the land was sold to a farmer.

Fort Langley was designated a National Historic Site in the 1920s, and now it is open to the public. Visitors can get into the spirit of the gold rush there by panning for "gold" (don't forget to pick up your licence!). Interpreters in period costumes tell visitors about the fur trade and the gold rush history of Fort Langley. As you leave the site, you can stop at the bronze statue of James Douglas and pay your respects to him for keeping things under control during a chaotic time.

—*Mike Starr, Parks Canada*

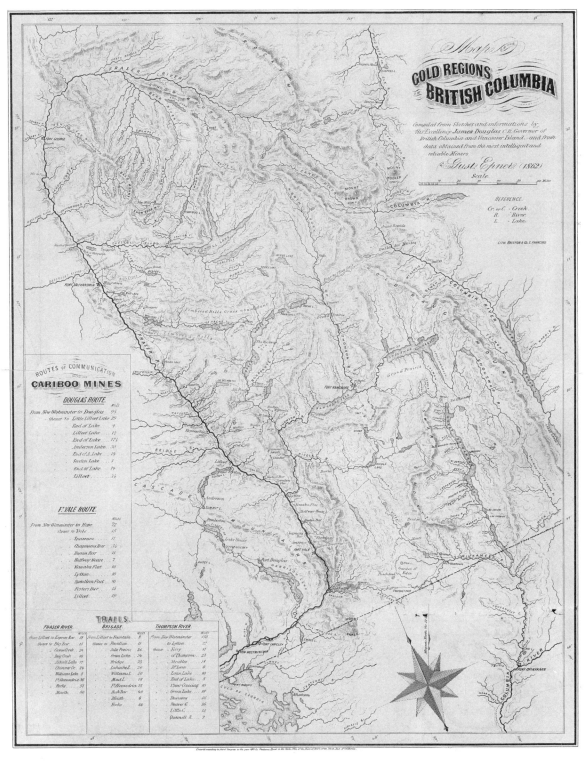

With the onset of gold fever, the world's mapmakers rushed to represent the geography of the province on paper. The results were not always accurate, as can be seen in this map from 1862, but they certainly captured the vastness of the new colony. *British Columbia Archives CMA-127-1862*

Afoul of the Law

Sep 16, 1859—Prisoners in Victoria Jail, Sep 14: Matthew Neil, manslaughter, 4 years penal servitude, 18th Apr; Jim (a Kanaka) aiding seamen to desert, 6 mo hard labor, Apr 21; Henry Hyde, aiding seamen to desert, 6 mo hard labor, Apr 23; An Indian, manslaughter, 6 mo hard labor, May 7; John Jones, larceny, 6 mo hard labor, Jun 15; George Becker, embezzlement, 6 mo hard labor, Jun 20; An Indian (in BC) assault with intent to murder, sentenced by Hon Judge Begbie, imprisonment for life, Jul 20; Charles Aubrey Angelo, misdemeanor, 1 yr imprisonment, Jul 25; Patrick Kearney, selling liquor to Indians, 2 mo, Jul 25; John Weymans, same offence, 2 mo, Jul 30; Timothy Blyon, same offence, 2 mo, Aug 9; Quantum, assault with intent to murder, 6 mo hard labor, Jul 28 (pardoned Oct 28); Stick-whe-lum, ditto; George Sandrie, assault, awaiting his trial (out on bail), Aug 29; Maurice O'Reilly, vagrancy and selling liquor to Indians, 1 mo imprisonment, Sep 3; John Donohue, selling liquor to Indians, fined £20 or 2 mo imprisonment, Sep 4; George White, R.M., striking a petty officer, 28 days imprisonment, 7 days of it solitary confinement, sentenced by Court-martial, Sep 8; Charles Weaver, debt, Sep 8; Thomas Martin, insane, confined for safekeeping, Sep 20; Matthew Kieth, an idle vagrant, 10 days hard labor, Sep 12.

—*from the* British Colonist, *selected by Leona Taylor*

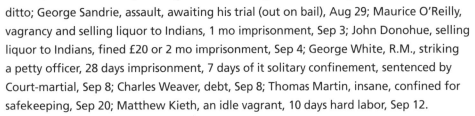

The miners kept coming. After acquiring provisions, they crossed the Strait of Georgia any way they could: aboard paddlewheelers, homemade boats and rafts, and in canoes bought from the Songhees people. Not everyone made it. Four years after the initial rush, W. Champness passed through Victoria on his way to the Cariboo goldfields, and he described the scene later in his book *To Cariboo and Back:* "It is a rapidly increasing town... Its appearance is not very prepossessing, as the houses are built in the most irregular manner, some being erected with their sides and gable-ends to the street, others at the same distance back, and small cottages side by side, 'promiscuously' with large hotels and government offices."

The unidentified author of a letter to the *Daily Telegraph*, Saint John, New Brunswick, provided fair warning to gold seekers:

There were about two thousand Canadians who came out here the same time I did, and the people in this God-forsaken town lived by gulling them. I believe the people here would starve to death if it was not for the piles of money which hundreds of deluded Englishmen and Canadians bring here every year. The country is not self-sustaining; it has no resources of any account. Last winter there were about fifteen hundred miners here in Victoria, most of them dead broke, and they could not get a day's work to do. They lived in miserable little cabins on one meal per day...the Government borrowed five thousand dollars from the Bank of British North America and set the men to work for one dollar per day pounding stones to repair the streets, when food and lodging at the meanest boarding house in town was seven dollars a week...The climate is very good here in the summer—it is very warm and dry; but the winters are ten times worse than in New Brunswick. There is little or no snow, but it rains more than half the time, and it is impossible to get around for mud.

The author had yet to meet the swarms of mosquitoes that awaited him on the mainland.

Life and Death

Died Nov 5, 1859 in the waters off Beacon Hill, Victoria, VI, Mr Edmund S Evans, aged 20, a clerk in the Treasury, s/o Rev E Evans, DD, Wesleyan Minister. He left home alone to go duck shooting; not coming back at the time expected, in a whole night's search he was not discovered. It is supposed that he entered the water to recover a duck he had shot, but becoming entangled with the seaweed, and not being able to swim, he was accidentally drowned. He was an only son.

Found murdered, Dec 5, 1859 at Victoria, VI, A half breed named Joseph Augur, who arrived here on the *Labouchere* from Ft Simpson. Found about halfway to the Indian rancheria at the N end of town, stabbed in the abdomen in several places. His coat, cap and handkerchief were carried away. No clue has been discovered.

—*from the* British Colonist, *selected by Leona Taylor*

2

GUARDED BY FIERCE MONSTERS

The Canyon Invasion and Resistance

As American miners scrambled up the Fraser River, they had very little on their minds other than a desire to get rich quick. But they soon learned that the river was not just another California stream. The author and journalist Bruce Hutchison painted a more accurate portrait of it in his book *The Fraser River*. Today it is considered one of the most beautiful rivers on the continent. But Hutchinson captured the spirit of 1858 when he called it a "ghastly trench bored out of solid rock… of all America's great rivers… probably the most unfriendly to mammalian life." The miners who came searching for gold would agree with him that the river was "forever mad, ravenous and lonely." It did not take them long to find out that the Fraser would not give up its treasures willingly.

Many of the first miners set out in poorly built canoes and drowned before they even reached the goldfields. Governor James Douglas wrote to the Colonial Secretary in early 1858: "Boats, canoes, and every species of small craft are continually employed in pouring

Opposite: Town of Yale. *Illustrated London News*, **May 12, 1865**

Yale, the centre of the Fraser River gold rush, was the last point on the river that steamboats could reach, and the beginning of the Cariboo Wagon Road. *British Columbia Archives F-08504*

their cargoes into Fraser's River, and it is supposed that not less than one thousand whites are already at work, and on their way to the gold districts. Many accidents have happened in the dangerous rapids of that river; a great number of canoes having been dashed to pieces, and their cargoes swept away by the impetuous stream, while of the ill-fated adventurers who accompanied them, many have been swept into eternity."

Some of them made it, and after they got a first tempting look at the rich bars along the river, high water submerged their diggings and did not retreat for weeks. "At present," one California miner reported in May, "the river is entirely too high to work, therefore I would not advise anyone to come here yet."

A Puget Sound newspaper reported: "It would seem that nature, miser-like, and if jealous of having her hoarded coffers ruthlessly assailed, has carefully locked up her precious treasures along fluted rivers, in canions, ravines, and mountain fastnesses." And a California newspaper reporter wrote from the Fraser: "There never was a gold field that offered so rich a harvest as this, nor was ever treasure guarded...by such fierce monsters."

The river was tough and so were the communities that sprang up along it. Yale, the new capital of the goldfields, was described as a "Sodom" that ran on a fuel of beans, bacon and rot-gut liquor. Men settled scores with pistols and bowie knives. Native women were terrorized and assaulted, and that torqued up tensions with the First Nations in the area. A journalist named David Higgins wrote of Yale:

> Every other store was a gambling den with liquor attachments. Ruffians of the blackest dye, fugitives from justice, deserters from the United States troops who strutted about in army overcoats which they had stolen when they deserted... vigilance committee refugees who had been driven from San Francisco under sentences of life banishment, ex-convicts, pugilists, highwaymen, petty thieves, murderers and painted women, all were jumbled together in that town and were free to follow their sinful purposes so far as any restraint from the officers of the law were concerned.

Gold Panning: Hard Labour

Gold mining techniques in New Caledonia were quite primitive before the arrival of the California miners, and no one was very good at it. It was relatively easy to recover bigger nuggets by sight. But the Californians brought their expertise in recovering smaller flakes and dust.

The pan was the most popular tool for separating gold from sand, dirt and river gravel. It was about the size of a small wok, with a flat bottom and slanted sides. A miner started by dipping the pan into a gold-bearing sandbar and swirling the contents around underwater. Then, by a series of rotations and shakings, both in and out of water, the lighter sand and gravel was "washed out," leaving the heavier dust-carrying residue—and, if they were lucky, gold flakes—in the pan. The gold was then picked out by hand or with tweezers.

In their haste, the miners often let finer gold escape in the washing process. That's why other miners, many of them Chinese, were able to come in later and recover more gold after the first wave of prospectors had moved on.

Above: Chinese miners were an integral part of the gold rush, patiently working diggings that others had abandoned. Here a Chinese miner uses a rocker, early technology to filter sand and gravel for gold without the back-breaking work of panning. *Library and Archives Canada PA-125990*

Left: The basic mining tool was the pan, and prospectors returned to the Fraser River year after year to see what the river had washed up. Even today, people search for gold by panning on the old bars where miners first struck it rich. *British Columbia Archives A-01958*

Panning was hard work. Prospectors squatted in icy mountain water for long periods, developing an early version of repetitive stress injury from constantly rotating the pan. It's little wonder that they soon started to develop the technology to streamline the washing-out process.

The rocker, or cradle, was one innovation. It was a wooden box mounted on cradle-like rockers. Sand and gravel were poured into a hopper mounted on the top of the box, which strained the gravel as the cradle was rocked. Other filters and screens could be added, and eventually the gold-bearing sediments ended up in a series of wooden bars or riffles in the bottom of the cradle. A pan was then used for the final "cleanup."

Other primitive gold-mining machines included the long tom and the sluice, basically long wooden chutes set at an incline with variations on the rocker's riffles and traps. Loads of gravel could be shovelled into the top of the chute and washed out with a continual stream of water, leaving the gold-bearing sediments trapped in the riffles. Both systems helped the miners recover more gold in a shorter period of time. More important, they reduced the time spent in back-breaking, knee-locking, wrist-twisting, finger-freezing labour.

—*Greg Dickson*

This photograph, taken in the Cariboo in about 1868, illustrates the kind of devastation mining brought to the landscape. Hillsides were stripped for wood to build flumes, and waterways were diverted without hesitation to help workers scour the slopes for gold.
British Columbia Archives F-08564

The Aboriginal people were not happy with this invasion of their territory—they knew what had happened to Native people in other gold rush sites. In California they had been almost completely exterminated during the plunder. And a war was still raging in the Washington Territory, where Native people were resisting the torrent of settlers and gold seekers headed for British Columbia.

During the summer of 1858, many altercations broke out along the Fraser between American miners and Native people. Ned Stout, who would later figure prominently in the Cariboo gold rush, was a member of a group that was attacked near China Bar: "They shot at us when ever they got a chance and we did the same. They did their best to cut us off and we had a very hard trip as we had to keep clear of the river as much as possible. I was shot in the arm and breast and a number of our men were killed and wounded...I do not know just how many white men were killed during these fights, but there were thirty six at least. The first notice which came of the trouble was one morning when nine bodies drifted down the river past Yale. The heads were severed and the bodies horribly mutilated."[Source to be inserted at a later time, using about this much space]

The so-called Canyon War came to a head in August, when American miners formed militias to track down and kill the Indians, Dan Marshall's account of the incident below.

Spuzzum

The name of this small Fraser Canyon commmunity, near the boundary between the Coast Salish and Nlaka'pamux (Thompson) people, means "little flat."

Grim Legacy

As a fifth-generation British Columbian, I well remember my earliest trips to the sublime landscape of the Fraser Canyon. On occasion I would accompany my father to engineering projects that he supervised, and the arid, desert-like climate—so scented with sagebrush and ponderosa pine—was unlike anything I had experienced in the rain-forested lands of Vancouver Island, for this is where my mother's family have lived since 1858, the year in which my Cornish ancestors travelled from California to the "New El Dorado."

During my childhood, I held many of the more popular conceptions of the gold rush: old sourdoughs making their trek north with pick, pan and shovel; paddlewheelers steaming by miners' camps; the instant tent-towns with saloons and gambling dens in full swing; and, of course, gold, the hidden treasure that spoke of instantaneous wealth! Indeed, this storied conception—all very true—was about adventure and, for a gold rush descendant, one in which we could be proud of our past. My great-great-great Uncle William was a 58'er who, among other pioneer achievements, worked with Walter Moberly as foreman of the Dewdney Trail. And yet, many years later while at UBC, I began to dig more deeply into the gold rush legacy (literally prospecting my way back to California through archival collections along the Pacific Slope), and I discovered a very different and, for indigenous peoples, tragic story still largely unknown. My romantic notions were quickly shaken as I discovered that these Fraser River-bound gold seekers had organized into large miner-militias that triggered Indian wars not only in Washington and Oregon, but also in British Columbia. In fact, the Fraser River gold rush not only broke the back of First Nations' control of their territories, but precipitated the formation of Indian reserves even before the Colony of British Columbia was established in the fall of 1858.

Native-white conflict became widespread. First Nations that inhabited the goldfields were (and still are) ancient peoples whose culture, trade, and food—particularly the salmon—all depended on the Fraser River itself. But with gold seekers arriving en masse, the environmental consequences of placer mining began to rival the salmon fisheries on these same contested grounds, and conflict was inevitable. In addition, before 1858 Native people were the discoverers of gold in BC, having both mined and profited from a resource of which they were increasingly dispossessed.

With the deaths of two French miners at the height of foreign occupation, non-Native miners organized for the express purpose of making war. Gold seekers had been expelled from Native territories and gold-washing grounds, and in response a military-like campaign was started to clear the path of Native blockades and armed resistance. In a scorched-earth policy typical of the exterminationist campaigns waged against Natives in California, a Texas ranger and his volunteer soldiers burned three Native villages at Spuzzum and massacred thirty-six Aboriginal people, including five chiefs. Many other violent acts occurred all along the Fraser and Thompson Rivers.

While the regular troops of the US army were engaged in fighting the Native peoples of eastern Washington, volunteer miners' militias, at least five companies in all, ascended the Fraser River in August 1858. Some set out to exterminate all Native people encountered; others offered to broker a peace settlement supported by a large show of armed force. One such company was the Pike Guards, commanded by Captain H.M. Snyder, a regular correspondent to the San Francisco *Bulletin*. In a lengthy letter to Governor James Douglas, Snyder told of his ten-day military-style campaign that concluded treaties of peace with chiefs from above Yale to present-day Lytton. It was at Lytton that Snyder encountered Chief Spintlum and subsequently reported to Douglas that he had entered into a grand council with 11 different chiefs gathered from throughout the traditional lands of the Nlaka'pamux. "We stated to them that this time we came for peace," related Snyder, "but if we had to come again, that we would not come by hundreds, but by thousands and drive them from the river forever." This certainly would not have seemed an idle threat considering that upwards of 1,500 US army troops were simultaneously engaged in a full-scale assault against the First Nations of the Columbia Plateau region (caused by the coming of Fraser River gold seekers).

The ethnographer James Teit, writing some forty years later after consulting Native elders, perhaps captured the great dilemma that confronted Chief Spintlum and his people:

Hundreds of warriors from all parts of the upper Thompson country had assembled at Lytton with the intention of blocking the progress of the whites beyond that point, and, if possible, of driving them back down the river. The Okanagan had sent word, promising aid, and it was expected that the Shuswap would also render help. In fact the Bonaparte, Savona, and Kamloops bands had initiated their desire to assist if war was declared. For a number of days there was much excitement at Lytton, and many fiery speeches were made. CuxcuxesqEt, the Lytton war-chief, a large, active man of great courage, talked incessantly for war. He put on his headdress of eagle feathers, and, painted, decked and armed for battle, advised the people to drive out the whites. At the end of his speeches he would dance as in a war dance, or imitate the grizzly bear, his chief guardian spirit. Cunamitsa, the Spences Bridge chief, and several other leading men, were also in favor of war. CexpentlEm [Spintlum], with his great powers of oratory, talked continually for peace, and showed strongly its advantages. The people were thus divided as to the best course to pursue, and finally most of them favoured CexpentlEm's proposals.

Clearly, the Nlaka'pamux had already decided for peace, prior to Snyder's ultimatum, in part because of Spintlum's considerable influence. In total, Snyder apparently concluded peace treaties with some 27 different chiefs, representing at least 2,000 Native individuals. But had Spintlum not urged peace, it is probable that an even wider conflagration beyond the immediate goldfields, involving a larger number of First Nations, would have occurred.

In 1927 a large stone monument was erected in Lytton to the memory of Chief Spintlum. The monument is largely unseen by the public and, like the Fraser River War, largely forgotten. And yet, an inscription etched in marble offers mute testimony to both this tragic event and the signal role played by this extraordinary Native individual in ending the war. In part it states: "When the White Men first discovered British Columbia the Indians were using the land and this caused bloodshed. David Spintlum did not want this loss of life and succeeded in stopping the war." We, the non-Native people of British Columbia, should be grateful for this man's actions. While it is important to mark the occasion of the province's sesquicentennial—to recognize many of the achievements of pioneer life—clearly the Fraser River gold rush was not only about the founding of this province, but ultimately a violent contest that dispossessed First Nations of their land and resources, a grim legacy that is still—150 years later—largely unresolved. Quite clearly, my ancestors were part of the colonization of British Columbia, but the greater danger today, perhaps, is that the romantic notions of our gold rush legacy, those I held in my youth, will continue to colonize the popular conscience of the non-Native public and, as such, continue the extraordinary injustice that continues to marginalize the First Nations of this province.

—Daniel Marshall, Department of History, University of Victoria, author of a forthcoming history of the Fraser River gold rush

After the Fraser River war, there followed an uneasy truce between First Nations and the miners. But life for Native people had changed forever. The old era of partnership with the fur traders was over. The struggle for the land itself gathered momentum as settlers and ranchers moved into traditional territories, renaming communities and landmarks and rearranging the landscape.

Fifty years later, when the gold rush was over, the Chiefs of the Shuswap, Okanagan and Couteau tribes wrote to Prime Minister Laurier, reminding him of the promises of the fur trade era and of what had happened to them since:

We speak to you more freely because you are a member of the white race with whom we first became acquainted and which we call in our tongue "real whites." One hundred years next year they came amongst us here at Kamloops and erected a trading post. After the other whites came to this country in 1858, we differentiated them from the first whites as their manners were so much different, and we applied the term "real whites" to the latter [viz., the fur traders of the Northwest and Hudson's Bay companies. As the great majority of the companies' employees were French speaking, the term latterly became applied to the designation for the whole French race]. The "real whites" we found were good people. We could depend on their word, and we trusted and respected them. They did not interfere with us nor attempt to break up our tribal organizations, laws, customs. They did not try to force their conceptions of things on us to our harm. Nor did they stop us from catching, fishing, hunting etc. They never tried to steal or appropriate our country, nor take our food and life from us. They acknowledged our ownership of the country, and treated our chiefs as men... We never asked them to come here, but nevertheless we treated them kindly and hospitably and helped them all we could...

Just 52 years ago, the other whites came to this country. They found us just the same as the first or "real whites" had found us, only we had larger bands of horses, had some cattle, and in many places, we cultivated the land... We were friendly and helped these whites also, for had we not learned the first whites had done us no harm? Only when some of them killed us we revenged them. Then we thought there was some bad ones among them, but surely on the whole they must be good... At first they looked only for gold. We know the latter was our property, but as we did not use it much nor need it to live by, we did not object to their searching for it. They told us, "Your country is rich and you will be made wealthy by our coming. We wish to pass over your lands in quest of gold." Soon they saw the country was good, and some of them made up their minds to settle it. They commenced to take up pieces of land here and there. They told us they wanted only the use of these pieces of land for a few years, and then would hand them back to us in an improved condition; meanwhile they would give us some of the products they raised for loan of our land. Thus they commenced to enter our "houses" and live on our "ranches…"

They have stolen our lands and everything on them and continue to use same for their own purposes. They treat us as less than children and allow us no say in anything. They say Indians know nothing and own nothing, yet their power and wealth has come from our belongings... This is how our guests have treated us—the brothers we received hospitably in our house.

Governor Douglas tried to protect First Nations from the miners, but the tide of Americans, kept coming. Thousands came not only through Victoria, but overland through the Washington Territory, by trail from the Bellingham area, up the Okanagan River along the old Hudson's Bay trail and any other trail they could find.

Portuguese Joe

My great-great-grandfather, Portuguese Joe Silvey, was born in the Azores on Pico, a volcano rising from the floor of the Atlantic Ocean, in 1836. He became a whaler like his father and brother before him. He was a young boy who had few choices for a career on a tiny volcanic archipelago in the mid-Atlantic. To board a whaler was to escape a life of poverty, and even though the sailing vessel was a hard living, Portuguese Joe Silvey chose it, seeking life and fortune in a new world.

Eventually Joe ended up in the Pacific Ocean. His father and brother had died as whalers, and Joe and five Portuguese friends left their whaling vessel and came to the Gulf of Georgia. All spoke Portuguese, and Joe could speak some English as well—an advantage in the British territory of Vancouver Island and mainland BC.

Joe and his friends arrived during the Fraser River gold rush. They saw some of the many thousands of boats crossing the strait, heading to an unknown destination in search of riches, and they had caught wind of tales of gold nuggets being plucked from the Fraser River streambed. They were bitten by the lust for gold.

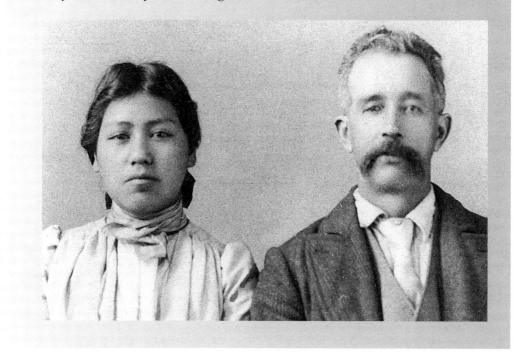

"Portuguese Joe" Silvey jumped ship with other young men from the Azores with dreams of finding gold. Like many others, he eventually went on to other pursuits, which included fishing, whaling and running a saloon in Gastown. Joe Silvey is shown here with his second wife, Kwahama Kwatleematt (also called Lucy), a Sechelt woman, in 1872. *Harbour Archives*

35

The men followed the flotilla of canoes, rowboats and other craft moving toward the mouth of the Fraser River. By the time someone on the whaler noticed they were gone, it was too late—they had timed the tides and winds and hidden among other boats and had slipped away.

They were deserters and thieves now. Fearful of being caught, they kept to themselves. But they were not caught by their captain or anyone representing the law, for they mingled with the hundreds of other gold seekers arriving from places all over the world.

Somewhere along their journey to the Fraser, Joe Silvey and his peers traded their small rowboat for a dugout canoe. Maybe it was at Musqueam or another Native village, before the river currents became fast. As they headed upriver, they stopped only to sleep, gather food and trade for simple gold-mining tools and an axe.

Just past Fort Yale on the Fraser, Joe and his peers stopped to set up camp and pan for gold. With their basic tools and a few gold pans, they set out to make their fortunes. My great-uncle Joe D. Silvey, the oldest grandson of Portuguese Joe Silvey, with the Silvey surname, told me that Portuguese Joe decided to build a cabin, not only for shelter but also for defence against the local Natives, who were said to be angry about the newcomers to the territory.

He chose to put the cabin door low to the ground, in case the local Natives decided to attack at night when all the men were asleep. The logic was that the Natives would have to crouch down and crawl in the door, and thus be vulnerable to the men's picks, axes and shovels, for they had no guns for protection. Joe D. Silvey told me that not long after Portuguese Joe and his peers had set up camp and commenced gold panning, a tragedy occurred. Some local Native Indians attacked the gold panners who were digging up the banks of the river, disturbing the natural order. The raid was so very close to Joe and his friends that they could hear the bloodcurdling screams of the miners just upriver. I was told that the yellowish river quickly turned red with blood.

Without a second thought, the Portuguese men abandoned their cabin, camp and gold-digging tools, taking nothing but the clothes they wore and their canoe. Paddling as fast as they could, and going with the swift current of the river in the canyon, the men pressed on until they neared the mouth of the river at the village of Musqueam.

At Musqueam, the local villagers and chiefs forced Portuguese Joe and his friends ashore. The men thought they were doomed to the same fate of the miners near Fort Yale, but it wasn't a hostile meeting at all. Joe and his peers were welcomed ashore at the Native village by Chief Kapilano. That is where Portuguese Joe met the Native woman who later became his bride, the granddaughter of Chief Kapilano. The two were married in the Native tradition. They settled at Point Roberts and opened a store, where they sold and traded food, alcohol and gold-panning tools to thousands of gold seekers who followed in Joe's footsteps to the Interior of BC. Portuguese Joe finally made his small fortune, not from gold, but indirectly through his store at Point Roberts and later, in his next venture—a store and saloon in Granville (Gastown).

—*Rocky B. Sampson, Great-great-grandson of Joe Silvey*

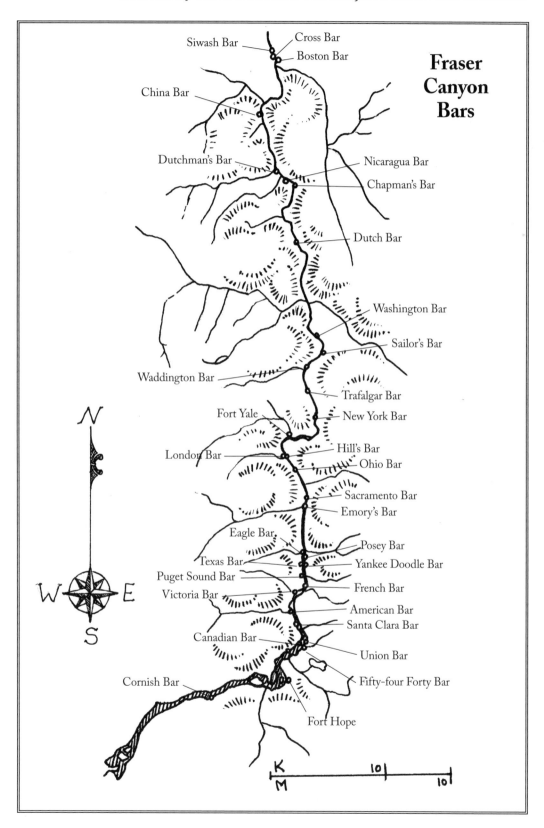

Fraser Canyon Bars

Siwash Bar
Cross Bar
Boston Bar
China Bar
Dutchman's Bar
Nicaragua Bar
Chapman's Bar
Dutch Bar
Washington Bar
Sailor's Bar
Waddington Bar
Trafalgar Bar
Fort Yale
New York Bar
Hill's Bar
London Bar
Ohio Bar
Sacramento Bar
Emory's Bar
Eagle Bar
Posey Bar
Texas Bar
Yankee Doodle Bar
Puget Sound Bar
French Bar
Victoria Bar
American Bar
Santa Clara Bar
Canadian Bar
Union Bar
Cornish Bar
Fifty-four Forty Bar
Fort Hope

N
W E
S

K
M
10
10

The names of the gold-bearing bars on the river reflect the American ancestry of the thousands of miners who flocked to the Fraser River: Boston Bar, New York Bar, Texas Bar, Yankee Doodle Bar, Sacramento Bar. Most miners in the early years were those who simply pulled up stakes in San Francisco and boarded ships for the Fraser River. They came from America, but many were recent immigrants from Great Britain, Germany, France, Italy, Spain and Poland. There were Russians, Swedes, Danes, Norwegians and Austrians and, of course, Chinese.

They brought California ways and attitudes with them. In San Francisco, vigilante committees had been set up to deal with unruly people and political enemies. And more than a few of the men on the Fraser were members of the vigilante committees or fugitives from their rough justice. They tried to settle scores in the California fashion.

Ned McGowan was one of those fugitives from "vigilante justice," an Irish American politician who narrowly escaped being lynched in California. By some accounts he was an honest reformer who had been libelled and framed by the corrupt vigilante committee in the bay city. Others saw him as an unrepentant political opportunist, a villain and maybe even a murderer. Whatever the case, McGowan was facing charges of accessory to murder in California and decided it would be wiser to head to the new Fraser River goldfields.

McGowan had been many things in his long career—a judge, legislator and political fixer among them—and he quickly became a leading citizen of Hill's Bar, the richest diggings on Fraser at the time. Men were making fifty dollars a day on the bar, a dream for most miners. McGowan bought into a claim and was soon running the place.

Hill's Bar

This Fraser Canyon gold site was named after Hill, the man who washed the first pan of gold there in 1858, touching off gold fever.

Governor Douglas was suspicious of his new American subjects and sought out loyal British citizens among the miners to serve as justices of the peace, gold commissioners and other functionaries. But British subjects were in short supply on the Fraser, and Douglas often had inferior material to choose from. The dregs of empire petitioned him for jobs. They knew the positions would be well paid to discourage desertion, and they were attracted by the opportunity to enrich themselves in less honest ways.

Water rights could be purchased for a "commission"; liquor licences and claim registration sometimes carried special "surcharges"; monopolies on supplies could be "arranged" for a price. Other officials simply enjoyed the privilege of lording it over the miners, issuing orders and making arbitrary rulings. Power corrupts, and on the Fraser River, British "peace, order and good government" did not always prevail.

Sometimes there was rivalry between colonial appointees in neighbouring communities. This was the case in 1858 in the neighbouring camps of Yale and Hill's Bar. Yale was the district supply centre, the head of navigation for river steamers and the centre of population and administration. Hill's Bar, just over a mile south on the other side of the river, was the most famous mining site on the Fraser. It was smaller, but it had the lion's share of the wealth.

Port Douglas

This small community at the head of Harrison Lake, where Governor James Douglas ordered work to begin on the Harrison–Lillooet route to the Interior, is long gone.

Peter Brunton Whannell, Douglas's justice of the peace in Yale, had been appointed in haste on the strength of a fictitious military record; but in fact he was a fraud artist who had skipped town in Melbourne, Australia. Whannell's assistant in Yale, Richard Hicks, was one of the most corrupt revenue collectors in the history of the gold rush. For a considerable period of time, Hicks ignored Victoria's orders to collect licence fees and instead illegally sold water rights, controlled liquor distribution and mishandled mining claim registrations.

Port Douglas in 1862

Our steamer, the "Colonel Moody," brought us in twenty hours to Douglas, a wooden-built town on a small lake at the north end of the larger and mountain-girt Harrison Lake. But we need not thus specially characterize any one lake in British Columbia, for every lake, pond, stream, or valley hereabouts is embedded in mountains; the latter, like pine trees and mosquitoes, are universal features and facts of the country.

Douglas derives its local importance from its position, at the commencement of the usual land transit up the country. Its principal trade consists in supplying emigrants with provisions and necessaries, and in forwarding such to the diggings. Hotels are springing up rapidly, such as, for instance, the "Columbia House" and "Cariboo Restaurant." Very recently a daily line of stages has been established to run in connection with the steamers on Lillooet and Anderson Lakes; but this is since our visit, when the necessary roads were as yet not completed.

At Douglas we united ourselves to a party of digging-bound emigrants... and laid in a supply of provisions for a four days' march of sixty miles, over mountainous and rough track...

—*W. Champness*, To Cariboo and Back in 1862

In nearby Hill's Bar, Douglas had appointed George Perrier justice of the peace. Perrier was a former sailor who was mining on the river when Douglas recruited him. "The governor asked Perrier if he understood the law," recalled one observer. "Perrier said he had read Blackstone. 'Tut-tut,' said the governor, 'it is not Blackstone you want here but just common sense.'"

Whannell and Perrier were rivals, and their jurisdictions overlapped in an inconvenient way. When Hill's Bar men went to Yale and committed offences, Yale men tried to enforce the law—when they could catch them. At Christmas in 1858, two white men from Hill's Bar

The gaol at Yale was a busy place during the gold-rush years.

picked a fight in Yale with the black barber of the town, Isaac Dixon, and pistol-whipped him at a dance. A few days later, Dixon went to Whannell to swear out a formal complaint.

Whannell sent a constable to Hill's Bar to apprehend the offenders. Perrier consulted with Ned McGowan, the real boss in Hill's Bar, and McGowan said that the men would not get a square deal in Yale and should be tried right there in Hill's Bar. Perrier didn't need much convincing. He sent his own officer to Yale with a warrant to arrest Dixon, as the chief witness.

This time it was Whannell's turn to defy a warrant. He arrested Perrier's constable and had Dixon locked up for his own protection. Judge Matthew Baillie Begbie, who had been appointed judge by James Douglas after the colony was proclaimed, later investigated the case. He reported to Douglas that "the gaol at Yale, which, being circumscribed in its limits, must when thus containing prosecutor, witness, and constable—everybody but the accused persons—have been rather inconveniently crowded."

George Perrier, Justice of the Peace

We are told that every genealogist finds a lawyer and a horse thief in "panning" for ancestors. Well, our information panning turned up both at once in my great-grandfather George Jean Perrier. My book *Ma's Father-in-Law—The Judge* will explain.

Before the gold rush of 1858, Perrier is mentioned by Frederic J. Howay, in his book *The Early History of the Fraser River Mines*, as having been a sailor. Howay also mentions that Perrier was "still mining on Hill's Bar" in February 1858.

In his book *McGowan's War*, Donald J. Hauka introduces George Perrier as one of a group of volunteer firemen from Engine House Number Eight in San Francisco, who were told by the superintendent of the San Francisco mint that the next excitement would be at the Fraser River. So Perrier, along with James Moore, then twenty-five years old, formed a company to go prospecting up the Fraser River.

The men left San Francisco on March 12, 1858. They travelled by steamer to Port Townsend, sailed on another boat to Fort Victoria and crossed the Strait of Georgia to the Fraser River in their own small boat. While this group of fifteen men were taking their meal among the gravel and rocks, Edward Hill noticed flecks of gold in the moss at his feet. Little did George Perrier know at that moment as he took up his gold pan and joined in the excitement that he would soon become justice of the peace at Hill's Bar. The Perrier Ditch company continued to mine for gold at Hill's Bar. In a letter to James Douglas dated November 30, 1861, Judge Matthew Baillie Begbie wrote: "Mr. Perrier who is well known to you shewed me $84 worth of nuggets, his dividend in respect of a day's work."

That was the lawyer—now on to the horse thief. No, it wasn't George Perrier. In a letter to Col. A. N. Birch, Secretary BC Explorations, November 1862, Perrier wrote that the horse Birch had left behind at Rock Creek had been stolen the next day by two French Canadians. Six days later the horse thieves came back across the river with "Old Charlie." Perrier employed a man to retrieve the horse, and when that didn't happen, he saw to it himself. "The men being residents of the valley I soon got on the track of them," he wrote, "but the horse being non-resident, it was rather more difficult to find him."

Old Charlie was found the other side of town in the possession of some Natives, who gave him up willingly, stating that two men had given them charge of him, and they were to have "five dolls" when they came back to get him. Perrier brought the horse to town and stated the case to the justice of the peace there, who desired him to retain possession of the horse and to look out he was not stolen again. Perrier allowed Old Charlie a bushel of oats every three days.

Thus Perrier gained custody of a horse and was paid for his services, and although the horse was stolen, he had legal possession and care of it.

—*Mabel F. Nichols, Great-granddaughter of George Jean Perrier*

Ned McGowan then came out of the shadows. He decided to go to Yale with a bag of gold dust and try to sort things out. McGowan offered to pay any fines, but Whannell's pride was smarting and he would not make peace. So McGowan returned to Hill's Bar with a new plan. He suggested that Perrier deputize him and authorize him to arrest Whannell for contempt of court!

"The operation was carried out with military precision," wrote Don Hauka in his book *McGowan's War*. McGowan went back to Yale with an armed posse, arrested Whannell in his own courtroom and released the prisoners from the Yale jail.

Whannell was hauled up in front of Perrier in Hill's Bar, fined 50 dollars for "his tyrannous and illegal acts" and sent back to Yale in humiliation. This was the genesis of "McGowan's War."

Whannell called in the cavalry. He wrote a letter to the commander of the Royal Engineers at Fort Langley requesting immediate military aid. Then he wrote to Governor Douglas: "This town and district are in a state bordering on anarchy. My own and the lives of the citizens are in imminent peril. I beg your Excellency will afford us prompt aid. I have applied to Captain Grant for assistance already as troops can easily be billeted in this town... An effective blow must at once be struck on the operations of these outlaws, else I tremble for the welfare of the colony."

It was an appeal that spoke to the governor's own belief that the American miners would use any excuse to take over the goldfields. He dispatched two of his most trusted lieutenants to the area: Colonel Richard Moody, newly arrived leader of the Royal Engineers, and Chief Judge Matthew Baillie Begbie. They quickly headed upriver with reinforcements.

Far From Home

Where mighty waters foam and boil
And rushing torrents roar,
In Fraser River's northern soil
Lies hidden the golden ore.

Chorus
Far from home, far from home
On Fraser River's shore
We labour hard, so does our bard,
To dig the gold ore.

Far, far from home we miners roam,
We feel its joys no more.
These we have sold for yellow gold
On Fraser River's shore.

In cabins rude, our daily food
Is quickly counted o'er.
Beans, bread, salt meat is all we eat—
And the cold earth is our floor.

Lonely our lives—no mothers,' wives',
Or sisters' love runs o'er
When home we come at set of sun
To greet us at the door.

At night we smoke, then crack a joke,
Try cards 'til found a bore.
Our goodnight said, we go to bed
To dream of home once more.

With luck at last, our hardships past,
We'll head for home once more,
And greet the sight with wild delight
Of California's shore.

And once on shore, we never more
Will roam through all our lives:
A home we'll find, just to our mind,
And call our sweethearts wives
—*dated July 1859, Emory's Bar, Fraser Canyon; from* Songs of the Pacific Northwest *by Phil Thomas*

What they found was relative tranquility, not a "war." But there was potential for violence. McGowan admitted later that he was prepared to fight if it came to that: "We had arranged a plan, in case of a collision with the troops, to take Fort Yale and then go down river and capture Fort Hope, and retreat with our plunder across the country into Washington Territory—only twenty miles distant. This would, we supposed, bring on the fight and put an end to the long agony and the public clamor—that our boundary line must be 'Fifty-four Forty or Fight!'"

Lillooet

First known to miners as Cayoosh Flat, Lillooet became Mile Zero for the Cariboo Wagon Road in 1862. The name was adapted from the proper name for the Lower St'at'imc people, the Lil'wat of Mount Currie.

Moody and Begbie were not looking for a fight. They charmed the miners along the way, complimenting them and wishing them well. The good feelings were reciprocated in a gunfire salute from the crowd in Yale, most of whom were Americans. McGowan too turned on the charm. He readily submitted to British justice and quickly paid a five-pound fine assessed by Judge Begbie. He then invited Begbie, Moody and their team to Hill's Bar, where he treated them all to a tour of the diggings and some expensive champagne. That was the end of "McGowan's War," a tempest in a teapot if ever there was one. The real victims were Perrier and Whannell, who lost their positions when the real facts became known.

McGowan later acknowledged that the restraint of Begbie and Moody had saved the day: "Fortunately, we fell into the hands of English gentlemen, and their presence and wise counsel saved many of us, no doubt, from a sad ending."

Lytton in 1862

Twelve miles below Nicomin is Lytton, named after Sir Edward Bulwer-Lytton, sometime Secretary for the Colonies. It is situated at the point where the Thompson unites with the Fraser. Here we received a kind invitation to spend the night in front of a blazing fire in a strong iron stove. After our usual devoirs to the 'weed,' we especially enjoyed our warm stretchout in such comfortable quarters, so secure from wind, rain, and cold; for winter was now fairly commencing.

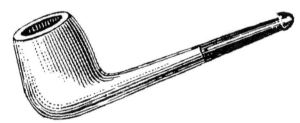

—*W. Champness*, To Cariboo and Back in 1862

McGowan sold his mining stake and returned to the United States shortly after. And for many years, BC history books were strangely silent on the more violent aspects of the Fraser rush. We may have Governor Douglas to blame for that: he and his colonial masters in London preferred a whitewashed version of the events, short on bloodshed and long on British fair play.

Cayoosh Creek

The name comes from *cayuse*, or Indian pony. A horse owned by Natives was said to have collapsed and died at this creek during a ride from Mount Currie to Lillooet.

In his dispatches, Douglas tended to play up his command of events. He insisted on a strong military presence, both at the naval outpost at Esquimalt and at the Royal Engineers headquarters at Sapperton. But in his official correspondence, he was careful to understate the significance of the Canyon War with First Nations and the Ned McGowan "war."

Lillooet in 1862

On the third day from Douglas we arrived at Lillooet, a young town, finely situated on a plain surrounded by lofty mountains, snow-covered even at midsummer; for it was now the 14th of June. Some attempts at gold-mining were being carried on here, chiefly by Chinese; their earnings were about three dollars a day.

We here held a council respecting our further route; and, after being informed of the rugged and mountainous nature of the trails from here to Cariboo (two hundred and fifty miles distant), and also of the very high price of provisions further up the country, we determined to lay in a large stock of flour, bacon, beans, and engage a team of seven horses for our enlarged party of twenty comrades. We further hired the services of an experienced California packer, who undertook to accompany us and securely pack our supplies on the beasts from time to time, at a uniform charge of thirty cents per pound on the whole weight of baggage... The prices here were thirty-five cents per pound for bacon, thirty cents per pound for beans, and twenty-five cents per pound for flour. Further up country the charges were still higher. An income of two hundred and fifty pounds per annum, in British Columbia, will not nearly produce the comfort which one hundred pounds would in England.

—*W. Champness,* To Cariboo and Back in 1862

Douglas was probably right to downplay the McGowan incident. But if the officials in London had examined the hostilities closely, they might have found that Douglas was largely to blame. By appointing incompetent officials in the goldfields, he had provoked the miners to take the law into their own hands. The results reflected badly on Douglas's judgement of character.

Harrison to Lillooet

For two years I lived in a small trailer on the Lillooet River—and stepped out every morning onto the Harrison-Lillooet Gold Rush trail! What an experience—the spirit of thousands of miners who slogged along that trail 150 years ago is still strong. This lesser-known early history of the BC gold rush is almost unknown, compared to the Cariboo Trail and Barkerville.

I have co-authored a book called *Spirit in the Land: Our Place of Prayer*, which is mostly about the Church of the Holy Cross in Skatin (formerly Skookumchuck). I'm always looking for more details about the people and events that preceded it, when the first non-Aboriginal people travelled through the valley on their way north to the Cariboo.

—*Sharon Syrette, Mission*

Douglas saw the First Nations as victims, and he would not stir up colonial fears about them. He negotiated treaties when he could to cement strong relationships. It was his inclination to protect the interests of Native people in preparation for the day when he might need their assistance to defend the colony against American territorial ambitions.

The first phase of the gold rush was nothing to write home to London about. It was improvised and chaotic. Douglas and his new team were determined to improve their record.

Girl of the Golden West: Two Views

These two perspectives on Puccini's *Girl of the Golden West*, set in the California gold rush, were presented at the Vancouver Opera Speaks forum in the fall of 2003.

Puccini Has Got It Right

Cole Harris, Professor Emeritus, Department of Geography, UBC

The effects of the gold rush on British Columbia were enormous. The gold rush was the crucial event in the province; it was really the onset of modern British Columbia. It ushered in the Crown colony of British Columbia, created quickly by the colonial office in the fall of 1858. It marked the demise of the fur trade in southern British Columbia, and it broke down Native resistance in British Columbia to a very large extent; partly because of the fire power, the sheer military might that comes in with the miners, also because following very shortly on the heels of the miners was the devastating epidemic of smallpox that raged through the province in 1862. In many parts of the province, smallpox killed half to three-quarters or more of the Aboriginal population, and Native British Columbia was thrown back on its heels. The gold rush was an overwhelming, traumatic event, and modern British Columbia was launched.

Any differences between this gold rush and the California rush? Perhaps two. The racism of the California gold rush was directed towards Natives and Hispanics; in BC, it was Native people and Chinese. There's also the question of whether the gold rush had got out beyond the institutional state-based forces of law and order. In British Columbia, Governor James Douglas, representative of the colonial office, was doing his best to manage this rush, but he had very little to work with. There were not many men, not many ships; there was not much that he could do. Eventually gold commissioners would be appointed, and justices of the peace would be named, but it was a frail effort. Really, in the summer of 1858, the gold rush is on its own in British Columbia.

Miners were left very largely to their own devices. There was a war in the Fraser Canyon; it was difficult to figure out exactly what was going on, but a good many Native people and some non-Native miners were killed. There was another war in the Okanagan, and a good deal of killing. The state couldn't deal with this, it was happening too fast. The miners had an enormous amount of fire power—they were bringing in six-shooters, invented by this time and very effective in mopping up Native people in the American southwest. The spiral-bore rifle had just been invented. An arsenal that Native people can't cope with was coming in. These people were Indian fighters; they knew how to deal with Native people—at least they think they did—and they organized themselves into posses and moved through British Columbian territory. But very quickly in BC, the government did get some hold on the situation, and overall the levels of violence in British Columbia were much lower than in California.

Basically I think Puccini has got it right. I think he understood a gold rush. I was moved by the opera—it's a powerful piece of work, if you're interested at all in the social commentary that is in an opera, and if you're interested in connecting that social commentary to the part of the world in which you live.

Sacred Sites of the River People

Albert (Sonny) McHalsie, Sto:lo Historian

The Sto:lo, the river people, were here when those 30,000 men came up for their gold. In the late 1700s there was a huge smallpox epidemic; in 1808 Simon Fraser, the first European to travel down the river, was chased back upriver by the Musqueam people; in 1827 Fort Langley was established; and then in 1858 there was the gold rush.

We had our own structure of society and ideas of ownership of property, like who owned fishing grounds, who owned ancestral names, how they're given, how they're taken away, how you're given access to resource sites to your extended family. All those rules and protocols were in place. Fort Langley was established in 1827, largely for furs, but they gave up trying to entice our people to go out and trap furs because we had a rich, strong salmon economy. Eventually Fort Langley switched to the salmon trade, because of the Sto:lo. They also started growing cranberries.

We also had arranged marriages. The men in Fort Langley were quite aware of that, and they followed the rules. Some men from the fort intermarried with the Sto:lo people. The chief at the local village still exercised his authority and treated Fort Langley as his resource, so when people came to trade goods there, he was like the middle man. He would stop and take his little bit and then trade with the fort, treating the fort as though it was part of his extended family ownership. But then in 1858, when the gold rush began, the men came from California, where there was a price on scalps. Those were the men who came up here. When they arrived, it was high-water time and the gravel bars were still covered in water. They couldn't do any mining. They brought alcohol with them and they introduced it to our First Nations people, and that brought its own problems. Then there was the mistreatment.

The Hill's Bar conflict took place at an important resource site for making sockeye oil, and one of our most important sacred sites was just downriver. It was a Transformer site, a place where children were shown rock and told the story. That probably had something to do with the skirmish at Hill's Bar.

This transformer stone, on the Fraser River near Yale, is believed by some First Nations people to have been human beings at one time. Long before prospectors and others flooded to the area in the 1850s and '60s and renamed every gold-bearing sandbar and turn in the river, these sites were well known to Aboriginal people and important to their cultures, and their Native names were hundreds of years old.
Mark Forsythe photo

3

PEACE, ORDER AND GOOD GOVERNMENT
Douglas Asserts His Authority

Governor James Douglas watched events unfold in his new mainland colony with both hope and anxiety. The rush for furs had ended and the rush for gold was on. Prospecting was a far messier pursuit and most of those who took it up had no respect for the First Nations, who had been full partners in the fur trade. American-style justice would prevail if British justice didn't get there first.

Douglas could take the temperature of the times. The frontier was being pushed back and the mainland would soon open to settlement. The governor didn't like settlement—American settlers in the Oregon territory had put an end to British interests there. And now the gold rush was bringing a new wave of American immigrants north of the 49th parallel. Would history be repeated?

With the cry of "Fifty-four Forty or Fight!" ringing in his ears, Douglas knew he would have to act. As if to mock his administration, there was even a mining site on the Fraser called the 54-40 Bar. Douglas began by proclaiming that there would be no settlement on the Fraser. In the spring of 1858, he met with one group of miners. "I refused to grant them any rights of occupation to the soil," he wrote, "and told them distinctly that Her Majesty's government ignored their very existence in that part of the country, which was not open for the purposes of settlement, and [they] were permitted to remain there merely on sufferance; that no abuses would be tolerated; and that the laws would protect the rights of the Indian, no less than those of the white man."

The American record in dealing with First Nations was nothing to brag about. Conquest and displacement had led to wars throughout the Oregon and Washington Territories. But Douglas still held onto a dream of White–Native partnership in the British colonies. In 1855 he wrote to the colonial secretary: "I am of the opinion that there must have been some great mismanagement on the part of the American authorities, or it is hardly credible that the natives of Oregon, whose character has been softened and improved by 50 years of commercial intercourse with the establishments of the Hudson's Bay Company, would otherwise exhibit so determined a spirit of hostility against any white people."

Like many HBC employees, Douglas lived what he preached. It started on the home front: his wife Amelia was half Cree. Intermarriage was a fact of life in the West, a practical as well as commercial bond. Church leaders sent out from Britain were appalled to find so many "country marriages" in the colonies and assumed they were partnerships of convenience. It was there that the Church was mistaken. Many of these marriages were lifetime partnerships that would not be sacrificed to the Church's European view of propriety. The Douglas marriage was a prime example.

One of Douglas's guiding principles as he faced the challenges of the gold rush of 1858 was certainly that the fragile coalition with First Nations must be protected. Douglas knew that if it came to a war with the Americans over his new colonies, he must rely on an alliance with Native people. He even suggested during the American Civil War that he could raise a Native army and retake the Oregon territory for Britain while Washington was distracted. He would pursue a policy of fair treatment of Native people and equal rights under the law, and he would negotiate treaties when he could.

Opposite:
Town of Douglas
from the *Canadian
Illustrated News*,
July 23, 1870

James Douglas, who served as governor of both Vancouver Island and British Columbia, was the most powerful man of the gold-rush era. He was autocratic but sensitive to the interests of First Nations and other groups.
British Columbia Archives A-01227

Below: Licences to prospect for gold, gathered into books like this one, were mandatory. They were an important source of revenue for Governor James Douglas's colonial government, and the certificates reminded American miners that the goldfields were British.

A Proclamation

The British Columbia Proclamation issued at Fort Langley: An Act to Provide for the Government of British Columbia (2nd August, 1858)

By His Excellency, JAMES DOUGLAS, Governor and Commander-in-Chief of Her Majesty's Colony of British Columbia and its Dependencies.

WHEREAS, by an Act of Parliament made and passed in the 21st and 22nd years of the Reign of Her Majesty Queen Victoria, Chapter XCIX, entitled "An Act to Provide for the Government of British Columbia," the limits of the said Colony were defined, and Her Majesty was authorized to invest the Governor thereof with such powers as in the said Act of Parliament are mentioned;

And whereas by a Commission under the Great Seal of the United Kingdom of Great Britain and Ireland, Her Majesty has been pleased to appoint JAMES DOUGLAS to be Governor of British Columbia; And the said Governor is required by the said Commission, amoungst other things, formally to proclaim said Act with the said Colony of British Columbia.

Therefore I, James Douglas, Governor of the said Colony, now proclaim and publish the said Act for the information and guidance of Her Majesty's subjects, and others whom it may concern, as follows:

ANNO VICESIMO PRIMO ET VICESIMO SECUNDO

Victorae Reginae,

CAP. XCIX

GOD SAVE THE QUEEN

Douglas would have preferred a mainland colony under the exclusive control of the Hudson's Bay Company. He was a company man first, and he hoped for HBC control over all trade and transportation in the goldfields. Officials in London were opposed to this course, and they appointed Douglas governor of the new colony on the condition that he sever all connections with the HBC. To give him credit for flexibility, Douglas took up the challenge, and so began a brilliant strategy to keep British control of the colony against overwhelming American odds.

To emphasize the premise that the gold belonged to the government, the miners were first licensed. Running a gold colony would cost money, and licence fees would pay for roads, courts and government. At first, Douglas dodged the issue of permanent miner settlements, but he was developing a backup plan. He wrote to London for support:

The opinion which I have formed... leads me to think that, in the event of the diggings proving remunerative, it will now be found impossible to check the course of immigration, even by closing Fraser's River, as the miners would then force a passage into the gold district by the way of the Columbia River, and the valuable trade of the country in that case be driven from its natural course into a foreign channel and entirely lost to this country... I would recommend that a small naval or military force be placed at the disposal of the Government, to enable us to maintain the peace and enforce obedience to the law... For the time being, all my efforts will be directed towards maintaining the peace in the gold districts... and infusing a British element into the population.

As the pace of the gold rush accelerated, so did Douglas's improvisations. If settlement was unavoidable, he must have authority to deal with it: "I think it therefore a measure of obvious necessity that the whole country be immediately thrown open for settlement, and that the land be surveyed, and sold at a fixed rate not to exceed twenty shillings an acre."

History Lost and Found

On a cold, rainy day in November 1858—the 19th, to be exact—at a ceremony at Fort Langley, the mainland Colony of British Columbia came into existence primarily as a response to the Fraser River gold rush and the influx of thousands of American miners. This date is considered the birth of the present-day province. James Douglas, governor of the Colony of Vancouver Island, was sworn in as governor and commander-in-chief of British Columbia. His authority to act in this position was derived from a commission issued by

Lytton, pictured here in 1867, was named for the colonial secretary of the day in 1858. Edward Bulwer-Lytton penned the famous opening line: "It was a dark and stormy night..." The original Native village was Kumsheen, and local First Nations resisted the invasion of gold miners, meeting violence with violence. *British Columbia Archives A-03551*

Queen Victoria. Now known as the 1858 Douglas Commission (to distinguish it from the 1851 Douglas Commission, which appointed him governor of Vancouver Island), it gave Douglas almost unlimited power and authority "to make ordain and establish all such laws institutions and ordinances as may be necessary for the peace order and good government of Our Subjects." Representative government was the long-term goal, but the colonial secretary, Sir Edward Bulwer-Lytton, felt that self-government would be too risky "among settlers so wild, so miscellaneous and perhaps so transitory." This suited Douglas, who was more inclined to despotism than democracy.

The commission is an impressive document. It consists of three large parchment pages, attached to the Great Seal of Queen Victoria. Presumably when Douglas retired in 1864, with a knighthood, he took both the 1851 and 1858 commissions with him. He died in 1877.

The commission of the first governor of Vancouver Island, Richard Blanshard, was eventually acquired by the Provincial Archives of BC, but the 1858 Douglas Commission was nowhere to be found and was believed lost or destroyed. None of the Douglas descendants knew what had happened to it.

Then, in the spring of 1953 in London, the secretary of the BC Land and Investment Agency, a company with ties to British Columbia since the early 1860s, was instructed to clean out a long-disused vault, which had survived a bomb in 1944, and destroy any records no longer of any value. In the process she came across an old brown paper bag. Fortunately, the secretary was conscientious and identified the contents as having belonged to the grandfather of two of the agency's clients, James A. and John Douglas. Apparently the documents had been "deposited … many years ago by a member of the Douglas family." This may have been James William Douglas, Douglas's only son, on one of his trips to London. One of the documents was the 1858 commission. James William Douglas died in 1883 at the age of 32, leaving two young sons—James A. in London and John in Victoria—who decided that it and the other material should be given to the Provincial Archives of BC. Nearly a hundred years after it was first brought to BC, the 1858 Douglas Commission returned. This unique and important historical document is now part of the collection of the BC Archives, which is fittingly located on the property where Douglas once lived.

—Frederike Verspoor, Archivist, Access Services, British Columbia Archives, Royal British Columbia Museum Corporation

....

Lytton

This small centre, located at the confluence of the Thompson and Fraser Rivers, was named after the secretary of state for the colonies, Sir Edward Bulwer-Lytton. Camchin, a Native village, was located at this spot as well.

....

As his official appointment as governor of the new colony approached at Fort Langley, Douglas outlined his plan: "To accomplish that great object of opening up a very inaccessible country for settlement, by the formation of roads and bridges immediately and pressingly wanted; to provide public buildings for the residence of the officers of the Crown; for the use of the judiciary, for offices of record; and, in short, to create a great social organization, with all its civil, judicial and military establishments, in a wilderness of forest and mountain..."

A few months earlier he had been contemplating how to keep the Americans out of the colony, and now he was taking steps to employ, police and transport the same people. Over the summer of 1858, when the miners were idle because of high waters, he hired and fed many of them as part of the first public works program in the colony. He then formed teams of miners to build a road from the Harrison River to Lillooet.

The project derailed rebellious activity in Victoria, and it proved a great success with miners, who were looked after until the Fraser could be panned again. It was a brilliant stroke and it bought Douglas the time he needed to put proper law and administration in place. His biographer, Derek Pethick, declared the action Douglas's finest hour: "Much had depended on him in this hour of trial; and much in this crucial time he had supplied. Possible disaster had by skill and resolution been avoided..."

Gold Rush Lillooet

Although Yale and (mistakenly) Barkerville are associated with the Fraser gold rush and its founding of the colony, the other main centre of the Fraser rush was in the area of today's town of Lillooet. In those days, downtown Lillooet was a shantytown, built amidst and on top of the main St'at'imc village, which became known as Cayoosh Flat, or simply Cayoosh. Across the river, just north of today's Bridge of the Twenty-Three Camels, were Parsonville (or Parsonsville) and the slightly smaller Marysville, and another boomtown at the confluence of the Bridge River a few miles upstream, also known then as the Lower Fountain(s), and known today as Six Mile. For thousands of years this location was the centre of salmon fishing on the Fraser: its Native name is Sat' or, in an older spelling, Setl.

The town of Bridge River (one of several communities by that name over the years) sprang up around a toll bridge constructed at the onset of the gold rush. This bridge replaced an age-old Native pole bridge—torn down by the miners—across the Fraser at the Bridge River Rapids, where Coyote is said to have jumped back and forth from shore to shore to create the rock ledges that form the narrow throat the Fraser is forced to roar through, and which form the platform for the ancient fishing stations and drying racks that line the rapids. Although busy, most traffic across the Fraser was by ferry at locations farther downstream. It was busiest at the mouth of the Lillooet Canyon, where the old Suspension Bridge is today (abutments and cable moorings associated with the ferry can still be seen), and others down nearer Parsonville and Marysville.

Also part of "gold rush Lillooet" or, as it was known in those times, "on the Upper Fraser." were the junction and roadhouses that sprang up at the Upper Fountain (Fountain today) a

few miles farther upstream, where the River Trail from the lower reaches of the Fraser met the trail from Lillooet (today's Highway 12 route was then impassable). The trail continued to parts that were little-known at the time—Fountain's importance as a junction increased with the onset of the Cariboo gold rush and the construction of the first road in the Interior, northward from Lillooet. Cayoosh, Parsonville, Marysville, Bridge River and the Upper Fountains all had a full range of services, from hostelries and saloons and barbers to brokers, freight companies and blacksmiths. All but Cayoosh Flat have vanished, and in 1860 the townspeople petitioned the visiting Governor Douglas to change the community's name to Lillooet, with the permission of the leaders of the St'at'imc and Lil'wat. For reasons unstated in the record, they found the name Cayoosh distasteful. This may be because of the recent Cayuse and Yakima Wars in Washington Territory, the aftermath of which many miners on the Upper Fraser had struggled through.

The immediate impact of the gold rush was drastic. Disruption of the fishery caused famine among the First Nations peoples of the Interior—all nations fished at Bridge River and the adjoining stretches of the Fraser, and some 10,000 people gathered food there during fishing season. As more and more miners and hangers-on arrived, the ancient village of the

Parsonville on the Fraser River, as seen in *The Illustrated London News,* December 17, 1864, was sometimes known as The Fountain. The community was one of the many boomtowns that sprang up along the river.

55

St'at'imc, where today's Main Street lies, was overwhelmed. There were already thousands of men on the Upper Fraser before Governor Douglas commissioned the construction of the Douglas Road or Lillooet Trail via the Lakes Route, which bypassed the Fraser Canyon. This trail was built partly in response to miners' fears of the Nlaka'pamux in the wake of the Fraser Canyon War, but also because of worries of impending starvation among the miners on the upper Fraser. It was nearly impossible to ship supplies via the Fraser Canyon's rocky and precipitous trails, and miners arriving by the Okanagan Trail and other inland routes were more likely to be looking for supplies than bringing them in. Others had come in, struggling through the brush and harsh climate of the Lakes Route, even before that route was formally opened. Once it was, the torrent was massive, with 20 or 30 thousand men pouring into the Upper Fraser area (and through it, eventually to discover the goldfields of the Cariboo, Big Bend, Omineca, Peace, Cassiar and Stikine). One journal estimated the "permanent" population of Lillooet as 16,000 at its peak, but as an associate remarked to the diarist, "if you took away all the Indians, there really aren't that many." Another visitor remarked, "it is extraordinary the number of French Canadians there are about," and the roster of names in the various historical registries of businesses and in diaries shows the presence of many Germans and other Europeans, as well as the dominant Americans and Chinese and a scattering of Britons. When Judge Matthew Baillie Begbie tried to convene a jury in Lillooet, he could not find 12 British subjects, in a town of thousands.

Most estimates agree with Alfred Waddington's guess that no more than 10,500 miners actually worked on the Fraser at any given time, and half of those were on the Upper Fraser, near Lillooet. But in a gold rush, there are always many more people in the area than the miners themselves—those who provide food and drink and other services, or find other ways (gambling, stealing, selling sex) to rid miners of their gold. Cayoosh Flat and its sister towns were, like Yale and other gold-rush towns, "lusty, brawling places," and as Ma Murray's daughter Georgina Keddell quips in *The Newspapering Murrays*, a biography of her parents, Lillooet was Gomorrah to Yale's Sodom in the social life of the canyon. In the typical BC goldfield, as many as a third of the total numbers were Chinese, and the governor himself said that within the white contingent, actual Americans numbered only about 20 percent relative to newly arrived Europeans, Britons and Australians, all of whom had originally come to British Columbia directly from California. Natives from other parts of the province also came to the gold-rush centres, but Lillooet already was an ancient focus of Native life—and politics—in the province.

The Fraser Gold Rush is most infamous for the Fraser Canyon War between the Nlaka'pamux and the miners' armed companies, but it was a different situation in the Upper Fraser, where all was quiet during the war and, despite the depredations caused by displacement of the fishery and the inundation of the country with a polyglot horde of foreigners of all colours, the St'at'imc were known as the Friendly Indians—quite opposite to one of the alternate names for the Nlaka'pamux—the Knife Indians, or "the Couteau" in Anglo-French. Journals of miners and other travellers through the country during the peak of the gold rush comment on famine among the Native people, and also on their suffering through recent wars. These wars were waged against the Nlaka'pamux and Secwepemc, and also (separately) the Chilcotin, and had decimated the St'at'imc and Lil'wat peoples for a generation after the massacre of Nicola's War, led by the Nicolas to avenge the killing of Chief Nicola's father by the chief of the Lakes Lillooet.

Among the new arrivals were people of many nations and colours, although the first formal evidence of that is from an 1861 census—one that includes Galicians (Ukrainians and Poles), Austrians, Hungarians, Sandwich Islanders (Hawaiians), Mexicans and other Latin Americans, and Mormons (listed separately from other Americans).

Port Douglas was another one of the Mainland's largest towns, along with Yale and what was to become Lillooet. All were larger than New Westminster or Victoria, from where steamers arrived daily to begin the arduous journey to Cayoosh. The series of portages involved all manner of cartage: mule trains and Chinese packers with bamboo poles and Native men using tumplines (carrying by headstrap) were complemented by busy steamer, sail-driven barge and Native-operated canoe services on Lillooet, Anderson and Seton Lakes. At both ends of all three lakes, booming port towns emerged—Ports Lillooet and Pemberton on Lillooet Lake, Port Anderson and Wapping on Anderson Lake, Flushing and Port Seton on Seton Lake. Flushing and Wapping were so named because they were busy enough to remind travellers of the London Tube stations of those names. Connecting them was the Short Portage (renamed Seton Portage on the gold rush's centenary in 1958), just over a mile and only 15 metres in elevation differential. It was traversed by British Columbia's first official railway—a horse- or mule-drawn affair, resembling an ore cart, which ran on wooden rails using the slight downward slope of the portage to carry goods eastward into the goldfields. (Luckily for the horses and mules, nearly all freight was eastbound, and the westbound carts were generally empty.) Also in the record was a toll road known as Dozier's Way, named after its proprietor, Karl Dozier, which competed with the railway for business.

—*Mike Cleven, who spent his early childhood in Lillooet and writes about BC history at cayoosh.net*

Bridge River

This river, which flows into the Fraser River near Lillooet, is named for a bridge built by Aboriginals, which was torn down during the gold rush. A new one was built by two enterprising citizens, who charged miners a 25-cent toll.

James Douglas was an astute observer. Even as he moved to counter American ambitions in the gold district, he could still stand back and judge the prospects of an uprising among the miners: "About two thirds of the emigrants from California are supposed to be English and French; the other third are German, and native citizens of the United States.

There is no congeniality of feeling among the emigrants, and provided there be no generally felt grievance to unite them in one common cause there will, in my opinion, always be a great majority of the population ready to support the measures of government."

Douglas relied on bluff and a small show of force to back up his administration. At first, he had only the aid of HMS *Satellite*, a Royal Navy ship, to keep the peace and help him collect licence fees from the thousands of miners who were now at work on the Fraser. But by fall, the first contingent of Royal Engineers was on its way to the colony to back up the governor's orders. Lord Lytton wrote from the colonial office to outline their duties:

> The superior discipline and intelligence of this force, which afford ground for expecting that they will be far less likely than ordinary soldiers of the line to yield to the temptation to desertion offered by the gold fields, and their capacity at once to provide for themselves in a country without habitation, appears to me to render them especially suited for this duty, whilst by their services as pioneers in the work of civilization, in opening up the resources of the country, by the construction of roads and bridges, in laying the foundations of a future city or seaport... they will probably not only be preserved from the idleness which might corrupt the discipline of ordinary soldiers, but establish themselves in the popular good will of the emigrants by the civil benefits it will be in the regular nature of their occupation to confer.

Noble Band of British Heroes

My gold rush history connection is through my membership in the Royal Engineers Living History Group, which commemorates the contributions of the RE to the existence of the Colony circa 1858–63. Due to the influx of thousands of expatriate Americans during the Cariboo gold rush, there was a grave concern about annexation by the US. What Governor James Douglas needed was the infrastructure for the colony and troops on the ground other than the Royal Marines onboard ships at Esquimalt. In five short years, the RE mapped, surveyed and built roads from Sapperton (now New Westminster) to Bella Coola.

We do re-enactments of "living history" from San Juan Island to Barkerville. Any character, historical or fictional, who might have been in the colony at that time is eligible. Your obedient servant, etc.

—*"Srgt. J. McMurphy RE," aka Todd Birch, Quesnel*

As educators, we use hands-on activities, period clothing and equipment and first-person representations to demonstrate what daily life was like in the gold rush colony. Histories of British Columbia treat the deeds of the Royal Engineers with awe. And the accomplishments of these soldiers, both in engineering and in public service, were indeed remarkable. Yet often the engineers themselves are portrayed as Victorian-era supermen, a "Noble band of British heroes" transforming the wilderness, a reverence that is obvious in the idealized 1967 oil painting by Rex Woods of the engineers at work. A careful examination of the letters, journals and archived documents of the engineers puts a human face on them. Officers squabbled and back-stabbed one another, enlisted men drank to excess and deserted regularly, and the work was plagued by accidents, many of them fatal. An 1859 photograph of the real engineers provides a striking contrast to the romanticism of the Woods painting. We strive to give the public a glimpse into the daily lives of the engineers and their families—to reveal the real people behind the legend.

—*"HRLuard, Captain, RE," aka Simon J. Sherwood*

Lord Lytton, the colonial secretary, was going to send his finest soldiers, but he did not intend them to be used for routine police work, as he made clear to their commander, Colonel Richard Moody: "Nothing can be more likely to sap the manhood and virtue of any young community than the error of confounding the duties of soldiers with the ordinary functions of police... the Colonists should be taught the necessity of providing against internal disturbance... they should learn to rally round the law, and create themselves a machinery for giving that law its ordinary effect..."

In addition to being colonial secretary, Lytton was an author. It was he who penned the famous opening words: "It was a dark and stormy night..." His reputation as an author outlived his legacy as a politician, but in BC, the town of Lytton is named for him.

The Royal Engineers

True to their motto, time but enhances their fame;
Hard though their task nothing could them restrain;
Ending their long sea voyage and on shore once again,
Robust, strong and willing, success their brightest aim,
On Fraser's mighty river bank their home a canvas tent,
You soon could hear the humming that saw the hammer sent.
A city stands upon the spot here, fifty years ago,
Lo! The Indian and the coyotes enjoyed their to and fro.
Every day they cut new trails where white had never been;
No grander road then Cariboo new country's ever seen.
Girtling streams with bridges, felling mighty pines,
Initial work in everything—even churches in their line.
Nobly did they do their work, BC will always tell,
Empire-builders surely! Their descendant offspring swell.
Esteemed by one and all are the few that now remain;
Remembered in all honour those who've left this earthly train.
Symbols of their motto, they upheld their glorious name,
BC admits that *Ubique quo fas et Gloria ducunt*, a motto without stain.
—*Thos. Harman. 8th March, 1909, courtesy of the Royal Engineers Living History Group, royalengineers.ca*

Lord Lytton was an avowed political opponent of the Hudson's Bay Company and, at first, a vocal critic of Governor Douglas. But during his short tenure as colonial secretary, he gained confidence in Douglas and eventually saw him as the only proper candidate to run the Pacific colonies. And he backed up Douglas on broader British interests as well. "The Colonists," he wrote, "… must not be left to suppose that against external aggression Great Britain would not render them the aid due to the dignity of her Crown, and the safety of her subjects in every part of Her Majesty's Dominions; for wherever England extends her sceptre, there, as against the foreign enemy, she pledges the defence of her sword…"

To the Engineers, Lytton issued instructions to be above reproach:

> You are going to a distant country, not, I trust, to fight against men, but to conquer nature; not to besiege cities, but to create them; not to overthrow kingdoms, but to assist in establishing new communications under the sceptre of your own Queen. For these noble objects, you, soldiers of the Royal Engineers, have been especially selected from the ranks of Her Majesty's armies. Wherever you go you carry with you not only English valour and English loyalty, but English intelligence and English skill. Wherever a difficulty is encountered which requires in the soldiers not only courage and discipline, but education and science, sappers and miners, the Sovereign of England turns with confidence to you.

And so the stage was set to create a new colony out of the wilderness. The engineers would build roads, lay out a new capital at New Westminster, survey many townsites, back up colonial authorities when there was any threat of insurrection, and eventually join the ranks of the immigrants who settled in BC.

Colonel Moody proved to be a difficult ally for Governor Douglas. The two men disagreed on the appropriate site for the new capital: Douglas wanted Derby, on the south bank of the Fraser River near Fort Langley, and had it surveyed. Moody rejected the site because it could not be easily defended against an American attack. Douglas wisely deferred to Moody's judgement. And while Moody did not stay in the colony when the engineers' work was done, he left the province a respected official and, along with Douglas, a central figure in the creation of British Columbia.

The other pivotal person among the new ruling elite was Matthew Baillie Begbie, soon to be Judge Begbie, sometimes known as "the hanging judge." While there were other magistrates in the province, Begbie came to symbolize British justice and the rule of law in the mining camps.

Begbie was well versed in the law and had been a successful lawyer in London before his appointment. But more of his rulings were based on common sense than strict interpretation of the law. And his courtroom addresses were notorious for their bluntness. After one jury brought in a verdict that disappointed him, he turned to the accused and declared: "You deserve to be hanged! Had the jury performed their duty I might now have the painful satisfaction of condemning you to death, and you, gentlemen of the jury, you are a pack of Dalles [Oregon] horse thieves, and permit me to say, it would give me great pleasure to see you hanged, each and every one of you, for declaring a murderer guilty only of manslaughter."

Judge Matthew Baillie Begbie's name has become synonymous with the dispensing of justice in the goldfields. He arrived in BC in 1858, held court in various locations around the colony and developed a reputation as the "hanging judge"— an exaggeration that he may have encouraged. *British Columbia Archives E-07841*

Judge Begbie on Natives

We found almost everywhere Indians willing to labour hard for wages and bargaining acutely, perfectly acquainted with gold dust and the minute weights used for measuring one or two dollars worth. These circumstances are inconsistent with an utter heedlessness for the next day's provisions. It was the uniform practice of store-keepers to entrust these Indians with their goods (for transport) and with provisions for their sustenance. Thefts were said to be unknown and great care was taken of their burdens. My impression of the Indian population is that they have far more natural intelligence, honesty and good manners than the lowest class, say the agricultural and mining population of any European country I ever visited, England included.

—*Charles Perkins, "When the Judge Came Riding"*

On another occasion, Begbie was said to have uttered these words to a group of miners: "Now boys, there must be no shooting, for if there is shooting, there will surely be hanging." Some historians believe the speaker was actually Peter O'Reilly, one of Douglas's peacekeepers in the Kootenays.

Whatever the case, Begbie's liberal use of invective is probably behind his reputation as the hanging judge. Certainly he used the gallows no more than any other frontier judge. And his actual record reveals a surprising streak of leniency. Fewer than 30 men were hanged under his jurisdiction. There could have been many more, but for at least ten of them, Begbie successfully argued for reprieves.

Murder in Cantwell's Bar

Judge Matthew Baillie Begbie's legacy can be measured in one of two ways. The first, favoured by weekend newspaper editions, recalls "the hanging judge," undemocratic, given to outbursts of anger, contemptuous and legally "challenged." The second must be sought in circumstance, in Begbie's personal letters and his accomplishments, and in the series of claim-jumping cases where the judge had recourse to the principles of equity, which confounded the "possession is nine points of the law" school of claim jumpers.

Matthew Begbie in his late thirties, when he was appointed chief justice of the colony, was extraordinarily cultured, urbane and courtly, a man fit to walk and talk with poets. With all his fine manners and good humour went a constitution like an ox, an inflexible dedication and a will of rawhide. In a formal sense he was also probably the best-educated man west of the Rocky Mountains on either side of the international boundary.

The shack town of Derby, three miles downstream from Fort Langley, was the gathering place for newcomers from California. Everyone who arrived was in a hurry to move on, so the place had a neglected look, as though it might disappear without regret—as indeed it did a few years later.

Cantwell's Place was the only structure of any consequence in Derby. It was a large building, about 9 by 15 metres, built of logs and rough lumber with two doors and no windows. Inside, lanterns hung from the rafters. A chest-high counter at one end of the room was used as a bar. A long roulette table ran along one side. On the other side there were round tables for card players and a dilapidated billiard table brought up from San Francisco. The lamps made pools of light and sent grotesque shadows dancing around the walls. At the end opposite the bar stood a rack of miner's clothes and a few bolts of cotton and canvas. Over this was a hand-lettered sign: DRYGOODS.

A man was shot to death in this room one night, or one day—no one was sure what time the shooting took place, for it was always more or less night in Cantwell's Place. There were 30 or 40 men in the saloon at the time.

Judge Begbie presided over this trial, his first case, in the trading room at Fort Langley. Ogilvie, one of the Hudson's Bay men, was the foreman, but Begbie insisted that since the

Derby's place in the limelight was short-lived. The town was Governor James Douglas's choice for colonial capital, but the Royal Engineers vetoed his plan and chose New Westminster instead. Derby is still part of a favourite BC walking trail. *City of Vancouver Archives Out P825N381*

accused was an American, half of the jury should be his compatriots. The incidents of the trial related here are taken, a good deal less than verbatim, from the judge's desk book.

The first witness was a man by the name of Brown who had been on the river for six months and was a friend of the dead man, Hartwell. They had been sitting together at the foot of the roulette table when Hartwell went to the bar and stood there arguing loudly with Neil. Something was said about two or three dollars.

Hartwell walked over to Brown and said. "Give me your pistol. Would you see me insulted when he's armed and I'm not?"

Brown, without any remonstrance, handed over his pistol, both barrels fully loaded.

Neil stepped away from the bar and the men faced each other about eight metres apart. Brown heard two shots with no time to cock between them, so he surmised each of the men had shot once. Then Neil shouted, "Murder!" and shot twice more.

Hartwell lay sprawled on the floor. He had been shot with three bullets.

Brown looked around for his pistol but could not find it.

Neil said, "It's over there by the door. He must have thrown it."

Brown found that only one barrel had been fired. Neil had not been touched.

Another witness, Lewis, the bartender, said he had heard the argument and had told Neil not to make a disturbance. He saw Hartwell walk down the room to Brown and get the pistol. Hartwell was about eight metres away when he raised the pistol with both hands. Neil said, "Shoot if you want." Lewis thought Hartwell lowered the gun before he fired and the bullet went into the floor, but Neil fired at almost the same time and then twice more. Hartwell was dead.

By the time the trial was over, judge and jury both knew that Neil was a deadly gunfighter and that Hartwell, for all his foolish bravado, was no real threat. However, the jury would likely have acquitted Neil if Begbie had not prodded them to a verdict he thought more just. They came back once, saying they could not arrive at a decision. The Americans were all for an acquittal, because in California, whenever two armed men faced each other—whatever the circumstances—a shooting was always done in self-defence.

"I found it necessary to withdraw from the jury all the capital parts of the case. The jury were a remarkably intelligent lot. I charged them pretty strongly for manslaughter; in fact it appeared to me a case too clear for them to require to turn around in their box. They could not come to any decisions on the evidence whether Neil had retreated as far as he could previously to firing which last was not to be wondered at, seeing that there was no evidence that he showed any willingness for the combat, but that he expressed his readyness, 'If that's your game', he cried, 'I'm in!' and advanced firing bullet after bullet with fatal precision, drilling the deceased at every shot."

Judge Begbie received the verdict late at night, saying that he did so only to relieve the discomfort of the foreman, who was suffering from a bad boil, otherwise he would have left them all night without coal, food or candle to help them make up their minds. Sometimes Begbie made those harsh-sounding remarks from the bench. They were remembered and repeated to form part of the legend and to give credence to the disparagement that followed him for years. There is no record that he ever did commit a harsh or unfeeling act, and it is more likely that such things were said to hide a strain of gentleness within him that he felt was scarcely fitting to his task.

After passing sentence for a term of imprisonment, the judge said:

Prisoner I am glad your case has drawn to this temporary Courtroom so many of your compatriots and I want to say a word to you and your friends who are within the sound of my voice. I am given to understand that miners in the western states think they can govern their country by the Bowie Knife and Colt's revolver. But that will not be tolerated for a moment under the British flag, where a man who behaves himself doesn't need and will not be allowed to carry these deadly weapons at all. Let me tell you what liberty means in this country. It means you can do what the law allows to be done; beyond that is licence and you cannot go in that direction. I have been appointed a judge to administer British law and I warn you all that anyone who comes before me, and who is guilty, will be severely dealt with by this court.

—*"When the Judge Came Riding" (unpublished manuscript), by Charles Perkins, a retired lawyer who lives in Langley*

The miners certainly knew Begbie, at least by reputation. He made a regular circuit through the goldfields whether there were cases to be heard or not. Begbie loved the British Columbia wilderness and was always pushing for another road trip. He described the BC back country in glowing terms in his diary and letters, and made many recommendations to the governor on how services could be improved. He liked to bake bread for his colleagues on the trail and was always full of stories and gossip.

Begbie on the Bench

When a man was sandbagged on the trail into Quesnel from the creeks a miner was charged with highway robbery and seemed sure to be convicted until the jury surprisingly acquitted him. Judge Begbie released him, saying, "Prisoner, you have escaped your just desserts. The jury in their wisdom have decreed that you are not guilty of sand-bagging that poor fellow, so you are free to go." And then he added, "I devoutly hope the next man you sand-bag will be one of the jury."
—*Cariboo Sentinel*

Homestead Murder

My great-great-grandmother, Ann Clinaculwhat Clark, was one of the first Songhees women to formally marry a European in Victoria, in the Colony of Vancouver Island in 1861. Very little information is recorded about women such as Ann. Her husband came to Canada from Scotland because of the fur trade, or perhaps the Gold Rush, but whatever the reasons, the family didn't venture very far during the short time they were together.

Ann and her family homesteaded on a 160-acre [64-hectare] allotment on Mayne Island, on today's Active Pass, and it was she who discovered her husband's body there in 1870. He had been murdered. She said that "he was at work making shakes," and "I saw his body lying there, was afraid, and ran away" to give the alarm. Ann needed to travel across Active Pass to Galiano Island in the only transportation available, a canoe or a rowboat, to get help. Huge ferries travel through this narrow channel now, and for anyone who has gone through Active Pass, it is almost impossible to describe how horrendous her experience must have been when she made that hideous discovery and went for help.

Ann was left alone with three small children. The murder trial was conducted by Judge Matthew Baillie Begbie. Six generations later, the records are a fascinating read. In Begbie's trial notes, Ann bears witness to the violent details of her husband's demise, and Begbie seems to regret that this trial must end in a hanging. The evidence against the accused was suspicious at best, but the murder of a settler wouldn't be tolerated. Tragic in its detail, the trial record is nevertheless a tiny glimpse into a time of extremes, and offers rare information about the life of one nearly invisible First Nations woman of the time.

Sadly, Ann lived only until 1871. Her infant son later became my great-grandfather, Fred Clark. He was born into dire circumstances, but lived to be nearly a hundred years old.
—*Susan Garcia, Vancouver*

There was bloodshed in frontier British Columbia, but the colony's reputation for "peace, order and good government" was not just legend. Douglas wisely appointed gold commissioners around the province to collect licence fees, register claims, settle disputes under $200, and serve as land commissioners, revenue collectors, Indian agents and coroners. Some of them, like Peter O'Reilly, William Cox and John Carmichael Haynes, became almost as well known as Begbie. They were sometimes forced to make up the rules as they went along. Cox is credited with resolving one claim dispute by having the rivals run a race from the courthouse to the claim they were fighting over. In *British Columbia: A History*, Margaret Ormsby writes that Cox once used his fists to convince an American that he did have the authority to act as a revenue officer.

Begbie and his team of commissioners may have cultivated their image as tough guys, because in the goldfields they had only their moral authority to back them up against guns and knives. But like Cox, Begbie did not shy away from threats of force. He wrote to Governor Douglas in 1859: "My idea is that, if a man insists upon behaving like a brute, after fair warning, and won't quit the Colony, beat him like a brute and flog him."

When the gold rush was starting to run out of steam and Begbie was thinking about his legacy, he wrote:

> The criminal statistics of the colony appear highly favorable when placed beside those of any other gold-producing country. Crimes of violence are extremely rare; highway robberies almost unknown... stabbing and pistoling, so common in the adjacent territories, are almost unheard of on the British side of the line; although the population is composed of the same ingredients. I should be sorry to have it supposed that I am vain enough to attribute this most fortunate state of things purely to myself. I know what is due to the Executive, in all its branches, particularly to the excellent and invaluable magistrates, who, scattered at great intervals, generally with only two or three constables apiece, enforce observance of the laws almost entirely by their moral influence.

Mount Brew

This point south of Lillooet was named after Chartres Brew, appointed the first Inspector of Police in the colony of British Columbia in 1858. Later he served as gold commissioner and judge.

Preserving the Peace

"Come here, please," Chief Inspector Chartres Brew called loudly to the man shovelling far out on a sandbar in the Fraser River. "Are you Herbert Hockings?"

"Why? And who are you?" the man shouted belligerently, then strode towards the bank.

"You can handle Hockings' bilking of Charley," Brew informed Peter O'Reilly, who, if he passed Brew's assessment of his abilities, was to be appointed one of BC's gold commissioners.

Yesterday, Charley Joe, a Sto:lo, whose people had lived in the Fraser Canyon for centuries, had complained that Hockings had not paid him for being paddled up the river. Instead, once the miner had his heavy pack on the bank, he had ordered Charley to leave or he would sink his canoe and shoot him. As the angry Sto:lo paddled back down the fast current, he decided that he would probably have to kill Hockings. But, first, he would talk with Brew, who had often told him when he rode in Charley's canoe that Queen's men are supposed to help an Indian man as much as a white man. Maybe Brew or one of his men could get his pay.

Fortunately, the head of the BC colonial constabulary had just arrived at the Yale detachment. In a muddle of Chinook and English, Charley Joe related what had happened. Brew decided that he and O'Reilly would locate Hockings, one less task for the three tired Yale constables, who were supposedly keeping law and order for the 20,000 miners scattered along the Fraser between Hope and Boston Bar.

Brew knew how overworked they were. Only last week, he had again pointed that out to Governor James Douglas. When Brew had said, "Sir, each constable is just one man...," the wily old governor had interrupted, "Well, Brew, so am I. But I certainly do not let that hamper me."

Instead, Brew had learned, Douglas relentlessly dictated his expectations and hoped they would be patched in, as best as possible. O'Reilly was a prime example. The governor had told the lad he was hired, almost as he got off the boat from Ireland, on the condition that he might be fired by Brew, if he was not found suitable. Which was why the chief inspector and the probationary gold commissioner were now miles above Yale, Brew assessing O'Reilly even as they waited for Hockings.

"Take over, Mr. O'Reilly," he repeated, as the miner waded through the shallows and approached them.

"This is Chief Inspector Brew and I am O'Reilly. Please show us your miner's licence," the novice ordered.

The massive man handed over a much-folded piece of paper. "Here. As it says, I am Hockings. What do you want?" He smelled fetid, his hair was as matted as his scraggly beard, his tattered jacket had split across his bulging shoulders while his pants were encrusted with mud and other matter.

O'Reilly announced with full authority, "Harold Hockings, unless you immediately pay the $20 you owe Charley Joe for your canoe trip, you are under arrest."

"That dirty Indian!" Hocking spat and swore.

"We'll have none of that, man. Act civilized and pay up," O'Reilly ordered. "Or you will be in jail by nightfall."

Hockings paid. O'Reilly wrote him a receipt.

As they rode away, Chief Inspector Brew summarized, "Certainly one of the lower class miners, wasn't he? Another x-welitems, just as Charley Joe called him, Gold Commissioner O'Reilly. That is a Sto:lo insult, it translates into 'hungry people.' Or, as I interpret it, greedy men."

—*Lynne Stonier-Newman, Friends of the BC Archives, from her book about O'Reilly, to be published by Touchstone in spring 2008*

So the early gold rush era passed in British Columbia without much violence. The Canyon War and the later Chilcotin War can be considered exceptions. As the Fraser rush gave way to the Cariboo rush, the administration of justice was refined, and the miners gained confidence in the ability of the legal system to solve their grievances. Yale did not develop into another vigilante town like San Francisco, and Barkerville was no Deadwood. Instead, a multicultural society grew up on the frontier with an unusual level of civility for the times.

4

OUTSCOURINGS OF
THE WORLD
A Multicultural Society on the Pacific

While some of our history books might paint a different picture, the British Columbia of 1858 was as multicultural as the province is today. And it wasn't by accident. The gold rush drew people from around the world, and Governor James Douglas encouraged immigration by blacks (most of them American), Europeans and Chinese.

Before 1858, about 700 non-Native and mixed race people lived in the British Pacific, most of them on Vancouver Island not far from Fort Victoria. The Native population at the time has been estimated at around 70,000, most of them living undisturbed on the mainland. The 30,000 miners who flooded into the goldfields in that first year threatened to overwhelm the fur-trade culture, and turn fur-trade country into another California.

Blacks

Starting with the first ship that brought miners from California, the *Commodore*, there were some surprises. Black settlers who feared repressive measures even in the western states saw British Columbia as a sanctuary from slavery. Governor Douglas wanted them to come north. His own mother was "coloured"—a Creole woman from British Guiana, where Douglas was born. But there was more than blood motivating him. He needed settlers who shared his wariness of the United States. And blacks from California had every reason to resist an expansion of American territory north of the 49th parallel.

California was not a slave state, but legislators there were enacting discriminatory legislation against blacks. The state was home to many southerners who supported slavery, and the Civil War was only a few years away. Neither North nor South had yet embraced the abolition of slave holding. Douglas saw his opportunity and extended full citizenship rights to black immigrants to attract them northward.

About 800 blacks came to British Columbia in that first year. The deciding factor may have been the arrest of Archy Lee, a fugitive slave who was apprehended in California in 1858, and whose story was followed closely by the California press. This article appeared in the *Sacramento Daily Union* on January 8, 1858:

A colored boy, aged about 18 years, who was claimed as a slave by a man named Stovall, a citizen of Mississippi, was arrested as a fugitive by Officer Coons at the Hackett House. From what we can learn of the case, Arch [better known as Archy] left Mississippi against his will and accompanied his young master Stovall to the state as a body servant... Stovall started for the Bay on Monday last with the view of returning to the East, but discovered en route that Arch had given him the slip. Arch contends that he did not wish to leave him, having always been well treated by him, but not finding him on the boat, left in search of him, and was unable to return in time to rejoin him. He also alleges that he does not wish to return to Mississippi. Whether or not he will be compelled to do so is to be decided probably today by Judge Robinson. This, we believe, is the first case of this kind ever broached in California.

Lee's master brought him into the "free territory" knowingly, and that may have helped the courts to decide to free Archy. But Lee and free blacks could see clouds on the horizon,

Opposite: Town of Hope, shown in the *Canadian Illustrated News*, May 18, 1872.

James Douglas, keenly aware of American territorial ambitions, encouraged the new black population in Victoria to organize into a militia for extra protection. This photograph of the Victoria Black Rifle Corps was taken in the 1860s.
British Columbia Archives C-06124

and many decided to leave for Vancouver Island. An account in the *Alta California*, one of the leading newspapers of the day, described their departure:

About one hundred and fifty Negroes, among whom the celebrated "Archy" figured conspicuously, were on board the Commodore, intending, as they allege, to colonize in the British possession. A number of Chinese also assisted to make up the motley group... these seemed to be genuine miners from the [California] interior, and some of them still carried the mud of their diggings on their clothes and boots. Several had well worn mining tools with them, showing that they were no raw recruits. On the starboard side of the after cabin was posted a rough map of the Fraser River, and the gold region, around which all interested crowd were gathered, some looking over the shoulder of others, and anxiously listening to one who pointed out the route...

Douglas did not just encourage the blacks to immigrate; he encouraged them to integrate. He enlisted a number of blacks to become Victoria's first policemen—a move that was less than popular with American miners in the city, some of whom were militant supporters of the Confederacy. Douglas also encouraged the black population to form their own militia, which he was prepared to use against the Americans should the cry of "Fifty-four forty or Fight" get louder.

A correspondent to the *San Francisco Bulletin* wrote disparagingly about Douglas's motives: "The [Hudson's Bay] Company do not want to see a white man arrive at Vancouver Island—least of all, the smart, enterprising Yankee... This may account, in some degree, for the patronage which Gov. Douglas is said to have so largely extended towards the coloured people who lately left this city."

Those early black British Columbians became farmers and businessmen, barbers and dentists in gold rush towns (for some reason, barbers seemed to develop an expertise in dentistry), teachers and lawyers. The early years were good for the black community. They suffered discrimination at the hands of American southerners in the colonies, but Douglas's government was supportive. In addition to recruiting them for police work, Douglas hired black labourers to build his Harrison route to the goldfields. It wasn't until the Civil War period and the end of the Douglas administration that a new "British" brand of racism took root and the early dream of equality faded away.

Europeans, Central Americans, South Americans

Douglas also wanted a broad mix of European and other cultures, people who would be different enough that they would be unlikely to group together into a pro-American block. He was glad to see a large German contingent, as well as French, Scandinavians, Slavs, Mexicans, South Americans and West Indians. These people were better candidates to become "British subjects." Like the black settlers, many found their way to British Columbia by way of California, where their prospects were now equally bad. Mexicans, Peruvians and native Spanish-Americans were leading players in the California goldfields—they were skilled gold prospectors. But the US miners dismissed them as "greasers." One Scotsman captured the mood there when he wrote to a friend: "[The goldfields] are loaded to the muzzle with vagabonds from every quarter of the globe, scoundrels from nowhere, rascals from Oregon, pickpockets from New York, accomplished gentlemen from Europe, interlopers from Lima and Chile, Mexican thieves, gamblers of no particular spot, and assassins manufactured in hell for the purpose of converting highways and byways into theaters of blood."

An economic recession hit California in 1857. "San Francisco is at this moment crowded with more unemployed... in proportion to her population, than any other city in the Union," one newspaper reported. The result was a general stampede to the Fraser River, summed up in a ditty of the time, "The New-Yellow Fever":

What's the matter? What a clatter!
All seem Fraser-river mad.
On they're rushing, boldly pushing.
Old and young, both good and bad;

Lawyers, doctors, judges, proctors.
Politicians, stout and thin;
Some law-makers, some law-breakers.
Rogues as well as honest men.
Hurly-burly! What a hurry!

All confusion! 'Tis a sin
To see the sacrifice they're making
For the Frazer river tin.

Women of the Fraser River Gold Rush

Whether they were First Nations or European, the women who took part in the Fraser River gold rush had difficulty adapting to the rough-and-tumble environment. Native women were the most vulnerable—prospectors from California brought with them racist attitudes that alarmed Governor James Douglas. To ensure good relations between whites and Natives, Douglas visited Hope and Yale in June 1858 to warn the miners that under British law, men and women of all races were treated equally.

Native women assisted in the gold rush by packing goods, guiding newcomers in canoes and gathering food to sell to the miners. They also took part in gold mining. At Yale, a Hudson's Bay clerk named Ovid Allard protected his Native wife Justine from unwanted attention, but she in turn had to keep an eye on her marriageable daughter. According to Donald Hauka's book *McGowan's War*, the notorious California prospector Ned McGowan said that the pretty girl was courted by three men: Justice of the Peace George Perrier, the physician Dr. Max Fifer, and "an Englishman." Justine was relieved when her daughter chose William Kirby (possibly the Englishman McGowan mentioned).

Twenty-year-old Georgina Henrietta Alford arrived at Yale in the fall of 1858. She soon became pregnant by her lover, Peter Brunton Whannell, whom Douglas had appointed justice of the peace and postmaster for Yale. Douglas was unaware of Whannell's bad reputation in Australia, where he had abandoned a pregnant wife and numerous children in order to elope with Georgina. Whannell lasted a year before being fired. He and Georgina returned to San Francisco, and eventually to Australia and India.

Johanna McGuire was Irish, and likely also a bootlegger. D.W. Higgins, who worked as an agent at Yale, described her as having a dual personality: polite and well-spoken when sober, but wild and foul-mouthed when drinking. She followed the gold rush from Yale to the Cariboo and appeared before magistrates numerous times. One magistrate, Henry Maynard Ball, claimed that she came from a wealthy family in Ireland. Johanna's life came to a sad end in December 1864 during a drinking spree, when she was beaten by her partner, Ned Whitney. She refused to lay charges with the Victoria police and subsequently died of her injuries.

Malvina Toy had enough gumption for ten women. She emigrated from Cornwall to the United States with her husband Peter, a hard-rock miner. Peter found work with many of his countrymen in the lead mines of Wisconsin and the gold mines of Grass Valley, California. In 1859, Malvina, Peter and their young daughter Mary Louise arrived at Hope to take part in the Fraser River gold rush. Most of the miners had found their way north to the Cariboo by this time, so Peter left Malvina in the care of his Cornish friend James Uren and headed for the Interior. Peter never returned, and Malvina and James became partners. Jane Elizabeth Uren was born at Hope in 1861, possibly the first white baby of the gold rush. The family moved to

Clinton soon afterwards and opened a hotel. By 1872, Malvina also owned a pack train that delivered goods from Yale to Barkerville. During this time she gave birth to four more children, but the couple did not marry until 1882, ten years after Peter Toy was presumed drowned in northern British Columbia. They spent their latter days at Savona, where they ran another hotel.
—*Marie Elliot, Friends of the BC Archives*

Growing Up in Multicultural Yale

Grace Gertrude Smith, nee Garraway, was the daughter of Gertrude Jenny Castle and Douglas Garraway. Grace was born—weighing in at 11 lbs., 12 oz.—on a sunny day at Boothroyd Siding, which no longer exists, in a CPR sidecar near Yale, BC, on April 7, 1915. She died March 15, 2007. Her mother's parents, Martin Castle and Monique Etasse, who were both half-Coast Salish, were from Victoria, BC. Martin had owned one of the first bakeries in Victoria, and Monique, aka Monica, had served as the first Native interpreter of Aboriginal dialects for the Victoria courts. Grace's mother Gertie was born in Yale in 1898. She was raised there, and was sent to St. Ann's Academy in New Westminster to be raised and educated by the nuns when her mother died early.

Grace was raised in Vancouver but spent summers visiting her cousins in Yale. She fondly remembers her friends—white and Chinese children and a few on-reserve Natives, who were considered by the others to have a lower social status. She spoke of the On Lee family, who owned one of the two general stores in Yale. Kim On Lee was her mother's friend, and she remembers the other family members. The elder men would sit in the porch entry smoking opium pipes for relaxation, and the mother would not do any housework, as it was beneath her position in a wealthy family. She dressed traditionally, had very long manicured fingernails and small, bound feet, and was expected to do very little. One of the On Lees' sons, who had a long ponytail as was the custom for Chinese boys and young men, was the subject of much discussion when some of his white schoolmates cut off his ponytail as a prank. This brought much embarrassment and disgrace to the family. Mom's mother learned how to cook some Chinese food dishes and taught Grace the same.

Grace remembers picking cherries and selling them in newspaper cones propped upright in cedar baskets woven by Natives. As children, Grace and her cousin would dress up and walk onto the train when it stopped in Yale and offer passengers the cherry cones for 5 cents each. Grace's mother called her *oolan*, apparently a Chinese word meaning "earth-mother," because she was always gardening.

Most of Gertie and Grace's male relatives worked for the railway, on the CPR trains. Her great-uncle, August Castle, purchased the home of Andrew Onderdonk, chief engineer for the CPR, and August lived there for most of his life. He died at the age of 109 in Surrey, BC, and his house was declared a BC provincial museum in the1970s.
—*Merle Smith, Coquitlam*

Aboard the immigrant ships, San Francisco toughs spent their time physically abusing and robbing black and Chinese passengers. The rowdies would force their way on-board without paying and then extort provisions from the other passengers. In his book *The Fraser Mines Vindicated* (1858, the first book published on Vancouver Island), Alfred Waddington dismissed many of the newcomers as the worst sort: "speculators of every kind... bummers, bankrupts and brokers... gamblers, swindlers, thieves, drunkards and jail birds... in short, the outscourings of a population containing... the outscourings of the world."

Hope

This community was established in 1848–49 by the Hudson's Bay Company. The "hope"—which was realized—was that an all-British route could be found to connect Fort Kamloops with Fort Langley.

They came to British Columbia from all over: "Americans were in the majority," Waddington wrote. "Then followed Germans, French and Chinese. Next came Italians, Spaniards and Poles [as well as] Russians, Swedes, Danes, Norwegians, Austrians. English, Scotch and Irish..."

Kanaka Bar

Gold seekers from Hawaii washed for gold at this site in the Fraser Canyon.

Hawaiians

The Hawaiians, or Kanakas, started to arrive as early as 1811 to work in the fur trade. They were discouraged by European control of land in Hawaii and threatened by European diseases. Kanakas represented about 10 percent of the non-Native population in the British Pacific in the 1850s. They helped clear land at Fort Langley and formed their own team to build the Harrison route to the goldfields in 1858.

My Mysterious Great-Great-Grandma

At the time of the 1858 gold rush, my large, extended family had already begun setting down roots in BC. Around 1848–1850, two of my Hawaiian great-great-grandfathers arrived in BC with the Hudson's Bay Company, working as seamen, longshoremen and labourers. One married a First Nations woman and started a family in Vancouver. Almost everyone's original Hawaiian name or First Nations name was lost or changed along the way.

Another Kanaka, as the Hawaiians were called, was possibly a Hudson's Bay Company employee whose daughter—Theresa Berra-Berra, my great-great-grandmother—was born around 1850 and grew up in Fort Langley area. Theresa's place of birth and her parents' names are unclear, but the women on her side of our family celebrated being Hawaiian, and still carry on the tradition of the hula. Aunts and great-aunts and grandmothers have taught the children to dance and to hold feasts and luaus, and continue to do so right up to the present day. Family stories tell how Theresa had fresh Hawaiian poi sent up to her from the ships that arrived in port. One aunt also remembered a "royal entourage" of Hawaiian visitors crossing the bridge to visit this same grandma in her South Westminster home 100 years ago.

Theresa married a black immigrant from the eastern USA who was said to have a Tahitian father. Her husband worked as an oyster cultivator in the White Rock area in 1874 and 1875, then as a barber in Yale in 1881. Only two of their four children survived past their teens—the other two drowned. Generations were only 14 or 15 years apart at that time. There were lots of children, and everyone—even children and teens—toiled hard on the farms and on the river, fishing or trapping for furs. The gold rush meant there was lots of work along the Fraser River, and the fur trade was dwindling.

As far as I know, none of my family caught the fever for gold. I heard that some Hawaiians panned for gold at Kanaka Bar in the Fraser Canyon, but I believe our family was not dreaming of these riches. They were weaving their roots with the First Nations, carrying on with some of their traditions, bringing Hawaiian traditions here, living always by the rivers and the inlets, and starting new traditions of their own. My great-grandma worked in the first BC fish cannery near New Westminster, and five generations followed every season until the canneries closed in the 1990s. Also, like the early Hawaiians, my grandpa, my father, many uncles and cousins worked their whole lives as longshoremen, and some continue to do so today.

The family of my great-great-grandma, Theresa Berra-Berra Browne, merged with the Clark family in about 1890, and a Clark married a Garcia in 1920. I am carrying on the story-sharing tradition, probing our past and enjoying the mysteries, digging for my own kind of gold: the stories, given out in pieces, to this one and that.

—*Susan Garcia, Vancouver*

Legend has it that a Hawaiian man may have been responsible for the first major discovery of gold on the mainland. An article in the *San Francisco Bulletin* in the spring of 1858 reported:

Wm Peon and Antoine Plant, two half-breeds, resident of Colville Valey, arrived in the Dalles [Oregon], lately, with about fifty ounces of gold, which they stated they had procured in the Shuswap country... They had about as much more dust which they had disposed of to Mr. McDonald, in charge of the Hudson's Bay Company, Fort Colville. They represent the Indians as quite hostile to Americans, and would not advise any venture into the country unless in large parties—fifty at least—well armed. The gold they washed principally from the banks of the river, and it was everywhere abundant, wherever there was earth to hold it.

This was the Nicomen River discovery, one of the major gold finds that drew prospectors to the Fraser and Thompson Rivers. William Peon was Hawaiian according to Daniel Marshall of the University of Victoria. Peon had been employed by the North West Company and was believed to be married to an Okanagan Indian woman. His enthusiastic reports of riches in the BC Interior started the rush of Washington and Oregon miners to the region.

Most Hawaiians intermarried with whites and First Nations people, and became part of the melting pot of colonial culture.

Chinese

Chinese immigrants played a larger and larger role as the gold rush spread. At first they came to California, where, like the blacks, they were not encouraged to share the wealth. In 1848 only a handful of Chinese miners were reported in the state. But within a few years, the numbers had grown to 20,000. They called California the golden mountain, but it was a hostile place. One account from the time reported that a villain by the name of Three-fingered Jack hanged six Chinese men by their pigtails and cut their throats.

Nam Sing, pictured here with some children at Barkerville, was the first Chinese miner in the Cariboo. At the height of the gold rush, the Chinese population in BC was about 7,000. *British Columbia Archives G-03059*

The Chinese Gold Miners

Despite racial prejudice, many white miners tolerated the Chinese, who often worked diggings abandoned by white miners or provided useful services as market gardeners, restaurateurs, launderers and storekeepers. The 1876 report of Oliver Hare, government agent at Forks of Quesnelle (British Columbia, Minister of Mines, Annual Report, 1876, published in 1877, pp. 420–21), reveals prejudice in the use of derisory terms such as "Chinaman," "Celestial" and "John," and in expressions of doubt about their truthfulness. But the report also shows that the Chinese were adaptable, and that contrary to popular opinion, they enjoyed a good standard of living. Hare wrote:

The Chinese… are by nature reticent and untruthful in their answers [about the amount of gold collected], especially when it touches their pockets; this I find to be the case more among new arrivals from California than those who have resided here any length of time… and [who] have found out they are no heavier taxed that the white miner… Owing to the severe cold the river fell unusually low in February and March last, giving the Chinese a good chance for working among reefs and shoals to advantage. They also adopted a new style of mining in the south fork; rafts of logs were moored in the stream on which were generally three Celestials, two of whom had shovels and picks with handles eight to ten feet in length, for scooping up the dirt from the bottom of the river, which the third person passed through his rocker; although a tedious process, they managed to get from three to four dollars per man per diem of only a few hours. I… feel quite safe in stating that at least $3,000 can be added to the estimated yield of the claims…

The Chinese have it all their own way; the white miner seems to have set his face against this part of the country, or rather than take the chances of four dollar diggings he will hunt till he nearly starves searching for better; not so with the Chinaman, if he gets a claim that will pay fair wages he sticks to it, and if it pays better, so much for luck; anyway it is better than running over the country after an uncertainty. Many persons suppose that a Chinaman can afford to work for less wages because his style of living is so much cheaper, but let me tell those persons that John is as fond of good living as they are. When I get to a Chinese cabin I can tell nearly at a glance if the claim pays by the number of oyster, lobster and sardine tins, also China wine and Hennessy brandy bottles lying around their domicile.

[Because of drought last year and flooding this year] many Chinese miners have left for other districts not being able to get work here, but most of them will be back again to winter quarters. The town of the Forks is their general rendezvous; last winter more than two hundred lived there and upon the whole kept themselves very peaceable. I had considerable trouble with gamblers… but succeeded in preventing them carrying on their games publicly. The whole of the trading at the Forks is done by Chinese; there are several good stores there, also two butchers, a blacksmith and a watchmaker; three of the storekeepers have liquor licenses and two of them opium ditto. On Keithley there are six

stores, five of which have liquor licenses. A vast quantity of spirits are consumed among the Chinese but strange to say one never sees a Chinaman intoxicated or quarrelsome in the streets.
—*Patricia Roy, British Columbia Historical Federation*

As they would later do in British Columbia, the Chinese in California worked abandoned claims and made them pay. The work was harder, but once white miners moved on to other claims, there was little resistance to deal with. The Chinese created their own society, a separate society. They preferred opium to alcohol, and their frugality and industry caused resentment among white settlers.

In 1858 and 1859, the Chinese turned their attentions to British Columbia. Governor James Douglas favoured Chinese immigration as part of his strategy to build up the population—numbers were dropping as Americans returned to the United States during the Civil War. By 1860, about 4,000 Asians were living along the Fraser River. They came in groups of 40 or 50 with each ship. "A detachment of thirty Chinese miners arrived yesterday," Douglas wrote in January of that year, "being it is supposed the pioneers of a larger immigration of that people."

The governor's enthusiasm for the new immigrants was not entirely free of the conventional racism. While he welcomed the Chinese as a potential boost to the colonial economy, he also wrote: "They are certainly not a desirable class of people, as a permanent population, but are for the present useful as labourers, and, as consumers, of a revenue-paying character."

Chinese Freemasons Society

The first Chinese came to British Columbia in 1858 to try their luck at hitting the jackpot during the Fraser Valley gold rush. They either came from California or fled China to escape poverty and/or persecution.

They spoke little or no English when they arrived, and they ended up creating their own community through the Chinese Freemasons Society in 1863. This group, the first and oldest Chinese association in Canada, had its roots in China more than 350 years earlier. There, it was a secret society formed to overthrow the Qing Dynasty, which was ruled by the Manchus. The Freemasons tried to drive out these northern invaders and restore the previous Ming Dynasty, but they failed. As punishment, many society members were executed, along with their families. Others escaped to British Columbia to start new lives.

The society's headquarters was in Barkerville, in a small wooden house that is still standing. There Chinese labourers could get help in their own language. When someone new arrived, he went to the society, and members would help him find a job and room and board. The society also had an important function as a banker. Its members couldn't earn interest, but the Freemasons stored their wages for them. When a member died, the society became executors of his estate, arranging and paying for the funeral and sending money to his family in China.

The Freemasons Society, or "tong men min zi dang," spread its network throughout British Columbia, to Quesnel, Victoria, Kamloops, Cumberland, Vernon, Salmon Arm, Revelstoke, Kelowna and Cranbrook, among many other places. More than 60 branches were organized across Canada.

At the time the Chinese Freemasons was established, there were fewer than 2,000 Chinese migrant workers, over 80 percent of whom were members of the society. Some had joined in China, and others applied in BC, through a recommendation by a member. According to Chuck Chang, the current president of the Freemasons, the induction ceremony involved recounting the revolutionary roots of the society, and new members had to swear to obey the rules before becoming "hong men" or freemasons.

The Chinese Freemasons also started the first Chinese newspaper, the *Chinese Daily News*, in 1907. The name was changed to the Chinese Times in 1915, and the paper continued until 1992. Today there are 19 branches of the Freemasons across Canada, with headquarters in Chinatown in Vancouver.

—*Bernice Chan, freelance journalist*

Chapters of the Freemasons Society, founded in BC in 1863, became centres of many Chinese communities in the province. The societies served as employment agencies, banks and social centres. This photograph, taken in 1910, shows a Chinese Freemasons parade in Kamloops. *British Columbia Archives B-03381*

Most Chinese immigrants who came to BC in search of gold were men, and they formed clan associations to overcome their loneliness and isolation. Barkerville had its own Chinatown, which is today preserved at the historic site. *British Columbia Archives A-03783*

In Search of Gold Mountain

- Barkerville's Chinatown was at the "upper" end of town, segregated from the Caucasian community. In it there were a few Chinese miner cabins, the Chinese association or clan buildings, two or three general stores that supplied Chinese goods, a butcher shop, a pig farm, vegetable gardens, an herbalist store, gambling dens, opium dens and other enterprises.

- The discovery of gold encouraged people to migrate to the Interior. Many of them were good citizens, hardworking and law-abiding. They were men and women of every walk of life, different nationalities and diverse careers. Among them, however, were outlaws, gamblers and opportunists who were ill-prepared for the hardships encountered in gold mining. There were also drifters, idlers, vagabonds and ruffians who loitered around the different mining camps. Rev. J.B. Good described Lytton as "a town which cannot be surpassed... for ungodliness, profanity and vice."

- The Chinese miners and immigrants also had their share of social issues—in the mining communities as well as their own. Attempts were made to stop the Chinese miners from reaching the goldfields. On June 16, 1861, the *Colonist* reported attempts "to drive them [the Chinese] back if they venture to ascend the North Fork (at Quesnel Forks). Violence will be used to expel them entirely from the northern digging." In 1869, Chinese miners applied for protection from the governor of BC before they ventured north to the Omenica.

- Chinese daily practices, customs and language were foreign to Caucasians, who often labelled the Chinese as barbarians, heathens, Celestials, Mongolians, Chinks and Chinamen. In Barkerville, Caucasians resented Chinese residents raising poultry and growing vegetables in their backyards, and accused them of corrupting "the drainage with animal and every kind of filth... it was the characteristic of a semi-barbarous race..."
- Most of the Chinese immigrants in that era were single men leaving their wives and families in China, and they were lonely and lost. Fortunately their friendship and kinship with one another motivated them to form clan associations such as the Oylin, the Wong, the Cheng Tsang and others to help one another overcome their feelings of isolation and abandonment, and give them a sense of belonging.
- As much as the early miners attempted to show caring, friendship and companionship to one another, nothing could replace the warmth, love and intimacy of a family. Some early miners lived with First Nations women, especially in the Omenica district. One of them, Chow Ah Lock, lived with Josephine Alexander, a Carrier, at Babine Lake near Fort St. James. Chow so loved Josephine that he decided to stay in Canada. They produced a son, David, who stayed in the region until he passed away at the age of 102 in the late 1990s.
- The flavour of the early gold rush towns has disappeared, except in Barkerville, which is today a living museum... The Chinese Freemason building (Hongman Min Zhi Dang), one of the oldest structures, erected in 1865, is still there. This building has been restored to provide visitors with glimpses of Chinese culture in the early days. A unique Chinese museum in Chinatown in Barkerville also displays a good collection of artifacts and other exhibits related to the life of the early Chinese miners in the region. The archives contain old newspapers and other documents that relate the stories of miners of different nationalities in the Cariboo region.

—from "A Survey of the Gold Rush Era," a paper by Lily Chow, Board of Directors, Barkerville Heritage Trust. The paper was presented at the 12th ACSC bi-annual Canadian Studies Conference & Symposium at Shandong University Canadian Studies Centre, Jinan, China, November 2006.

American miners pushed for special taxes on the Chinese, and the idea of a "pigtail tax" surfaced in BC as it had in California. Governor Douglas resisted. The Chinese in turn provided the desired economic boost, and while they did not participate in the economy to the same extent as white miners, their purchase of mining equipment in Victoria provided a much-needed shot in the arm for local merchants. As American miners left behind claims on the lower Fraser for richer prospects upriver, the Chinese moved in, and made a living working over the same ground.

Judge Matthew Baillie Begbie wrote that in British Columbia, "alone of all mining countries you will find Chinamen, not protected, but standing in no need of protection, unmolested." This was not strictly true. At Rock Creek in the Boundary country, where a gold rush had broken out in 1859, miners tried to exclude Chinese miners from the diggings by establishing their own code of laws.

The cultural practices of the early Chinese brought much suspicion and hostility. Judge Begbie spoke up in their defence:

> Their laws and customs of marriage and divorce, as in all non-Christian nations are widely different from ours. They are much more simple and arbitrary. A wife is usually purchased in a very direct way, without any of the circumlocution which too often veils similar transactions among whites [Begbie was a lifelong bachelor]. Divorces are effected by mere expressions of will. A miner who feels no shame in purchasing the possession of a female for a single night for $20.00, is scandalized when a Chinaman pays $500.00 for the possession of a female for six months, or until they disagree. No disgust is felt by Europeans when parents make a sine qua non on consenting to their daughter's marriage that the husband shall settle ten or twenty thousand dollars upon her; but it is infamous if a Chinaman purchases the consent of parents or guardians for one thousand dollars.

Begbie also appreciated that the Chinese were law-abiding residents. Only three Chinese were convicted of murder during the colonial period. One was hanged, but Begbie pressed for reprieves for the other two.

Lost in the Crowd

"Never perhaps was there so large an immigration in so short a time into so small a place," wrote Alfred Waddington (in *Fraser Mines Vindicated*, 1858) about the gold rush to BC beginning in 1858 and extending through the early 1860s. Of the 30,000 or more new arrivals, some came in groups but most were on their own and could become lost in the crowd.

Many men simply disappeared from view. The route to the diggings ran through unmarked terrain of dense forest, precipices and treacherous bodies of water. R. Byron Johnson wrote, in *Very Far West Indeed:* "We soon found ourselves in the quandary of not knowing where to go; one advised one thing, one another, and a third another, all equally certain to be 'a dead thing,' until we were fairly puzzled." Another prospective miner, J.J. Benjamin, mused: "Will the number ever be known of those who met death in that dangerous [Fraser] river or on its inhospitable shores?" Some men wore out, particularly as the gold rush moved north into the Cariboo. "Number of men on foot passed during afternoon, blanket on back, seeming halting & footsore, unsuccessful miners on way back I presume," Walter Cheadle wrote in his journal in 1863. The wealth acquired by the lucky few disoriented others, who, as Donald Fraser wrote in the *Times,* "lost their time, and their strength and health in their restless wanderings." In only a few cases was a man able to alert others to his likely fate, as when a party of miners "observed a handkerchief hanging to a tree." Going closer, they reported discovering "the decomposed remains of a man wrapped up in a blanket, his head on a log, and close by his side a tin mug, with the following words faintly scratched on it: Donald Munro; lost in the wood; is from Inverness, Sct, b, Jun 1825" (*British Colonist).*

Other men chose to lose themselves in the crowd. Only because he died accidentally and an inquest was held do we know about one man's attempt to reinvent himself. Edward Brande Fisher was a genteel young Englishman with an inheritance sufficient for him to book "First Class Cabin Passage" to British Columbia, but instead of making for the diggings wooed and wed a young Aboriginal woman with whom he settled down on Piers Island not that far from Victoria. At first "dearest Teddy" deflected his mother's entreaties that he "tell us more what you do," but then, her letters attest, he gave up writing at all. The small gilt-edged leather notebook found on his body contains unsent pencilled drafts and also, tucked in it, his mother's increasingly desperate entreaties to let her know "how do you manage your farm—have you any one living with you." Establishment London and British Columbia of the gold rush could not be reconciled, and young Fisher simply disengaged. His mother likely learned of his death through the colonial governor of Vancouver Island, to whom she had sent her last letter so "that I may be sure it reaches you."

Most families left behind were not so fortunate. Notices routinely placed in the newspapers, such as these two appearing on May 1, 1860, in the *British Colonist*, testify to the ambiguity that marked many miners' lives:

Information Wanted—Robert, James or William Dugan, late of Aus, John Wilson would like to hear from you. John Wilson, Cooper, San Francisco, CA

Information wanted of Felix Hagan or John Quinn, who left Prairie City, Sacramento Co, CA, for Fraser R, Jun 1858. Was last seen Apr 1, 1859 on the forks of Fraser and Thompson, going to either the Fountain or Canoe diggings. Any information of them will be thankfully received by Charles Hagan.

Two years later, on November 3, 1862, it was a wife—more likely a widow—who pleaded for information:

Information wanted of the whereabouts of Joseph Giles, n/o Plymouth, Eng, who came to Victoria in HBC steamer Labouchere as butcher, 4 years ago. His wife is most anxious to hear from him, if living or dead; Nov 6—We are informed that Joseph Giles was drowned in Swift R in 1861. He was in a dugout canoe.

The gold rush needs to be remembered, not just from the perspective of those who survived to tell their stories but also those who by choice or chance got lost in the crowd.

—*Jean Barman, professor emeritus in the Department of Educational Studies at the University of BC and the author of numerous books, including the award-winning* Stanley Park's Secret. *For more on Edward Brande Fisher, see below, and see Barman's* Maria Mahoi of the Islands.

Tragedy in Cowichan Bay

In December 1862, at 20 years of age, my great-great-grandfather Edward Brande Fisher left London, England, for (as he put it) "the diggings." With his inheritance he bought a first class ticket, and he embarked on his journey with 40 cubic feet (1.2 cubic metres) of luggage and a line of credit for £500.

Once he was in Victoria, his plans changed. He pre-empted land on Piers Island, near today's Swartz Bay ferry terminal on Vancouver Island, and later 60 hectares near Cowichan Bay.

Fisher received letters from London, but like many young men, he never took time to write his mother—who admonished him for not writing. In her letters she warned him against spending foolishly, reminded him of life's dangers and sent updates on family matters. They are warm letters, expressive of a loving mother.

Fisher married a young Cowichan woman named Sarah in January 1864, and later became a father when Sarah gave birth to their son George. Tragically, shortly after the birth, Fisher shot himself to death while climbing a fence. There was a question of murder, so an inquest was held at the John Bull Hotel in Cowichan, presided over by Alexander Caulfield Anderson, but the evidence showed no wrongdoing. Fisher is buried at the Catholic Church in Cowichan Bay, at what came to be called the Butter Church.

Young George was put into a Catholic orphanage in Victoria and Sarah remarried, changing her name to Annie. I am the first descendant of Edward Brande Fisher to hold his mother's letters, now in the BC Archives.

I am proud of my ancestry, and thank my ancestors for the connections.

—*Larry Bell, Cowichan*

Aboriginal People

The first people watched all these developments with concern. With the co-operation of the Hudson's Bay Company, they mined the first gold, and while it had little value in their culture, they appreciated its importance. And they certainly knew through communication with southern tribes what the discovery of gold had cost other Native people. The Digger Indians of California had been all but wiped out. This account from *California Sketches* by O.P. Fitzgerald (1878) sums up the attitude of the California miners:

The shooting of a "buck" was about the same thing, whether it was a male Digger or a deer.

"There is not much fight in a Digger unless he's got the dead-wood on you, and then he'll make it rough for you. But these Injuns are of no use, and I'd about as soon shoot one of them as a coyote."

First Nations people were the first to find gold in BC. When gold seekers from everywhere else flooded in, First Nations prospectors defended their right to work alongside others on the Fraser River. *British Columbia Archives D-06815*

The speaker was a very red-faced, sandy-haired man, with blood-shot blue eyes, whom I met on his return to the Humboldt country after a visit to San Francisco.

"Did you ever shoot an Indian?" I asked.

"I first went up into the Eel River country in '46," he answered. "They give us a lot of trouble in them days. They would steal cattle, and our boys would shoot. But we've never had much difficulty with them since the big fight we had with them in 1849. A good deal of devilment had been goin' on all roun', and some had been killed on both sides. The Injuns killed two women on a ranch in the valley, and then we set in just to wipe 'em out. Their camp was in a bend of the river, near the head of the valley, with a deep slough on the right flank. There was about sixty of us, and Dave was our captain. He was a hard rider, a dead shot, and not very tender-hearted. The boys sorter liked him, but kep' a sharp eye on him, knowin' he was so quick and handy with a pistol. Our plan was to git to their camp and fall on 'em at daybreak, but the sun was risin' just as we come in sight of it. A dog barked, and Dave sung out: 'Out with your pistols! pitch in, and give 'em the hot lead!'

"In we galloped at full speed, and as the Injuns come out to see what was up, we let 'em have it. We shot forty bucks—about a dozen got away by swimmin' the river."

"Were any of the women killed?"

"A few were knocked over. You can't be particular when you are in a hurry; and a squaw, when her blood is up, will fight equal to a buck."

The California miners brought their prejudices with them, asserting that the "only good Indian is a dead Indian." The Indians in return tried to force miners off the diggings. And the Indians of the Fraser and Thompson goldfields were much tougher rivals than the miners had encountered in California. This account in the *San Francisco Bulletin* in May 1858 speaks to the Aboriginals' resistance to the miners: "I would recommend the voyager to procure the aid of Indians, both for the purpose of managing the canoes, and to prevent being fired upon by the predatory and savage tribes who have hitherto had but little intercourse with the whites, and are both physically and mentally vastly superior to the Diggers in California. Like all aboriginal races, they never let a wrong go un-avenged, and an 'eye for an eye,' and life for life, is their motto."

A letter printed in the *San Francisco Times* gave further evidence of the hostility miners might encounter in the BC goldfields:

The Indians in the British possessions entertain not very friendly feelings towards white Americans. This is also the case towards the Chinese. This latter people will no doubt suffer severely from the Indians, would they come into this country in large numbers. This enmity towards these races is no new thing; the Indians have always cherished a little hatred towards what are called Boston men, mixed with no little feeling of contempt. It has grown out of the general treatment they have received from the people of the United States, as compared with the British. These races despise the Chinese, and will shoot them as soon as they would a deer. But a short time since a party of Americans were stopped while attempting to ascend the Fraser River in a whale boat, and all their provisions and tools taken from them. At the same time coloured Americans are not molested, especially those in company with the English. The Indians understood that they have been obliged to leave American territory to escape oppressive laws, and naturally feel sympathy for them, and refrain from molesting them. At the time the whale boat was sent back, a party of coloured men, having Indians or English with them, were quietly suffered to pass. The Indians say "Boston man, church man no good, King George man very good."

Alone and Lonely

Some of the thousands of men who joined the gold rush to BC were already married or settled into single-sex sociability, many others were soon alone and lonely, for newcomer women were few and far between. An anonymous Cariboo miner lamented how "there must be at least two hundred men to every woman" (*Cariboo: The Newly Discovered Gold Fields of British Columbia*).

Many, possibly most, miners were men in their early 20s. They were in their sexual prime in a historical time period when the common understanding in most of their home societies was that men had irrepressible drives that needed to be satisfied one way or the other. These

Lonely miners found that single women were a rarity. **Miss Brown and Miss Irving, the only two unmarried women of New Westminster in 1868, had their picture taken on the road to Spuzzum from Yale.**
British Columbia Archives H-02913

young men's options were limited. They could pay for sex, and there were both newcomer and Aboriginal women willing to respond. They could get a moment's comfort by frequenting dance halls, which operated both in Victoria, where many men wintered, and in the goldfields. Such pleasures were ephemeral. The hurdy-gurdies who danced with miners in the boomtown of Barkerville set clear boundaries as to other favours:

> They danced at nicht in dresses light,
> Frae late until the early, O!
> But oh! their hearts were hard as flint,
> Which vexed the laddies sairly, O!
> —from "The German Lasses," by James Anderson

In October 1865 the *British Colonist* reported how at the end of the mining season the women left "on their way below, having reaped during the season a rich harvest of dollars and specimens from the lovers of the terpsichorean art and the admirers of the fair sex."

Men who began to think of settling down, rather than moving on as most miners were wont to do, faced particular difficulties, as reported in the *Times* in 1862:. "There is probably no country where the paucity of women in comparison with men is so injuriously felt... Without them the men will never settle in the country." A contemporary mused how "I never saw diggers so desirous of marrying as those of British Columbia" *(Cariboo)*. A lucky few could afford to "send money over to England for the passage out of an English girl or Scotch lassie he has known, more or less" *(Cariboo)*, but most did not have the means to do so. Measures taken to ameliorate the situation, as with two "brides' ships" arriving from England in 1862–63 under the auspices of the Anglican Church, were a drop in the bucket—the hundred marriageable women who came on them were quickly snapped up.

In these circumstances it was young Aboriginal women who some alone and lonely miners watched and wanted. Notions of race determined that these women would be appraised for the extent to which they approached White notions of beauty and dress. A ditty penned in 1862 indicates that some passed with flying colours:

> Her elastic bust no stays confined,
> Her raven tresses flowed free as wind;
> Whilst her waist, her neck and her ankles small
> Were encircled by bandlets, bead-wrought all.
>
> Her head as the wild deer's, erect and proud,
> To superior beauty never bowed;
> Like the diamond sparkling in the night,
> Her glistening black eyes beamed with light...
> —from "The Maid of Lillooet," Press, 1862

Some such liaisons were brief and instrumental on both sides, but others endured for a lifetime. The several hundred long-lived relationships that can be traced through oral testimony and such printed sources as vital statistics, censuses and memoirs, tended to be based in agriculture. A miner cum settler took up land, sometimes near his wife's people and often in proximity to other interracial families. Favoured locations were the Gulf Islands, the Okanagan and Nicola Valleys, and the routes to the goldfields. At the time British Columbia entered Canadian Confederation in 1871, about 10,000 non-Aboriginal people were strung out across the entire province, and it is indicative of the magnitude of this phenomenon that in the area extending from the Fraser Canyon through the goldfields, more mixed-heritage than white children attended the newly established public schools. Men once alone and lonely were forging an interracial British Columbia.

—*Jean Barman*

Multicultural Dream

Governor Douglas encouraged a multicultural society as the best defence against American domination. He himself had a mixed-race background, so his policy also insured that his own family would not be marginalized in the emerging colonial community. By building a multicultural society, with equality for First Nations, blacks and Chinese, whose loyalties were to the new colonies first, Douglas hoped to create a bulwark against American ambitions on the Pacific. But over time, his multicultural dream would fade, and with it much of the early promise of interracial co-operation.

5

THE SECOND RUSH
The Cariboo

Americans led the charge to the Fraser River goldfields in 1858. The Fraser turned into a little bit of the United States in the heart of British Columbia, but the Cariboo rush was different. Many of the Americans had lost interest in the "humbug" of BC gold by 1859 and were headed for discoveries south of the 49th parallel. Some ended up fighting in the Civil War that soon engulfed their homeland. And while some Americans made their way up to the Cariboo from the Fraser diggings, the new argonauts came directly from other parts of the globe.

Many Americans felt BC was played out; the rush was over. They were wrong. The next big strikes came on the Quesnel River and on Williams Creek in the Cariboo. There the leading prospectors were Cornish, English, Welsh, Scots, Irish, Dutch, German, French, and Chinese.

Opposite:
The Cameron claim on Williams Creek, from *The Northwest Passage by Land*, 1865.

Cariboo's First Discovery at Horsefly

Rumours began reaching the men on the Fraser that on a river farther North—the Horsefly—there was evidence of "blue clay" similar to the stratification they had found in California at the sites of the large lodes. Sometimes called the Blue Lead (pronounced *Blue Leed*), after a well-known rich deposit of gold in California, the gold in the Horsefly River was said to present the same indications, and a rich stratum of the "Blue Lead" extended north and south across the Horsefly River. There is ample verification for claims that the first gold found in the Cariboo came from the Horsefly River in 1859. However, there are questions as to which party of men was actually the first to arrive—we have accounts of at least four groups finding gold there.

Much gold was found in the Horsefly River at the time, but it served only to stimulate the miners in their search for more gold, and they pushed farther North to the next stream and then the next. From the Horsefly River, men went north to Keithley and Antler Creeks, and then they reached Barkerville and made rich strikes there in 1861.

Horsefly has earned its proper place in the history of BC—it was there that the first gold was discovered in the Cariboo, and 1859 was the year!

—*Horsefly Historical Society*

These goldfields were also a lot farther away from the United States—and from Victoria, for that matter. The cattle trail to the Cariboo was rugged in the summer, muddy beyond belief in the spring and fall, and impassable in winter. It required a far heartier breed of miner than the Fraser. A handbook for gold-seeking emigrants published in London in 1862 hinted at the hardships and privations to come:

THOSE WHO OUGHT TO GO.

Capitalists, Artisans, Mechanics, Labourers and Able-bodied Men of every description. Unmarried females.

THOSE WHO OUGHT NOT TO GO.

Persons of a weak constitution, of no particular trade or calling.

Women of every description were welcome. At the peak of the Cariboo gold rush, passage would be arranged for any single English woman prepared to go to the Pacific colonies with the object of matrimony. *Wives for our Bachelors!* That was a headline in the Victoria *Colonist* in the early 1860s. The bachelors of the goldfields certainly did need wives. In their rush to get to British Columbia, they had given little thought to the domestic life ahead—virtually no female companionship was available to them. The First Nations were highly suspicious of these invaders, not least because First Nations women had been cruelly victimized by the early wave of miners on the Fraser. For those who were serious about marriage and family, there would have to be another solution.

Antler Creek

In 1861 the *British Colonist* reported that "new and rich diggings have recently been struck" at this spot near Barkerville, and that "a pair of very large antlers were found on its bank."

In Victoria and England, societies formed to encourage women to emigrate for the purposes of matrimony. The Reverend John Garrett, secretary of the Columbia Mission Society, wrote in the London *Times*: "Reliable information has reached this country, through various channels, of the inestimable value which a careful stream of emigration of industrious women from Great Britain would prove at the present stage in the rapid progress of the colony of British Columbia. It is an essential element in the sound growth of a new colony that the men who first open it out should be able to settle and surround themselves with the humanizing ties of family life."

Keithley Creek

"Doc" Keithley struck it rich here in July 1860.

The Mission societies were looking for respectable lower-class women for the most part, women who might start out in domestic service and then marry under congenial conditions with the blessing and guidance of the church. The societies hoped to rescue some women from a life on the streets of London and other large British cities. And they hoped to rescue other souls in the goldfields by bringing the two groups together.

The women found passage on a variety of "bride ships" headed for the colonies. On-board conditions were sometimes appalling, and not all of the women were of high moral fibre. A

Royal Navy captain who witnessed the arrival of one bride ship reported: "One woman was carried up helplessly intoxicated, and two or three more were evidently the worse for liquor... There is not a shadow of a doubt in my mind... at least one or two of the women are thoroughly bad and must have been so before leaving England."

....

Cariboo
Governor James Douglas wrote that this name was adopted because it is the "favourite haunt of that species of the deerkind."

....

One woman who left a permanent and much more positive legacy was Margaret Faucette, who came out on the *Tynemouth* in 1862. She became a teacher and married John Jessop, the man considered the father of BC's public school system. The Jessops were a formidable couple, committed to improving the way children were taught in pioneer British Columbia. Many of BC's first families started with the marriage of women who came over on the bride ships and found husbands in the Pacific colonies.

More ships arrived over the next few years, but few of the women made it to the Cariboo goldfields. The ships docked in Victoria, and that is where most of the passengers found husbands.

Loneliness was the least of worries, however, for the men who made the trek into the Interior in the 1860s. One miner from New Brunswick wrote home in 1864 about the hardships he had encountered on the trail to the Cariboo:

We left the next day at noon for Fort Yale, about 100 miles up the Frazer, and arrived there about the middle of the following afternoon. (That is a hard old river. The steamer had to make four or five attempts before she could run some of the rapids.) As we drew near Fort Yale we passed two snow capped mountains, the magnitude of which it would be impossible for me to give you an idea. We left Fort Yale on the 30th of April (1863) with four animals packed with grub, and arrived in the Cariboo on the 30th of May. The first 60 miles of our journey were through the Cascade Mountains, where if a person had a taste for wild scenery, he might get completely gorged. It is about 400 miles from Yale to Cariboo, and yet hundreds of men pack 60 to 70 pounds at that distance on their backs. The people in New Brunswick have no idea what hard work is. I have stood in the town of Van Winkle, on Lightning Creek, and seen a crowd of men leave for William's Creek, most of them with 100 pounds on their backs, when the snow was so deep that horses could not travel. They had a high mountain to climb at the start; and it was a hard site to see them winding their way up the trail, gasping for breath every step. These men were employed by merchants and packed by the pound. It is about 14 miles from Van Winkle to William's, and it is called a day's work to pack a load that distance and walk back light. Yet hundreds of men would have been glad of the chance to pack at any price, for it requires as much influence to get employed in Cariboo as it does to get a government office in St. John.

Keithley's Creek in 1862

Our small party reached Keithley's Creek in two days from the Forks, passing along the shore of Cariboo Lake. There we paid half a dollar each to cross the deep stream in a boat; and it was money well expended, as it saved us a weary circuit of three miles, no trifling matter when burdened with fifty or sixty pounds of baggage. Keithley's is one of the most dull and gloomy places on the route, consisting of rude log-shanties of the roughest description. We stayed for several days here. The little stock of provisions we had brought with us (of beans, bacon and flour) was eagerly bid for by the store-keepers. We were offered twenty sovereigns for about half a hundred-weight of this supply; but we would have refused double that sum; for gold is not to be preferred at the risk of starvation. Not one pound of flour was obtainable at Keithley's, except that which we had brought. Beans and bacon were here "the staff of life."

—*W. Champness,* To Cariboo and Back in 1862

The miners didn't come to the Cariboo to pack groceries. They came believing the newspaper stories that said they could strike it rich. Unfortunately, most of the gold was well below the surface, some of it under a band of clay 4.5 metres thick. That gave experienced miners the clear advantage.

Lightning Creek

This place near Barkerville took its name from a Yankee slang term for hard work. Miners found it especially tough going in this creek.

The Story of "Cariboo" Cameron

As children, my brother and I frequently spent the summer with our grandparents in Prince George. On one such trip, we paid a visit to Barkerville and the gravesite of John "Cariboo" Cameron. He was my grandmother's uncle and the source of both pride and embarrassment to his many descendants in this conservative family. It was fascinating to hear of the quest for golden riches and the strange journey with Sophia's embalmed body from Barkerville to Ontario.

Over the years we heard many fascinating stories of my grandmother's childhood in Cornwall, Ontario, but the tale of Cariboo Cameron was by far the most intriguing.

—*Susan McLoughlin, Peachland*

John Angus "Cariboo" Cameron struck it rich in the goldfields, then went home to Cornwall, Ontario, and married his childhood sweetheart Sophia Groves. (The couple, centre, posed for a photograph with their wedding party.) In 1862, the couple and their young child made the arduous journey to the Cariboo, via Panama and Victoria, but the child died, and later that year Sophia died as well. Today Cameron is as well known for transporting her body back to Cornwall—which took more than a year—as he is for making his fortune in the Cariboo. *British Columbia Archives A-01158*

This chronology of John Angus "Cariboo" Cameron's life was compiled from public records by Wanda Story, a listener.

1858

John Cameron and two brothers, Alexander and Roderick, travelled to the Fraser gold rush in the Cariboo. John had two good gold strikes and made $20,000 (about $500,000 today). John returned to Cornwall and married Sophia Groves, his childhood sweetheart 12 years his junior.

1861

John and Sophia had a daughter, Alice Isabel.

1862

John and his family arrived in Victoria on February 27. The long trip via Panama was hard on young Alice and she died at the age of 14 months, 5 days, after the family arrived in Victoria. The couple then met Robert Stevenson, who offered them a partnership in the Antler Creek Store in the Cariboo, so John and Sophia travelled to Antler Creek. Soon they staked claims at upper Williams Creek. John later moved downstream, nearer Stout's Gulch.

A partnership was formed between John and Sophia, Allan McDonald, Richard Rivers, and Charles and James Clendenning. The group became known as Cameron & Co. and staked six claims. John and Sophia had another child, but it was stillborn. The winter was hard and typhoid was rampant. Sophia died of typhoid fever, then called mountain fever, on October 22 or 23, when the temperatures plummeted to −35°C. Her dying wish was that her body be taken back home to Ontario. She was temporarily buried at nearby Walkers Gulch. Two months later, on December 22, a mile below the Barker claim, the partnership struck gold.

1863

John Cameron and James Cunning established the first cemetery in the area. John Cameron offered $12 a day (about $200 today)—and, at the end, a bonus of $2,000 ($33,000 today) to any man who would help him carry out Sophia's coffin from the William's Creek to Victoria. It was a tough trip, with blizzards, rough terrain and temperatures dipping to 45 below, and it took them 36 days. After burying Sophia temporarily in Victoria, John returned to his Cariboo claim. He bought out the Clendenning and two other adjacent claims, and he commenced mining operations with as many men as he could hire. The town of Cameronton grew up around the claim. In October John returned to Victoria with $300,000 worth of gold ($7.5 million today). On November 8 he boarded a ship and took Sophia's body around South America and back to Glengarry, in Ontario, Canada. Sophia's father asked to see his daughter's face when the coffin arrived, but John refused and she was buried again. He shared his good fortune, believed to be eight pack horses laden with gold, with his five brothers.

1865

John, now 45 years old, married Christy Anne "Emma" Wood, and built her a lavish mansion. He invested in timber, the construction of the Lachine Canal and some eastern mines.

1872

Rumours had spread that John had sold his first wife, Sophia, into slavery and that he had taken the coffin home filled with gold. After nine years, John gave in to pressure. He had the coffin raised and drained out the alcohol, which had helped to preserve Sophia's body. The rumours were laid to rest, but grass never again grew over Sophia's grave where the alcohol had been spilled. Sophia was moved and buried for the last time at Summertown, near the mansion that had been built by the Cariboo gold.

1881

John and Christy Anne Cameron are listed in the census of Charlottenburg, Glengarry, Ontario: John as farmer and 60 years old, Christy Anne as his wife, 39 years old and born in Ontario but of German descent. They are also listed with young Mary McPherson, 12 years old. Alexander Cameron, brother of John, is listed in the census as a gold miner, 51 years old, born in Scotland.

1886

With his gold fortunes now reduced, John returned to the Cariboo with his second wife in search of more gold. But the easy-to-reach gold was gone. He worked in the Big Bend mines for a time.

1888

In September, John returned to Barkerville. On November 7, at the age of 68, John Angus "Cariboo" Cameron died of a massive stroke. He was buried in the Cameronton Cemetery.

1992

Around this time, the descendants of John Cameron had a plaque placed in his memory in Summertown.

The Cariboo claims were the richest strikes yet, and those who got in early were making more than $100 a day (about $1,650 today). Their names still conjure up visions of incredible wealth: Billy Barker, John "Cariboo" Cameron, Ned Stout, Dutch Bill Dietz, Ned Campbell, William Cunningham. In May 1862, Cunningham wrote to a friend:

> Dear Joe,
>
> I am well, and so are all the rest of the boys. I avail myself of the present opportunity to write you a half dozen lines to let you know that I am well, and doing well—making from two to three thousand dollars a day! Times good—grub high—whiskey bad—money plenty.
>
> Yours truly,
>
> Wm Cunningham.

Quesnelle Forks was the first of the Cariboo gold camps. For a time in 1860, it was the largest "city" on the mainland. In fact, the town's original name was the more pretentious Quesnelle City. In his wonderful book *Ghost Towns of British Columbia*, Bruce Ramsey includes a newspaper account of the town written by a character who went by the name of "Cariboo." It describes a Christmas meal:

> We had all to lend a hand in preparation of the feast, yet there was not so much to be done. Pork and beans was our chief dish, but not our only one; for we had some beef, boiled, roasted, stewed and fried. The boiling pieces were knocked off with an axe, as were those intended for the stew pan, but the steaks were cut with a saw. So solid was the original junk frozen that we could scarcely tell whether we were working through bones or flesh until the frost thawed out. Then we had plum duff, without plums; plainduff we called it. Next came slap jacks or pancakes, tea and coffee, whisky hot and whisky cold, brandy neat and two tins of sardines between ten of us. This was our first course. The second and third were without variation and like unto the first. It may be noted, however, that on this particular occasion, neither tea nor coffee was in great demand.

The Cornish Wheel, a large wooden wheel with shelves, was a common miner's tool in the gold rush days. This one was located at the Davis claim in Williams Creek. Water from flumes turned the wheel, which was used to pump out the mine shaft.
British Columbia Archives A-00558

Antler Creek in 1862

So we reached Cariboo at last; for Antler Creek is one of the principal places in the Cariboo district. We found the miners generally as dispirited as the accounts received on our upward journey had represented them to be. Many were trooping away. Yet both here and at the neighboring diggings of William's Creek, Lake House, Lightning Canyon, Last Chance, Peterson's, Davis's, and Cunningham's Claims, much gold was being found. At the latter place, two hundred ounces per diem were said to be taken out. Indeed, there is good reason to believe that this season fully a ton of gold has been here obtained. But at what cost! The expenses are enormous; for the mines hereabouts are not mere surfaceworks, like many of those in Australia or California, but involve heavy outlay and deep exploration.

Altogether, the experience of gold-mining in British Columbia hitherto has been some brilliant success, but much, very much disheartening failure, and the latter far preponderating over the former.

—*W. Champness,* To Cariboo and Back in 1862

The gold rush gave rise to the establishment of the Bank of British Columbia in 1862, which eventually opened branches throughout BC and parts of the western US. It merged with the Canadian Imperial Bank of Commerce in 1901. *British Columbia Archives G-00693*

Vigilante to the Cariboo

My great-great-uncle John Shepherd arrived in Lillooet around 1858–59. He was a vigilante and gunman who had to get out of Pully Dam in the US, as he would have been hung. Finding Lillooet a good place for gold mining, he sent for his brother, Edmund C. Shepherd. Edmund arrived in 1859–60. He and a number of white men stopped to prospect, but found mainly quartz. He did, however, hit one gold mine: he found his Native wife, a Lillooet princess. They travelled to William's Creek and later Barkerville. According to reports from the Minister of Mines (housed in the Langley Archives), the only discovery made in the district that season was by Mr. E.C. Shepherd and partner, on the stream that flows into Antler Creek, now known as 88 Shepherd Creek. Oral history has it that John would get up at 3:00 each morning to stake his claim. It's not known how well he did. The *Enterprise* (first paddleboat used on the upper Fraser River) was taken up to Fort George in 1871; by this time Edmund was piloting paddlewheeler boats. A newspaper article from Quesnelmouth in December 1871 reports: "There arrived 40 men from Omenica at Fort George, ice being so thick... they hauled their boats and attempted to cross Quesnelmouth on foot. E.C. Shepherd found a canoe in the Canyon and picked up Dunlevy, Guichon, Tom Harper and Barlow. All of the 40 men were saved, although they lost horse, mules etc."

—*Donna Sweet*

Quesnelle Forks soon became just another stop on the road to the goldfields. But it got a second life when the Chinese miners moved in to clean up the claims abandoned by others. By 1862, when W. Champness passed through, Quesnelle Forks was a supply centre for the great mines on William's and Antler Creeks. In his book *To the Cariboo and Back in 1862,* he wrote:

> This place is the principal depot for provisions and materials for the mines, being located about fifty miles from the gold regions of Antler Creek and adjacent part of the Cariboo. The town at the Forks consists of general stores (mostly kept by Jews) and drinking shops: it is prettily situated, and the climate is milder than in many parts of the surrounding region.

> Here, too, we met with many returned miners encamped. Their accounts were deplorable, and their manifest condition confirmed the worst. Yet, here again, all admitted the existence of rich deposits at the mines. Their complaints were of the excessive dearness of provisions and stores, the impossibility of getting many necessaries, even for money; and beyond all, the intolerable difficulties of the soil and the tracks. Whilst waiting here we saw two packers from the mines. One of them carried with him a bell, such as is fastened to the foremost mule of a pack.

> Suspecting some disaster, we inquired after their animals, and received for reply a statement that they had started thence to Antler Creek with a train of thirty mules, not one of which had reached the destination, all having fallen down, at different places, into the precipitous ravines, along the perpendicular sides of which the narrow trails lead them. Sometimes a single such stumble involves a fall of a thousand feet. This, to an animal burdened with three hundred pounds weight of goods is, of course, certain death.

Robert Stevenson and the Cameron Claim

Robert Stevenson, my great-great-grandfather, was born in 1838 in a small township near Ottawa, Ontario, and arrived in BC in 1859. Over the next years he was involved in numerous mining ventures in the province and held various positions, including customs inspector and gold commissioner. In 1914 he was one of only two living veterans of the Boundary–Similkameen gold rush some 55 years earlier.

He was, however, best known for his involvement in the Cariboo gold rush. Judge Matthew Baillie Begbie once said of Robert Stevenson that he knew more about Cariboo mining than any other man.

Stevenson was also known for his long-lasting friendship/partnership with John "Cariboo" Cameron. The two men had known each other in Ontario, and in the winter of 1862 they ran into each other in Victoria. Stevenson helped Cameron get $2,000 worth of supplies on credit (about $41,000 today), and they went their separate ways.

When Stevenson heard of the strikes in the Cariboo and learned that horses were in short supply, he bought 100 head in Osoyoos and drove them to Lillooet, where they were sold for more than $10,000 ($200,000 today). Stevenson was one of only 10 men who took money into the Cariboo.

On August 22, 1863, a company was formed consisting of Robert Stevenson, John and Sophia Cameron, Richard Rivers, Allan McDonald, and Charles and James Clendening. Ground was staked on Williams Creek, a short distance downstream from Billy Barker's claim.

On October 23, Sophia Cameron died of typhoid fever. The temperature was −35°C, so she was buried temporarily in a tin coffin, which was placed in an abandoned cabin. Her last wish had been to be buried in Ontario.

Shortly afterwards, the men struck gold and the Cameron Claim eventually proved to be the second richest claim in the Cariboo.

On January 31, in bitter cold and two metres of snow, with 22 kilograms of gold borrowed from Billy Barker, Cameron and Stevenson set out for Victoria on the first leg of a trip that would end with Sophia's last wish granted.

In the words of Robert Stevenson: "A little after daylight on the last day of January 1863, we left Richfield with the coffin bound in strong canvas and strapped firmly to a toboggan and fifty pounds of gold dust tied on the top of the coffin, which made it top heavy, but we had no other place to put it."

Stevenson and Cameron journeyed 960 kilometres on snowshoe and by horse and steamer. They passed safely through communities devastated by smallpox and wore out three horses in the process, and they arrived in Victoria on March 7. In Victoria, Cameron had the tin coffin filled with alcohol to preserve the body and buried it again.

Stevenson and Cameron then returned to their claim, which turned out to be very rich indeed. Stevenson remained in the Cariboo until 1877, at which time he married and settled in the Fraser Valley, in Sardis. His farm of 120 hectares became a showpiece, and he held claims throughout southeastern BC and as far afield as Cassiar.

Robert Stevenson died in 1922 in Vancouver.

—*Bill Carmichael, Vancouver*

Some legendary miners also passed through Quesnelle Forks, among them "Dutch Bill" Dietz and "Doc" Keithley. In February 1861, Dietz set out in the deep snow from Antler Creek and stumbled on a new stream. An account from the Victoria *Chronicle* of November 1863 picks up the story:

> They found prospects on the northwest side of the creek varying from ten to thirty cents to the pan near the bedrock. After that one of the party sunk a hole on the east side... and obtained a similar result. Night coming on, and much time having been lost through only having one pick... they abandoned their work for that day and lit a fire to cook supper. But Dutch William, restless and enterprising, left the others basking before the burning logs, and travelled up the creek until he found the bare bedrock cropping up in the stream. He tried one panful of gravel, but obtained none of the precious metal.

He tried another taken from the side near where there was a high ledge, and to his great delight found himself rewarded with a dollar a pan. The gravel was frozen hard to the rock and when detached with difficulty thawed in the cold stream. Time passed quickly and he was soon obliged by darkness to return to the campfire. He showed his companions the prize he had obtained, but they, possibly, hardly believed his statement, for they determined to return to the Forks. Leaving his companions to bring up stores, he started back at daybreak for his new creek—making the distance in the wonderfully short time of three hours over an unblazed trail. But his strenuous exertions were unavailing; the whole population of Antler had tracked his steps, and within two or three hours after his arrival, the whole creek was staked off into claims over ground covered with eight feet of snow.

The creek would soon have a name, William's Creek—named not for Billy Barker, as is sometimes assumed, but for Dutch Bill. Sadly, his claim was one of the worst, and he died in poverty in 1877.

A Bet to the Death

An advertisement in the *Cariboo Sentinel:*

The Parlour Saloon

Barkerville

Spirits, Wines, Ales and Seegars

First Class Reading Room

A harmonic Meeting held every Week

Theatrical Entertainment

will be given once a week

by the

Cariboo Amateur Dramatic Association

Artists of alleged international renown occasionally made appearances, but it was their own bards and thespians who drew the greatest appreciation and applause. "This establishment has received a machine for manufacturing soda water and one for making sarsaparilla, both of which articles we are now prepared to supply to our customers," read Adler & Barry's Saloon ad in the *Cariboo Sentinel.*

But life in the saloons of Barkerville was not all dominoes and sarsaparilla. Card sharks with tidy fingernails never lacked for willing victims. Chance was a compulsive way of life—and death. O.J. Travaillot, one of Governor James Douglas's first gold commissioners, was an inveterate gambler. He lay in Barkerville's one-room hospital beside a man called Malanon, who had once played first violin in the Paris Opera and now made music for dancing with the hurdy-gurdy girls and was paid enough for a small daily stake into any game where he could find room. Both men knew they were dying so they made a wager—$50 (about $800 today) to the survivor. The game was

played out in front of the other patients. They saw Malanon raise his head as his voice rang out clearly, "Captain Travaillot, you win. I lose. I die now!" and his head dropped as he spoke.
—*Charles Perkins, Langley*

Another town on Williams Creek became the gold capital of BC. It was Barkerville, where Billy Barker struck it rich in 1862 by digging down 12 metres to find pay dirt. In 10 hours, it is said, Barker took out about $20,000 worth of gold (about $500,000 today), and that was just his share. His total take from the mine was said to exceed $500,000 (some $12.5 million today). The story was that he could be found hanging around the bars, singing this ditty:

> I'm English Bill,
> Never worked, an' never will.
> Get away girls,
> Or I'll tousle your curls.

Top: Billy Barker left his home in England for the California gold rush, then migrated north and, in 1862, struck it rich on Williams Creek. The instant town of Barkerville rose around his claim. Barker spent or gave away most of his earnings, estimated at $500,000 ($12.5 million in today's dollars). He died a pauper in Victoria. *British Columbia Archives A-01144*

Above: In 1862 Billy Barker struck gold just above bedrock at 12 metres. The deposit continued to 16 metres and required a windlass to haul the diggings above ground. *British Columbia Archives A-03858*

105

The "hurdy gurdy girls" arrived on the Barkerville scene in 1865. These young Dutch-German women were a rare treat for miners used to the company of other men in rustic circumstances. The girls would dance with the men for a dollar. *British Columbia Archives G-00817*

The Hurdy-Gurdy Girls

Messrs Adler and Barry's large saloon was crowded on Saturday night with the boys who had collected from every nook and corner of the creeks to have a peep at the hurdies who had made their debut on that occasion.

Here the hurdy-gurdy damsels are unsophisticated maidens of Dutch extraction from poor but honest parents and morally speaking they really are not what they are generally put down for. The girls receive a few lessons in the terpsichorean art, are put into a kind of uniform, generally consisting of a red waist, a cotton print skirt and a headdress resembling somewhat in shape the topknot of a male turkey.

The hurdy-gurdy style of dancing differs from all other schools. If you ever saw a ring of bells in motion you have seen the exact position these young ladies are put through during the dance. The more muscular the partner, the nearer the approximation of the ladies pedal extremities to the ceiling and the gent who can hoist his gal the highest is considered the best dancer. The poor girls as a general thing earn their money very hardly.

In passing up Broadway in the evening you may hear the hurdy-gurdy fiddlers letting off steam as if their lungs were made of cast iron and the notes forged with a sledge hammer.

—*Cariboo Sentinel*

A successful ladies' man Barker wasn't. Like Dutch Bill, he died a pauper after marrying a widow in Victoria who took him for everything he had—at least that's the legend. Richard Wright in his book on Barkerville disputes those stories, citing research by Ken Mather, a recent curator of the historical site. According to Mather's research, Barker did winter in Victoria in January 1863 and did marry a local widow. But he returned to Barkerville the next spring and made more money from his claim. Like many miners, he sunk money into other claims and lost most of what he made. His wife left him, but he continued to prospect into the 1870s, moving farther and farther into the wilderness in search of gold. He was 77 when he died of cancer in 1894.

Walking to Barkerville

My paternal grandfather, Joseph Guichon, walked to Barkerville, via Victoria, in 1863–64. He worked with Cataline, the famous packer, in 1865. My maternal grandfather, Pierre Bilodeau, was involved with the gold rush in Emory Creek, BC, and my mother was born there in 1883. Both families played important roles in BC's history. I am the daughter of Dr. Lawrence Guichon and was born in Merritt, BC, in 1921.

—*Marcelle J. Delesalle, Victoria*

Barkerville on Fire

Cries of "*Fire!*" were drowned in the roar of runaway flames on September 16, 1868, as the heat of the great Barkerville fire set structures alight. Great gusts of hot air carried burning shakes aloft and sent them spinning along to land on other roofs or to fall into the narrow openings between buildings, where in the next instant there was the crackling and then the roaring of a new conflagration. In minutes the whole main street was afire. Men and women ran for their lives. The heat seemed to suck the air out of the narrow valley. Many people collapsed and were dragged to safety. Miraculously no one died.

Within a week the *Cariboo Sentinel* published this report from Quesnel:

The remains of Barkerville, one day after a fierce fire wiped out the town in September 1868. A week later, 30 homes were being built on the still-smouldering site and a fire brigade had been formed. *British Columbia Archives F-08566*

Long ere this news of the conflagration of the town of Barkerville has flashed across the wires to all parts of the civilized world. No one but an eyewitness can form any conception of a scene so fraught with disastrous results, universal as far as Barkerville is concerned but not one that will retard the prospects or permanent interests of the Cariboo. Only a few days since we, with pride, spoke of the order and neatness of Barkerville and our ink was scarcely dried before the town was smouldering ruin; charred timber and heaps of rubbish marked the spot where stood the metropolis of Cariboo. In just one hour the merciless element had turned the tenants of 120 houses roofless into the streets and many with no more property than covered their persons.

When the last roof fell and the destruction of Barkerville was complete, fleeing hundreds with goods snatched from the flames sat upon their rescued plunder and wiped perspiration from their brows.

A week later, 30 houses were being built on the still-smouldering site. But the enormous energy and excitement after the fire only obscured the fact that Barkerville's heyday ended in flames on that afternoon. What followed was a reluctant and respectable descent into half a century of obscurity.

—*Charles Perkins, Langley*

Williams Creek quickly earned the title of richest creek in the world. Claims were earning $2,000 a day, $6,000 a day, and on rare occasions over $30,000 a day (about $620,000 today). For a lucky few, it was a bonanza.

But for the late arrivals in 1862 and 1863, the pickings were slimmer. Our New Brunswick correspondent was disheartened:

> The only creek in Cariboo that is worth a row of pins is William's; the whole country is depending on it, but even there the paying claims are few. Not more than one man in forty has made anything who have taken up claims there. I know some parties who have spent nineteen thousand dollars to the interest in buying in and working claims on William's flat. Some few men have made money by taking up claims and selling out and leaving the country at once. A Canadian of my acquaintance who was one of the first to strike gold on William's flat, had forty thousand dollars in his possession which he took out of the Canadian claim (which you may have read of), and instead of leaving the country at once, he invested it all on William's, and when I left in the fall he could not raise one thousand dollars. On the whole, I do not think that the Cariboo has turned one dollar for every ten that has been expended there.

Was Ever Luck Like Thine?

James Anderson, a Scotsman, was the Robert Service of the Cariboo gold rush. In his ballads he captured the spirit and characters of Barkerville during its heyday from 1863 to 1871.

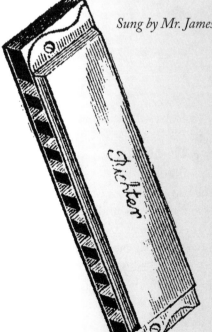

The Rough But Honest Miner
Sung by Mr. James Anderson, at the Theatre Royal, Barkerville, 13th Feb. 1869.

The Rough but Honest miner,
Wha toils night and day,
Seeking for the yellow gold,
hid among the clay—
Hawkin' on the mountain-side,
What he does there—
Ha! The auld "dreamer's"
"Buildin' castles in the air."
His weatherbeaten face,
An' his sair-worn hands
Are tell-tales to a'
O' the hardship that he stands;
His head may grow grey
And his face fu' o' care,
Hunting after gold,
"Wi' its castles in the air."

Hard Luck

Last night I sat and watch'd
Beside a comrade's bed—
An' a' was still, within an' out,
Save the watch-beat overhead:
My thochts gaed back and fore,
Frae now to "ould lang syne,"—
Till a' resolved to this at last,
"Was ever luck like mine?"
A voice then struck my ear—
Sae weary an' sae wae—
In words I couldna choose but hear,
And "helpless," thrice did say;
I mark'd the sufferer's face,
Read pain in ilka line—
A taunting spirit in me asked,
"Was ever luck like thine?"
This touch'd me to the heart—
I weaken'd richt awa—
I couldna thole to see my case
Compared wi' his ava.
And sae a lesson's taught,
that we should never tine—
However hard your lot may be
There's others waur than thine!

The food was boring and sometimes just plain awful—"Beans and bacon! Bacon and beans," in the words of one pilgrim. And the prices for supplies were exorbitant. The 1862 diary of S.G. Hathaway, who had come north from the California goldfields, lists some of the prices:

Aug. 6.–Nelson Creek–Cariboo.Got in to the new town of Van Winkle on Lightning Creek, on Saturday, July 18th. Provisions dear and scarce. Flour $1.25 a pound—tea $3.00, salt $5 for a 3 pound bag, Nails $3, a pound & hardly any to be had. [A dollar in 1862 was the equivalent of about $16 today.] My partners growled all the way up because I thought best to bring some nails along, —they wish now we had brought all nails! Sold Billy Mule at once for $140, & I found on dividing our goods that I had provision enough to last me 5 or 6 weeks. Next day, Sunday, we rested, & on Monday I took blankets & grub for two weeks, stored the rest in a cabin at $1 a week, & came over to Nelson Creek to prospect for diggings. First bought a license to mine, good for a year—$5 for that. My partners got discouraged in a day or two & went off, & I expect

Essentials for all seasons were near at hand for some placer miners. This well-supplied cabin was at Manson Creek, northwest of Barkerville, where the Omenica gold rush was ignited in the 1860s and 1870s. *British Columbia Archives D-07433*

they are out of Cariboo by this time. I then went in with two sailor boys from Martha's Vineyard who traveled part of the way up with us & came over to Nelson at the same time. Found some men who have been prospecting on the creek for 2 months, sinking shafts (wells, you would call them) trying to hit upon the deepest part of the channel where the gold always settles. They have the best looking chance on the creek, & as they had just got out of money & provision, they offered us an equal share with them if we would join them & feed two of them two weeks. We concluded to do so; so here we are, hard at work, the two weeks nearly up, & nothing certain as yet. Yesterday I went back to Van Winkle & packed over all my things—70 pounds. If anybody thinks that it is fun let them try it. —8 miles & back, over a mountain, deep sloppy mud nearly every foot of the way, & big logs to straddle & climb at every ten steps, it seems, & sometimes two or three of them together at that. Walk over that road in the morning & stagger back with a load of 70 pounds in the afternoon, & almost any lazy man would be satisfied with his day's work.

I am afraid Cariboo will swamp me as it has thousands of others. There are some few men who are getting out gold fast. Some few claims are yielding as high as 150 pounds a week—report says more; but the great majority are getting nothing, most of the crowd, in fact, have been driven back by the high prices eating their money up before they had a chance to try for diggings. I have almost a mind to go back to California if I find nothing where we are now, but I hate to give up while there is yet a chance, however

111

slight,—I have still about $440, left out of $613 that I had on leaving Suisun, & I can manage to stand it here for the balance of the season & have enough left to pay my way back to California & there begin anew. Not a pleasant prospect at that, but I suppose I shall have to stand it. However, if I stay here I shall not fail through lack of trying.

Men huddled in windowless cabins or worse, tents. Judge Matthew Begbie, who came to the Cariboo on his regular circuit, was one of those:

The climate of the Cariboo is at times exceedingly wet, as in all high mountainous regions, and it is not unusual to have torrents of rain for a week together without intermission. The tent... although it answers very well in tolerable weather, or even a few days of rain and where the camp is changed from time to time, I find that my tent becomes occasionally covered with mildew in the inside, while it is impossible to keep the books, etc., dry, and all writing and recording is carried on at the greatest inconvenience. Besides, the ground being constantly cold and damp, there being no opportunity of approaching a fire without going out into the heavy rain, all cooking and drying of articles of apparel becomes extremely irksome...

The Old Never Sweet

These excerpts from the memoirs of Samuel Drake, born June 18, 1838, in Devon, England, tell the story:

We arrived in Victoria, BC, and stopped there a week buying cooking utensils, pack straps, etc., as we decided to try our luck at the goldfields in the Cariboo. We went to New Westminster where we stopped at the Jolly Highlander. We were standing on the dock on Sunday morning waiting for a boat to take us up the Fraser River when we heard a band playing in the distance. It was playing Annie Laurie in quick step time. We learned it was the Sappers on their way to church. New Westminster went up 100 percent in our estimation.

We took a boat to Douglas Town on the Lillooet Butte. We had to pack everything overland until we hit Pemberton Lake, a trek of 24 miles. We took a boat for 30 miles, then more packing for 16 miles. We ran into some road men who said we were two weeks too early for the gold mines. I was offered a job as road foreman on the Cariboo Highway—the Yale route. Hosking said he would push on. I worked there until I had enough money to repay Mr. Bluett for the money he had loaned me. It was a load off my mind. I had my ups and downs on that road, men coming and going. Some of them had the idea that the road would build itself while they sat around, swapped yarns and smoked. The contract was up in October, so after spending two years in that country I went back to Victoria. It was a wonderful two years as I had made a lot of friends.

In April 1864 I left once again for the Cariboo. All I had to my name was my blankets, gum boots and my cornet. John Hosking and Bill Sampson met me. We worked on the West Briton claim, which didn't pan out very well. We then turned to the Lily of the Valley. We got a crew to sink a shaft and put in a drain. We went down to clay, but did not puddle enough gold to make assessments, so we abandoned that claim.

I next got a half interest in the Watson claim. From the first we took out enough gold to pay expenses. We worked until fall and made a nice haul. Things were going well until we got into a lawsuit and an injunction was put on the claim. We won the case and had started to work, when our opponents took us to court again, and once more we won the case. We were put in a court of equity and compelled to stop work once more. The court was held in New Westminster once a year in the spring. We had to eat, so started looking around for a job. We went to the Ruby claim and started work at $10 a day. Two weeks night shift and two weeks days.

In 1866 we heard we were likely to lose the Watson claim so sold out for $500. Joe Hugo and I prospected around Wilson Gulch for a time, then went back to the Ruby claim until March 1867, when it was rumored good pay had been struck at Muskitta Creek. Joe Hugo and I started for this creek. We met Bob Davis, who offered us 90 feet of ground as he and his partner had 700 feet higher up. Hugo and I considered the offer, but decided it was too small a piece and passed it up. It was the worst pass we ever made, as it was the best 90 feet ever opened on Muskitta Creek. We both deserved to have our pants kicked.

I started work at Williams Creek on the dump box on the "Wake Up Jacks." One day while working I heard a woman scream. I looked up to see smoke pouring through the roof of the dance hall. I called to the men, who came running, but we could do nothing. There was a strong breeze that blew the fire from one building to another. Goods were thrown into the street, but powder and oil became ignited and we were forced to stand back or get blown to smithereens. In a short time Barkerville was no more than smouldering ruins. It was a terrible but magnificent sight to see those flames licking up hard-to-get, useable material.

Immediately there was a scramble for lumber to rebuild the town. I was approached to start digging a foundation for a house up at Richfield, while George Shaw went to locate lumber. One day, while working, I was unconsciously whistling "Lift up your heads, O ye gates" from the *Messiah*. I looked up to see a gentleman standing watching me. He said, "Where did you learn that piece you were whistling?" I told him I had gone right through the *Messiah* as a bass player in Devonshire.

It turned out it was the foundation for his house that I was working on, and that he was a Church of England minister, Rev. J. Reynard. He said I was just the man he was looking for, as he had some instruments in Victoria and if I would undertake to start an orchestra he would send for them. I told him to get those instruments up here pronto and I would attend to getting players. We sawed lumber into January and February until the cold was paralyzing. So we went back to rocking our dirt in the old Never Sweet, where we did very well until spring. Then I went to Last Chance and Joe Hugo went to the old Ruby mine.

On New Year's Day I was invited to Mr. Reynard's for dinner and to inspect the instruments which had arrived with his family. There was a violin, a tenor viol, a fine harp, clarinet, bassoon, bombardon and flute. I decided to try the bassoon, and soon found players for the other instruments.

In 1871 Hugo and I got hold of a piece of ground from the old Cameron claim. It was a claim that promised well, but didn't amount to anything. In the fall the bishop sent for Mr. Reynard to go to Nanaimo to take charge of the Anglican Church. We were mightily sorry to see him go. My Partner and I always agreed that Mr. Reynard had a wonderful way with young men, and through his musical ability and his choir orchestra he kept us so busy practising that we were probably kept out of scrapes and fights. That was a country of rough, tough men composed of every nationality and nearly every tongue.

We had a very good orchestra and choir, with two women members. We gave concerts, with the proceeds going towards the building of the new church. By this time we had an organ. As the Methodist Church wouldn't allow their choir to put on a festival, a number of the young men asked if they could join our choir. I was delighted, as they were all good singers. At our Christmas service you may be sure the choir, accompanied by the orchestra, sang "Lift up your heads, O ye gates."

—*Beverley Sherry, Nanaimo*

Cataline

Jean Caux, known as Cataline, was born in France in about 1830. He came to the Fraser Canyon from Oregon in 1858, along with many other men. Cataline was not put off by the difficulties of getting to the gold diggings in the Cariboo. Unlike the overwhelming majority who departed BC almost as soon as they came, the young Frenchman from the Pyrenees turned the rough terrain to advantage by packing in needed goods and mining supplies over the steep, narrow trails on mule back. As roads were constructed, Cataline shifted his base of operations north to Hazelton, and for a time to the Omineca. He never stayed in one place for long, but he did have short-term relationships with Native women that produced several children. His daughter Clemence was educated at St. Anne's Catholic convent school in Victoria. Known for his colourful personality, Cataline sustained the colony of BC and then the young province for a good half-century with his pack trains. He died in 1922 in Hazelton, and he is remembered with a statue in Williams Lake.

—*Jean Barman*

Known as Cataline, Jean Caux was born on the border between Spain and France, came to BC in 1858 and went on to become BC's best-known Cariboo packer. His crews were Mexican, First Nations and Chinese men. By the time he retired in the Hazeltons, he had been packing for 54 years.
British Columbia Archives A-03049

Governor James Douglas was a Cariboo booster. In his letters to London, he waxed eloquent about the potential of the new discoveries beyond the Fraser: "Every successive discovery indeed tends to confirm the impression that the gold fields which have been struck at Rock Creek and Quesnel River or Cariboo, are but two points in a range of auriferous mountains containing incalculable wealth... a theory which, if correct, opens a magnificent vista of future greatness for the colony."

....

No More Bunkum

Come, boys, let's sing a song;
For the day it won't be long,
When united to our country we will be;
Then the "Maple Leaf" entwined,
And the "Beaver," too, combined
With Old England's flag shall float upon the sea.

Chorus:
Tramp! Tramp! the New Dominion
Now is knocking at the door,
So, good-bye dear Uncle Sam,
As we do not care a clam
For your Greenbacks or your bunkum any more.
—*from the* Cariboo Sentinel, *June 16, 1869, quoted in* British Columbia:
A Centennial Anthology

....

Hiking the Old Douglas Trail

In 1858 the British sent the Royal Engineers to British Columbia to help protect the new colony, survey land for cities and build roads. In 1859–60 the engineers helped in the construction of the Harrison–Lillooet gold rush route from Port Douglas on Harrison Lake to Lillooet on the Fraser River. The route bypassed the much more difficult trails in the Fraser Canyon. In 1862 the Royal Engineers were also involved in the surveying and partial construction of the Cariboo Wagon Road. When the regiment left the colony in 1863, most of its members chose to stay in British Columbia, where they formed a volunteer military force to protect the colony. This force eventually became the Royal Westminster Regiment, the regiment my father joined in 1940.

This personal connection, and my desire to make Canadian history more interesting to my grade 10 students, led me to take students hiking on the routes used during the gold rush. Since 1976, I have led or accompanied groups of 40 to 80 students on an annual hike along the Harrison–Lillooet trail. A six-day hike on the road constructed by the Royal Engineers gives the students an opportunity to follow the route taken by Richard Clement Moody, James Douglas, Matthew Baillie Begbie, Cariboo Cameron, Bill Barker and other gold rush legends. The remains of wagons, oxen and buildings, as well as the wagon road itself, make

the trip through one of the most beautiful valleys in BC something the students are not likely to forget. Native speakers and the folk songs of Phil Thomas, Jon Bartlett and Rika Ruebsaat have added to the experience at various times over the years.
—*Charles Hou*

The trail was heavily used from 1858 to 1864. It was replaced by the Cariboo Wagon Road in 1864. The Harrison–Lillooet route involved the intensive handling of cargo and delays in transportation (paddlewheel to Port Douglas, 46 kilometres by wagon or stage to Little Lillooet Lake, boat to the north end of the lake, wagon or hike to Lillooet Lake, paddlewheel to Port Pemberton, 48 kilometres by wagon or stage to Anderson Lake, paddlewheel to the end of the lake, 1.5 kilometres by rail (BC's first "railway") to Seton Lake, paddlewheel to the end of the lake, eight kilometres by wagon to Lillooet, ferry to the other side of the river, wagon or stage to Barkerville (hence Lillooet is mile zero). The Cariboo Wagon road was far more efficient. Paddlewheel to Yale and wagon or stage all the way to Barkerville.

California was the benchmark, and Douglas believed the Cariboo would reach it. The proud governor determined that a discovery of that magnitude merited a much better route, a wagon road up the Fraser, along the Thompson and due north. He decided to press ahead with the new colony's most ambitious public works project yet, the Cariboo Road: "To provide for the wants of the population becomes one of the paramount duties of the government. I therefore propose to push on rapidly with the formation of roads during the coming winter, in order to have the great thoroughfares leading to the remotest mines, now upwards of 500 miles from the sea coast, so improved as to render travel easy, and to reduce the cost of transport, thereby securing the whole trade of the colony from Fraser's River and defeating all attempts at competition from Oregon."

Strikes It Rich, Dies a Pauper

Here we have the grave of Billy Barker. He probably didn't have any marker, not even a wooden one when he was first buried—unless some of his friends thought of it. This marker is a plaque put here by the Historical Society; there is a slight error, he was not Cornish. He came from Cambridgeshire in England. He travelled around a bit before he got up to the Cariboo—he actually came late to it. Unfortunately old Billy went the way of so many gold rush guys who struck it rich: it just disappeared. I often say to the kids who visit, "Imagine if you won the lottery and all the friends you'd have the next day." People like Billy Barker would have dozens of friends who were dead broke—even starving. So of course he'd give the money to them. He didn't end up in Victoria until he was quite elderly and sick. And there used to be an old men's home in what is now the corner of the cemetery—it wasn't actually in the cemetery at the time! He died there, and was buried down here in the potter's field."

—*from a tour of Ross Bay Cemetery guided by Yvonne Van Ruskenveld, volunteer with the Old Cemeteries Society*

Young Overlander Laid to Rest

In 1862, a group of more than 250 people now known as the Overlanders set out from eastern Canada to travel 5,600 kilometres overland to the Cariboo goldfields. It was the only organized immigration from eastern to western Canada prior to the era of the railways. Among them was a young man of 19 years named Eustace Pattison. He is my connection to the gold rush, being a relative on my mother's side.

The Overlanders crossed the Rocky Mountains through the Yellowhead Pass and reached the Fraser River near Tete Jaune Cache in late August 1862. By this time they were nearly out of food and some of the party killed their oxen and horses for food. The temperature was dropping to near freezing at night. As soon as they got there, they began building huge rafts on which to float their oxen, their supplies and themselves down the Fraser River to the gold-fields. According to Rev. F.E. Runnalls, in his book *A History of Prince George*, one such raft was only 85 x 22 feet (25 x 7 metres) in size, yet it carried nine head of oxen.

Because of the shortage of supplies, 36 of their number volunteered to venture south

The treacherous Grand Canyon on the Upper Fraser River has claimed many lives, including some members of the Overlanders party in 1862. *British Columbia Archives D-07686*

to the headwaters of the North Thompson River from Tete Jaune Cache. They eventually reached Kamloops and continued downstream to Lytton, where they arrived on October 25, 1862. They drove 130 horses through this southern route, as Richard Thomas Wright reports in his book *Overlanders*. Two members of the party were drowned on the journey.

The main party, of which Eustace Pattison was a member and which was led by Thomas McMicking, started down the Fraser River at Tete Jaune Cache on September 1 that year. McMicking wrote in his journal that the weather was very cold, wet and uncomfortable throughout the river journey. The flotilla included several rafts, half a dozen canoes and even two bull boats of green hide stretched on willow. William McKenzie, James Carroll and Eustace Pattison were the first to leave the Cache, paddling a canoe they had purchased from the Natives. Young Pattison was ill. For several days he had felt a general malaise that was now concentrated in his throat. The trip had not gone well for him in general. The guide, Rochette, had deserted and had stolen Pattison's gun; then Pattison had lost his horse. He had been carrying a letter from J. Richard Stevenson to his brother Edward Stevenson in his pocket for four months and had only realized at Tete Jaune that the Dr. Edward Stevenson of his party was the addressee. Unfortunately, in delivering the mail, he did not ask for medical attention.

McKenzie, Carroll and Pattison were the first to arrive at the Grand Canyon of the Fraser River, located 160 kilometres upstream from Fort George. They realized it could not be run safely, and they attempted to line their canoe around, but the current caught the boat and swept it away. The canoe filled with water and sank, taking all of their provisions with it. The men now huddled on shore to await help. It was two days before the first raft party reached them—two days of cold and rain, without food, extra clothing or shelter. By the time rescue came, Pattison was so sick he could scarcely talk or swallow.

Eustace Pattison died on September 8, the day he arrived at Fort George. He had contracted diphtheria, and there was little that Dr. Stevenson could do. A small canoe was cut in half to make a coffin, and at 10:30 a.m. on September 9, 1862, he was "slowly and sadly" lowered into his grave.

Thomas McMicking reported in his journal that Eustace Pattison was 19 years of age at the time of his death. He was a shy, quiet young man and a "keen student of biology." Born at Launceston, Cornwall, England, he was the son of Samuel Rowles Pattison, a London solicitor. Eustace Pattison was also the first white man known to have been buried at Fort George. His unmarked grave is contained in the First Nations burial ground, located in what is now known as Fort George Park in Prince George.

—*Patrick Stapleton, Prince George*

RIP: Rebecca Gibbs, Black Pioneer

Rebecca Gibbs was the poetess of the Cariboo. The front of her grave marker says that she was a nurse, a laundress and a poet. She was one of the black pioneers who came through

Victoria and ended up going to Barkerville. She lived there for many, many years and had her own business, as well as being published quite extensively in the *Cariboo Sentinel*. Her most famous poem, "The Old Red Shirt," which is on the back of her grave marker, is key because it really represents what life was like for most of the miners—most of them went completely broke. She says:

> He said that the old red shirt was torn
> And asked me to give it a stitch;
> But it was threadbare and sorely worn,
> Which showed he was far from rich.

Then she goes on to exhort miners with good-paying claims and traders who wish to do good:

> Have pity on men who earn your wealth,
> Grudge not the poor miner his food.

The Victoria newspapers at the time show that all kinds of local fundraising was going on, organized by local women involved in social services. Of course in those days it was the prominent and privileged women who did those things—raising money for the poor, starving miners of the Cariboo.

—from a tour of Ross Bay Cemetery guided by Yvonne Van Ruskenveld, volunteer with the Old Cemeteries Society

There was one area of competition that Douglas would have to accept, if not actively encourage if the miners were not to starve. That was the provision of beef. British Columbia did not yet have an established cattle industry. The nearest supplies of any quantity were in the Oregon and Washington Territories, and so the Cariboo rush opened up one of the legendary cattle drives of western history.

Douglas had imposed a tax on imported beef, but he wrote to one of his gold commissioners, William Cox, that nothing should be done to discourage American cattlemen from supplying the Cariboo market:

> The great number of miners now traveling by Fraser's River towards the Cariboo mines will rapidly consume the small stock of food in the country—and great distress must necessarily ensue unless supplies of meat and breadstuffs are brought into the country with dispatch and regularity. It is almost hopeless to expect that food in sufficient quantities to satisfy the multitudes that will this year resort to the Cariboo, can be carried into that distant region on mules or horses. The means of transport are clearly insufficient for the large demand that may be anticipated... Mr. Cox is therefore instructed to encourage as much as possible the importation of sheep and cattle from the Southern Boundary and to be careful not to permit any obstacle to be thrown in the way of persons driving cattle from the US Territory for the purpose of being sent to the

Cariboo. Two or three thousand head of live cattle driven into the mines would effectually relieve us for the present year and I expect that number of cattle at least.

Ranchers in the Willamette, Dalles and Walla Walla regions saw the need and determined that cattle could be driven along the Columbia, up the Okanagan River system and into the Cariboo—at a profit. In fact, a cow purchased in Oregon for $10 (about $165 today) could easily be sold for 10 times that price in the goldfields. The trail was rough and the mosquitoes terrible, but the grazing was excellent and the cost minimal, only the price of hiring a team of drovers to get the cattle to the Cariboo.

In 1862, more than 4,000 head of cattle crossed the border. In 1863, many fewer were brought to the Cariboo, forcing prices up. But over the next few years, the annual drives averaged 3,000 head.

The boardwalks of Barkerville protected residents from frequent flooding and the filth of the street below. Fortunes were made delivering beef on the hoof to hungry miners and other townspeople.
British Columbia Archives A-03783

Ranch Country at Clinton

Once a busy junction on the wagon road leading to the Cariboo and Barkerville goldfields, Clinton was originally known as The Junction and Cut Off Valley, before being renamed in 1863 to honour the Colonial Secretary, Henry Pelham Clinton, the 5th Duke of Newcastle. A historical cairn in Clinton marks the junction of two routes to the Cariboo gold mines: the original 1859 Cariboo Trail from Lillooet, and the Cariboo Road through the Fraser Canyon, built in 1863 by the Royal Engineers (see Chapter 6). Situated halfway to these goldfields, Clinton was an ideal place for weary travellers suffering from gold fever to stop for food, rest, entertainment and even encouragement. Clinton grew with the demand for these services.

True to its rawhide roots, Clinton's Main Street still exudes a Wild West flavour, with

Clinton was an important junction. Two routes to the goldfields met here—one from Lillooet, the other from the Fraser Canyon. The town was named in 1863 in honour of Lord Henry Pelham Clinton, the colonial secretary of the day.
British Columbia Archives A-00346

many buildings boasting their original storefronts, and restored to retain the early western atmosphere and character. The area surrounding Clinton is known as the Guest Ranch Capital of British Columbia. From historic Hat Creek Ranch to Kelly Lake, Big Bar Lake and Jesmond, many guest ranches offer the genuine trail-ridin' cowboy experience.
—*Anne Freeman, Big Bar Ranch, Clinton*

Eventually, six men—the Van Volkenburgh brothers, Jerome and Thaddeus Harper and Edward Toomey—formed a company and set up stores in Barkerville, Richfield and Cameronton, controlling the cattle trade and establishing some of the province's major ranches. By 1870, the big drives were over, because the BC cattle industry was sufficient to supply the Interior market.

Horsefly

This town was originally called Harper's Camp after the pioneer rancher Thaddeus Harper. Horseflies are plentiful here in the summer.

Gold Rush Businessmen

Merchants and speculators from San Francisco were quick to join the gold hungry hordes bound for the Fraser River, in the spring and summer of 1858. They were ready to try anything from delivering mail and building toll bridges across roaring creeks to serving the finest cigars and whisky in ramshackled saloons. Some entrepreneurs remained only until winter set in, then left for good, but others, like Billy Ballou, the Barry brothers and the Chinese merchant firm of Kwong Lee helped to lay the commercial foundation for the new Colony of British Columbia.

Hudson's Bay Company clerk Ovid Allard was sent to Yale from Fort Langley to reestablish the abandoned store soon after American bootleggers first appeared at Hill's Bar. Backed by a relative who owned a wholesale and retail liquor business in San Francisco, Tom and James Barry with Sam Adler opened a saloon on Front Street at Yale that first summer. When the search for gold proceeded further north in 1859, James remained to operate the saloon, while Tom and Sam packed goods in to Quesnel Forks. They built a saloon at the Forks and a toll bridge across the Quesnel River. Two years later they went to Barkerville to open a much grander establishment. Sam liked to be on the cusp of gold discoveries so he spent the rest of his life following rushes to Atlin, the Kootenays and Granite Creek.

Billy Ballou had delivered mail during the California rush and was able to quickly establish his express business at Yale. Although two other express companies offered competition, Ballou extended his service throughout gold country by connecting with Dan Braley's Pony Express at Lillooet, which went as far north as Horsefly and Quesnel Forks. James Batterton helped Ballou service the many mining sites along the Fraser and Thompson Rivers.

The firm of Kwong Lee was based in Victoria and imported goods from companies in San Francisco and China. Besides carrying the usual provisions it also manufactured opium. Kwong Lee followed the development of the gold rush with stores at Yale, Lillooet, Quesnellemouth, Quesnel Forks and Barkerville. Their merchants joined the miners in signing numerous petitions to the colonial government for better roads and services.

Native men and women became business people too, making money from all these merchants. They packed in their provisions, built and sold canoes, and transported them up and down the rivers. Many native men were employed by the numerous packtrains that carried tons of goods to the Interior of the province during the short travelling season from April to October.

—*Marie Elliot, Friends of the BC Archives*

Eighteen sixty-two was also the year of a serious smallpox epidemic throughout the province. Native people were hardest hit. Those who came to Victoria to trade took the disease back to their communities in the Interior and on the North Coast.

The Smallpox Crisis

When staying at "The Lakes," we had seen a spot where about twelve wretched Indians had been buried by some of the settlers in the neighbourhood. All had been seized with smallpox, and, immediately on the appearance of the disease amongst them, their fellow-countrymen had abandoned them to their inevitable fate. The dread of disease by the Indians far surpasses their fear of violent or sudden death. The manner in which the sick and dying are thus forsaken by their companions is merely amongst the numerous illustrations of the degradation and depravity of human nature, when not enlightened by the blessed influence of the Gospel, prompting at self-risk to seek the good of others... In case of the abandoned Indians just referred to, they all died one after another, and remained unburied for days, until their bodies attracted the attention of some white neighbours, who, by means of long poles and rakes, managed to thrust the remains of the poor wretches into one common grave, dug for them hard by the scene of their desolate death.

—*W. Champness,* To Cariboo and Back in 1862

The Kipp Connection

During the gold rush years, Henry Kipp travelled from Ontario through the Panama Canal to the west coast, to Victoria and New Westminster. From there he canoed to Yale, and then he walked from Yale to Barkerville just when the Cariboo Road was completed. In Barkerville he found no gold riches, but he did make money playing violin in Professor Carpenter's orchestra for $25 per night.

After two years of work there, Henry travelled to Chilliwack to farm with his brother Isaac, whose wife was the first Caucasian woman on the Chilliwack Prairie and whose daughter was the first Caucasian child in the valley. Kipp Road in Chilliwack is named after these Kipps, and Kipp Road in Kamloops was named after their grandson Walter. In another story of Kipp adventurers, Walter's son Bob holds two records—destroying four German aircraft in a single night, as pilot of his Mosquito, and leading the first aerobatic Air Force squadron in Canada, the group now known as the Snowbirds.

—*Paul Kipp, Kamloops*

The Civil War would soon be raging in the United States. But in Victoria, Governor James Douglas was not sympathetic to the powers now engaged in an epic battle for survival of the union. He was an abolitionist, but it was not clear to him whether President Abraham Lincoln was an ally. In the early years of the war, Lincoln was still resisting emancipation of the slaves. His prime objective was to bring the rebellious states back into the union, even if it meant preserving slavery. Douglas, who had provided sanctuary for free blacks in Victoria in 1858, was equally pragmatic. If Lincoln could defend slavery to save the union, Douglas could advocate war to right a historic wrong against British North America. He had an audacious plan: an all-out assault on the US northwest to retake the Oregon Territories that the British had lost in the 1840s. In December 1861, Douglas proposed to catch the Americans off guard while they were preoccupied with their own war: "I conceive that our only chance of success will be found in assuming the offensive, and taking possession of Puget Sound with Her Majesty's ships, reinforced by such bodies of local auxiliaries as can, in the emergency, be raised, whenever hostilities are actually declared, and by that means effectually preventing the departure of any hostile armament against the British Colonies, and at one blow cutting off the enemy's supplies by sea, destroying his foreign trade, and entirely crippling his resources, before any organization of the inhabitants into military bodies can have effect."

Britain was not at war with the United States and did not want to be. The two countries came close in 1859, when a dispute arose over the San Juan Islands south of Victoria. American troops occupied the islands and Douglas responded with a proclamation of British ownership. He had the fighting spirit. But he did not have the support of British naval officers stationed at Esquimalt. They discouraged his sabre-rattling, knowing that London would not support any military adventures on the Pacific. The Navy brush-off was a rebuke to his authority, but Douglas was ready to try again in 1861:

Should Her Majesty's Government decide, as lately mooted, on sending out one or two regiments of Queen's troops, there is no reason why we should not push overland from Puget Sound and establish advanced posts on the Columbia River, maintaining it as a permanent frontier.

A small naval force entering the Columbia River at the same time would secure possession and render occupation complete—there is not much fear from the scattered population of settlers, as they would be too glad to remain quiet and follow their peaceful avocations under any government capable of protecting them from the savages.

With Puget Sound and the line of the Columbia in our hands, we should hold the only navigable outlets of the country, command its trade, and soon compel it to submit to Her Majesty's rule... This may appear a hazardous operation to persons unacquainted with the real state of these countries, but I am firmly persuaded of its practicability.

It was Douglas's last effort to reclaim lost territory, and there was no encouragement from London. But there would be other triumphs. One of his greatest accomplishments still lay ahead: the Cariboo Road.

6

ALL-BRITISH ROUTE UP THE FRASER

The Cariboo Road

The Cariboo Wagon Road was the colonial engineering marvel of its time, no less impressive than the Trans-Canada or the Coquihalla. It was 5.5 metres wide and 492 kilometres long, and it stretched from Yale—the head of steamboat navigation—to Barkerville. And it was built in a few short years during the gold rush by a remarkable cast of characters.

The Cariboo Road was also the most enduring legacy of the gold rush era. It was built for the express purpose of getting prospectors and hangers-on to the goldfields, but long after the gold seekers had gone home to eastern Canada, Europe and the US, the road was still used by those who decided to stay and make a home here. Between 1862 and 1865, colonial officials, with the help of the Royal Engineers and some extraordinary private contractors, designed and built a highway system that stretched north to the Cariboo, and another route east to the Rockies.

In proposing the Cariboo Road, Governor James Douglas was building on his first major transportation project, the Harrison Route (Douglas Trail) from the head of Harrison Lake to Lillooet, on the Fraser River. That project had been built in 1858 with public money,

Opposite: On the road from Yale, seen in the *Canadian Illustrated News*, January 6, 1872

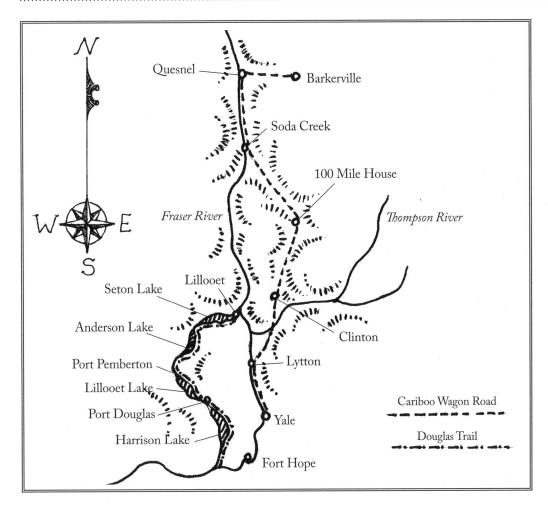

employing black, Chinese, Hawaiian and American expatriate miners who were out of work. The route served two purposes. It provided jobs for miners who might otherwise become a public nuisance, and it provided a safer transportation network of shipping, portages and trails to the Fraser River above Yale.

The Harrison Route had its drawbacks. The repeated transfer of materials from boat to packhorse and back to boat again proved complicated and expensive, and it only solved one problem: access to the upper Fraser. Now the Cariboo was opening up as the new centre of the gold rush, and Governor Douglas needed an "all-British" route up the Fraser. The Americans, he knew, were anxious to challenge the new colony's virtual monopoly on selling supplies to the miners, and he needed to discourage them from establishing alternative shipping routes that would channel revenues south of the border.

Douglas had big dreams for his new colony. His network of roads would connect the lower mainland with goldfields in the Cariboo, the Boundary Country and the Kootenays, but that was only the beginning. Ultimately, he was dreaming of a "trans-Canada" highway, "part of an overland communication with Canada by a route possessing the peculiar advantages of being secure from the Indian aggression [peace with the First Nations was still far from secure, and Indian wars raged south of the border], remote from the United States frontier, and traversing a country exclusively British, and which from its position, character and general resources can hardly fail, in the ordinary course of events, to become the seat of a large population."

A wagon road up the Fraser River to the Cariboo would transform the river where nature had refused passage. Ever since the Hudson's Bay Company had lost the lower Columbia to the Americans, Douglas had bemoaned the fact that the river he was left with, the Fraser, was much less hospitable. It connected the colony, but it was far too treacherous to navigate by boat or steamer. No human feat of engineering could change that, but a wagon road along the river could create a new artery on land.

One continuous route would also overcome the ruinous costs of shipping to the Cariboo. In 1860, the cost of shipping a ton of supplies from Victoria to Alexandria, one of the gateways to the Cariboo, was over $800 ($20,000 today). Miners trying to open up the new goldfields turned away when they saw just how much basic necessities cost on the ground. Douglas intended to remedy that, and he would soon have the funds on hand to build a new, more efficient route.

The new colony was starting to make money. Customs duties, miners' licences, tolls and land sales were on the rise. And while the Colonial Office in London was reluctant to finance any big projects on the Pacific, Douglas was soon able to secure a loan locally for £50,000. The Cariboo Wagon Road was a go!

In the spring of 1862, the number of miners heading for the Cariboo approached the records set in the opening months of the Fraser rush. Some 4,000 miners took the Harrison and Fraser routes, and another 1,000 followed the Hudson's Bay Brigade trail through the Okanagan. They were headed for towns with magical names: Richfield, Lightning, Van Winkle and, of course, Barkerville. And Douglas was building them a road.

The plan was that the Royal Engineers would build two strategic sections, and the rest

Teaming Up the Cariboo Road

Here comes Henry Currie, he's always in a hurry
Teaming up the Cariboo road
He makes his horses go through the dust and through the snow
Teaming up the Cariboo road
You should see him sprintin' to the ball at Clinton
Teaming up the Cariboo road
He makes his horses dance just like the ladies prance
Teaming up the Cariboo road

Chorus:
When you hear that whip a-popping, You bet he's got a load
When you hear that sweet voice singing
Stand up rowdy on the Cariboo road

Pete Egan as a rule to his horses he is cruel...
He beats them with a rail puts fire in their tail...
Old Pete can look so wicked when you ask him for a ticket...
At the sight of half a dollar he will grab you by the collar...

Well the driver's on the deck with a rag around his neck...
While the swamper in the stable makes sure the teams are able.
When the roads are in a mire then the freighters earn their hire...
But they can beat the weather when they all pull together...

—recorded by the late Phil Thomas, who collected, wrote and sang folk music in British Columbia for more than 50 years. "This song is a reworking of the 1885 Tin Pan Alley minstrel song, 'Climbing Up the Golden Stairs'," he wrote, "made to fit the Ashcroft Barkerville trunk road after the construction of the CPR. It is based on two oral fragments, the major one with the chorus sung for me by Gerald Currie, Chase, BC, in 1963."

would be constructed by private contractors, who would win the right to collect tolls. The road project would be a public-private partnership in the truest sense.

Ships of the Desert

Talk about invasive species. In April 1862, twenty-three camels arrived by ship at Esquimalt on Vancouver Island, to be used on the Cariboo trail as pack animals. It seemed like a good idea at the time; camels could haul twice as much freight as horses and go for days without water. However there were problems. The trail mules and horses were terrified of the Arabian interlopers, and stampedes often ensued with supplies flying everywhere; some

Camels were brought to BC in 1862 for use during the gold rush, to pack supplies into the Cariboo. But they frightened the other pack animals and were soon sold off and turned loose. At least one survived on the open range until the turn of the 20th century. *British Columbia Archives A-00347*

animals fell over cliffs to their deaths. It got so bad the government outlawed camels on the Cariboo Trail. In addition, the camels' soft hooves, which were adapted to fine sand, didn't fare well on the rocky terrain.

Some camels were sold to ranchers; others were released into the wild. The sighting of one was reported from a farm at Grande Prairie, Alberta, in 1896. The camels are still remembered in Lillooet, where the Bridge of Twenty Three Camels crosses the Fraser River. Janet May, a CBC listener in Powell River, salutes them in this poem:

Lament of a BC Pioneer
I am the graceful dromedary.
I dislike all things ordinary.
The common mules go marching by,
With manners that would make you cry.

One day along the canyon side
I met a mule, the nasty snide.
He backed and snorted, then he cried,
"Pink ink, you stink!" and I replied,
"Egad, but you're a horrid mammal
And I am such a with-it camel.
I feel your backpack is too small,

And if I trip you, you will fall.
Look down, you see the Fraser wide,
And if you do not hide your pride
And hastily step to one side,
I'll pitch you in the foaming tide!"

He didn't, I did, and now
He's died!

Work on the road began at Yale in the spring of 1862. The process was particularly slow and laborious on the lower Fraser and Thompson Rivers. That route had to be blasted out of rock, or built up with cribbing to hang a road from the cliff faces. George Hills, the new Anglican Bishop of British Columbia, travelled widely through his diocese, and in summer 1862 he witnessed the work near Jackass Mountain:

The especial difficulty now was the blasting operations of the road makers, high up on the mountain side, from which came down, with tremendous force and fury, whole avalanches of rocks and smaller debris, shooting over and past the trail, and utterly blotting it out. We were told we could pass when the workmen ceased their labours for the day; so we waited patiently, and about seven o'clock started to cross this dangerous point. On coming up to where the road was, I saw at once there was a great risk for our animals, which would, having to cross the mass of loose stones, be sure to lose their footing and probably be rolled with their packs; so I determined to take the lower trail, which, though very bad, avoided that particular difficulty... A huge rock, however, precipitated from above, some twenty yards ahead only of the spot where I stood, made me conclude it would not be safe until the blasting was over. That being the case, we proceeded... the train passed on, missing a turning upon which they should have gone, and went forward to a most dangerous and impassable trail... The narrow pathway, on which ten horses (seven of them bearing packs) and six men were now standing, had not in some portions of it ten inches of footing. Above was the perpendicular mountain and below was a chasm down to the torrent, some 800 feet... By God's mercy, we succeeded in turning each horse, and after considerable anxiety and exertion regained the right path and continued our journey till dark.

··

Jackass Mountain

At this site in the Fraser Canyon, the Cariboo Road drops some 250 metres to the river below. Before it was widened into a road, a jackass loaded with miner's supplies stepped into the abyss.

··

The bishop's account gives just a small glimpse of the perils encountered by the miners before the Cariboo Road was completed, and shows what an engineering miracle the road was. In the fall of 1862, by which time the road had reached Lytton, Governor Douglas made

The Cariboo Wagon Road, built in just a few years (1862–1865), was called the Eighth Wonder of the World. It was punched through steep, rocky terrain that was better suited for mountain sheep. The switchbacks and steep dropoffs of Jackass Mountain, photographed in 1868, shook the confidence of many travellers. *British Columbia Archives, A-03879*

his own inspection of the work completed so far: "In smoothness and solidity [the roads] surpass expectation—Jackass mountain. The Cleft. The Great Slides. The Rocky Bridges and other passes of ominous fame, so notorious in the history of the country—have lost their terrors. They now exist only in name being rendered alike safe and pleasant by the broad and graceful windings of the Queen's Highway."

It is difficult to believe that the new road was as pleasant as Douglas described it, because the work would go on for several more years, and there were many interruptions and dangers along the way. But even this stage was a major improvement, and Douglas was satisfied with the first year's progress. He hoped that it would be a tribute not only to the men who built it,

This British Columbia and Express Company stagecoach, photographed near Clinton in 1880, was driven by Stephen Tingley in the late 1850s. Eventually he bought the company and ran it for three decades. At one time "the BX" operated the longest stagecoach operation in North America, serving points between Yale and Barkerville. The best time logged was a non-stop journey 611 kilometres long that took 30 hours. It usually took the stage about four days to cover that distance. *British Columbia Archives -03074*

but also to his vision in those first difficult years of colony building.

The governor's project may have been popular with the miners. But at home in Victoria, Douglas was no hero. The newspapers were having a field day, skewering him for his authoritarian ways. Some of his key appointees also proved to be bounders. The acting postmaster of Victoria put his hand in the till and left the country for Germany. The acting harbourmaster proved to be a bad bookkeeper too. And the colonial treasurer was charged with embezzlement. Amor de Cosmos, editor of the Victoria *Colonist*, saw a pattern of mismanagement and laid the blame at the governor's square-toed boots: "Sooner or later the administration of Gov. Douglas will break down—will end—and a new administration will be inaugurated in its place. The elements of dissolution abound. Its glaring blunders, its sins of omission and commission, and above all its scandalous disregard of moral and legal right, preclude the possibility of its ever becoming popular or successful, but, on the contrary, holds out the uninviting prospect of being continually and justly execrated."

Riding with the BX

Both my great-grandfathers heard of the gold rush in BC and joined the many people heading west via the isthmus of Panama.

In 1858 my paternal great-grandfather, Stephen Tingley, left New Brunswick at age 19. He ended up in the Cariboo, working with F.J. Barnard, who had started the BC Express Company, known as the BX. He became a partner, then bought out Barnard and ran the BX

133

for the next 30 years. Much has been written of his skill as a stagecoach driver and his business interests in the Cariboo region.

Of the many important events of his life, two that took place in 1868 are recorded in his diary of that year. In January he left the Cariboo and made his way down to California, to purchase additional horses for the burgeoning transportation company. In mid-August he returned, having driven 500 horses overland to Vernon, BC, where the BX ranch was started. On November 7 he left Victoria and travelled by steamer to San Francisco, then overland by train to Boston, then up to St. John and Sackville, and he got married on February 24, 1869.

A few short years later, he took the same route back to Sackville with his two young sons and his wife's body in a lead-lined coffin. She had died in a buggy accident near Yale. The two boys remained in New Brunswick and were brought up by relatives. When they finished their schooling, they returned to BC to join their father in the business.

During the years they were apart, father and sons kept in touch through heartfelt and touching letters. One letter from my great-grandfather, enclosed in a black-edged envelope and postmarked 1875, states: "I am anxious for you to learn to write so you can write me letters… Clarence will remember something of BC of your Yale home and of your Dear Mama… Freddie cannot as he was so young so you must tell him as he gets big like you what a Dear Mama he and you had… I think of you always and am trying to do the best I can for you but this is a rough hard country."

My maternal great-grandfather, Charles G. Major, arrived in BC in June 1859 and spent two years working for the BX. He was one of the drivers of the first BX passenger stagecoach on the winding Cariboo Road.

In 1862, after clearing land for the townsite of New Westminster with John Robson, he headed to the Cariboo. He returned to New West in 1864, went into business and became a well-known member of that growing community.

—*Lael Hamilton, Bowen Island*

Tingley Creek

This creek, which flows into the Fraser River near Marguerite, was named after Stephen Tingley, the most famous stagecoach driver on the Cariboo Road, who later bought the BX company.

Douglas's new road turned out to be more expensive than he expected, and he had to go to the Colonial Office for permission to raise another £50,000. He wanted to borrow £100,000, but that was vetoed. Still, the positive reports from the goldfields could not be ignored: close to $3 million produced in 1862 and, by some estimates, more than $6 million in 1863 (almost $1 billion in today's dollars). There was no way of knowing just how much gold was being taken out of the ground. Some observers claimed the unreported amount was much higher.

For a privileged few, the gold rush brought incredible wealth. For many, there was great disappointment. But because of the new road project, there were new opportunities. Men could now earn good wages working for one of the many contractors building the Cariboo Road.

Thompson River

Simon Fraser named the river in 1808, after David Thompson, an explorer who worked for the Hudson's Bay Company and the North West Company and who travelled an astounding 128,000 kilometres. His precise maps were used for decades.

Joseph Trutch, who built the road between Chapman's Bar and Boston Bar, also became famous for constructing the Alexandra Bridge, a suspension bridge across the Fraser near Spuzzum, and later he served as the province's first lieutenant-governor. Walter Moberly and Charles Oppenheimer had the contract to build the road between Lytton and Spences

The original Alexandra Bridge, 20 kilometres north of Yale, was a suspension bridge built in 1863 by Joseph Trutch for the Cariboo Wagon Road. It is shown here in 1870. The bridge was washed out in 1894 and replaced in 1926, and is now part of a provincial park. *British Columbia Archives A-03928*

Bridge. They ran out of money and had to bring in new investors, and they turned to Chinese labourers, establishing a practice that would be repeated a few years later when the Canadian Pacific Railway was built along the same route. Between Clinton and Alexandria (formerly Fort Alexandria), Gustavus Blin Wright was at work on the road. He was given the right to charge tolls and worked hard to complete his section by the fall of 1863.

Palmer's Route

In 1862 Henry Palmer, a Royal Engineer, was given the task of surveying an old Native trail from the Bella Coola valley up to and across the Chilcotin plateau to the old Hudson's Bay Company Fort Alexandria on the Fraser River. It was a shorter land route than the Fraser Canyon wagon road, also being explored in 1862 (which became the Cariboo Wagon Road).

The trail was being used by miners at the time. It was generally level but had one major difficult piece, up the "precipice," as the men called it, from the Atnarko valley in Tweedsmuir Park. This obstacle was bypassed in 1955 by the Freedom Road, built by local residents with an 18 percent grade.

Packhorses and footwork were the mode of travel on the path. Some wagons were used on the plateau, but the going was very difficult: it took Palmer 25 days to cover a distance of 450 kilometres. Not only was the terrain rough, but also there were clashes of cultures when the surveying party met remote groups of First Nations people. The smallpox epidemic was reducing whole Native villages from hundreds of residents to a few individuals, and the stench of death was appalling.

The path crosses the Chilcotin plateau near Charlotte Lake (west of Anahim) and the Dean River at Towdystan, then goes to Puntzi Lake, Alexis Lakes, Palmer Lake and Narcosli Creek to the Fraser River at Fort Alexandria. The men arrived with one day's food left.

This route was used by miners, fur traders and others until the 1930s, but it was gradually reclaimed by nature, and now little evidence of it remains. During a new survey by F. Swannell in 1925, a blazed tree was found near the western end; this is the only confirmed site location of the original survey. (The blaze and message are housed in the BC Archives.)

Eight years ago, Tory Exshaw, a local rancher, led me to a spot on Palmer's route at the crossing of the north fork of Narcosli Creek. It consists of three pits in a triangle with a mound in the centre. This was a method of marking survey spots where trees or rocks were hard to find (metal pins were not in use at the time). The spot is flagged to prevent adjacent logging activity from damaging it. I have not been able to verify who erected the marker, as it is not recorded in archaeological records or land surveys.

Wildfires and logging have removed all other evidence of the original survey on the plateau. Palmer Lake, near Alexis Creek, is named for Henry Palmer, whose trail followed the shore. An S- bend between the Alexis Lakes is another marker of the trail.

In those days, a trail was viable only if hay and pasture were available nearby, to feed the horses. Neither was available in quantity for this route, thus the Fraser Canyon became the route to gold.

—*Andy Motherwell, Alexander Mackenzie Trail Association, Quesnel*

100 Mile House

A roadhouse was built at this spot along the Cariboo Road in the 1860s, 100 miles (160 km) from the start of the road at Lillooet.

Road building wasn't easy anywhere along the route, but at Lytton the work became less arduous as the road left the river and went overland, through Clinton and 100 Mile House. In his book *The North-West Passage by Land*, Walter Cheadle wrote about travelling the Cariboo Road in 1863:

> We crossed the Thompson at the foot of Kamloops Lake, which is about twelve miles long and not more than half a mile in breadth, and surrounded by fine rocky hills; then, leaving the river, we kept on to the valley of the Bonaparte, where we struck the road from Cariboo to Yale, as yet only partially completed.
>
> Soon after we again reached the Thompson, we came to a place where a portion of the road was not yet made, and led our horses over high rocky bluffs, which at first sight appeared completely to bar all passage. The trail was a mere ledge of rock a few inches in width, and conquered the precipitous ascent by a succession of windings and zig-zags. The path was so narrow that it was quite impossible for horses to pass one another, and as the river rushes hundreds of feet immediately below, and even a slip would be certainly fatal, it is necessary to ascertain that the road is clear before venturing over the dangerous precipices.
>
> Along this part of the road we met a number of Chinamen at work levelling the road, and their strange faces, large-brimmed hats, and pig-tails, caused intense amusement to our unsophisticated [Indian guides]. Further down a party of engineers were engaged in blasting the rock where the road was to pass around the face of a bluff, and eight or ten miles more brought us to the point where the road crosses the eastern bank of the Thompson. At this place, called Cook's Ferry [now Spences Bridge], we stayed the night.
>
> From Cook's Ferry the road continues to follow the eastern bank of the Thompson to its junction with the Fraser at Lytton—twenty-three miles; it is then continued along the same side of the Fraser for thirty-eight miles, or within thirteen miles of Yale, where it crosses the river by a beautiful suspension bridge. The road from Cook's Ferry to Yale, especially the part below Lytton, is probably the most wonderful in the world. Cut out of the mountain-side of the gorge, it follows the hills as they recede in "gulches," or advance in bold, upright bluffs, in constant windings, like an eternal letter *S*.

Wells

A new era of gold mining in the Cariboo began in the 1930s, when Fred Wells developed the Cariboo Gold Quartz Mine. Wells is named after him.

Cariboo Mail by Dogsled

Each year for the past 15 years, the Gold Rush Trail Sled Dog Association has organized the Gold Rush Trail Sled Dog Mail Run. Teams of sled dogs, along with skiers, skijorers and snowmobilers, travel over much of the Cariboo Wagon Road from Quesnel to Barkerville and Wells, passing through the locations of seven existing or former post offices as well as the sites of several other former gold rush settlements and roadhouses. The Gold Rush Trail Sled Dog Mail Run is almost the last endeavour on the earth in which "official" mail is actually transported along its regular route toward its final destination by sled-dog team.

Mail was first delivered to the Cariboo region of British Columbia by canoe and occasionally by dog team in the early 1800s. The North West Company—and, after 1821, the Hudson's Bay Company—maintained a tenuous supply line stretching from Fort Edmonton through Fort McLeod in the north and east, and along the Oregon Trail connecting Fort St. James in the heart of New Caledonia with the mouth of the Columbia River in Oregon to the south and west.

In the early 1860s, mail was carried on foot over a rough-hewn route to the Cariboo goldfields. With the improvement of the Cariboo Wagon Road, horses quickly assumed the role of major transporter, and at the same time, transportation companies took on the role of postal authority. Now that British Columbia was a colony the government took some responsibility for the mail, but it was the transportation companies that still "filled the bill"—they even created their own postage stamps. When British Columbia became a province in 1871, post offices as we now know them were established, under the responsibility of the federal government.

There are many heartwarming stories associated with Sled Dog Mail Run deliveries. An elderly man in a South Carolina nursing home gathered the other residents around when his envelope was delivered by the letter carrier so that they could all "see the snow fall out of it when it was opened." A woman tells of visiting her son in Zambia almost at the same time that the postie arrived to deliver an envelope "Carried By Dogteam" over the Gold Rush Trail.

—*Jeffrey Dinsdale, Quesnel*

By the spring of 1864, Francis Barnard was running four-horse stagecoaches between Yale and Soda Creek, where a steamer took miners on to Quesnel. The Royal Engineers pushed through the bush to make a trail from Quesnel to Barkerville. Margaret Ormsby wrote in *British Columbia: A History*: "The colony of British Columbia had a great inland highway, acquired at the price of a bonded debt of only 112,780 pounds, as well as permanent agricultural settlements."

Walter Cheadle described the "stage" in 1863:

[It was] a light open wagon, and besides ourselves and one other passenger, carried nearly a ton of freight. But we started with a team of five horses, two wheelers and three leaders, and for the first day went along famously. "Johnny," the driver, was a capital whip, and quite a character. He was a regular Yankee, and his Californian hat of hard felt, with a low steeple crown, and immensely broad brim, gave him a ludicrous appearance in our eyes. He was like all his race, a most unquiet spirit, always engaged in talking to us or the horses, chewing, spitting, smoking, and drinking, and at the last he was especially great; not a house did he pass without two or three drinks with all comers. But in justice to Johnny, who was a very good fellow in his way, it must be stated that he assured us that he was generally a "total abstainer," but occasionally drank for a change, and then "went in for liquor bald-headed." He was in the latter phase during our brief acquaintance.

Cheadle went on to describe one particularly hair-raising stretch of the journey:

> The road then went up rapidly, and brought us to the top of the famous "Rattlesnake Grade." We found ourselves on the brink of a precipitous descent of 2,000 feet, and in full view below saw the road following the configuration of the hill, with the numberless

windings and zigzags which had given rise to its name. Cut out of the mountain side, and resting for several feet of its width on overhanging beams, it was not broad enough to allow two vehicles to pass in safety, except at the points of the turns, nor was there any railing to guard the edge of the precipice.

Every one immediately volunteered to ease the poor horses by walking down, but Johnny negatived the proposition at once, and drove us down at a furious rate, the heavily-laden wagon swinging round the sharp turns in a most unpleasant manner. The giving way of the break, or of a wheel, or the pole, must have been fatal; but all held together, as of course it was likely to do, and we reached the bottom safely.

Cheadle had an opportunity to stay at some of the many roadhouses along the way to the Cariboo. But he was not impressed:

The accommodation along the road was everywhere miserable enough, but after leaving Clinton it became abominable. The only bed was the floor of the "wayside houses," which occur every ten miles or so, and are named the "Fiftieth" or "Hundredth Mile House," according to the number of the nearest mile-post. Our solitary blankets formed poor padding against the inequalities of the rough-hewn boards, and equally ineffectual to keep out the cold draughts which whistled under the ill-fitting door of the hut. A wayside house on the road to the mines is merely a rough log hut of a single room; at one end a large open chimney, and at the side a bar counter, behind which are shelves with rows of bottles containing the vilest of alcoholic drinks. The miners on their journey up or down, according to the season... come dropping in towards evening in twos and threes, divest themselves of the roll of blankets slung upon their backs, and depositing them upon the floor, use them as a seat, for the hut possesses few or none...

After supper and pipes, and more "drinks," each unrolls his blankets, and chooses his bed for the night. Some elect to sleep on the counter, and some on the flour sacks piled at one end of the room, whilst the rest stretch themselves on the floor, with their feet to the fire. Occasionally a few commence gambling, which, with an accompaniment of drinking and blasphemy, goes on for the greater part of the night.

At Soda Creek, Cheadle and his company took the steamer for Quesnelle Forks, glad to be finished with roadhouses. But worse was to come as they tried to navigate the trail into Barkerville (that stretch of road was yet to be completed):

At Quesnelle Mouth we slung our rolls of blankets on our backs, and started on foot for William's Creek. The road was very rough, a narrow pack trail cut through the woods; the stumps of the felled trees were left on the ground, and the thick stratum of mud in the spaces between was ploughed into deep holes by the continual trampling of mules. The ground had been frozen, and covered with several inches of snow, but this partially melted, and rendered the surface greasy and slippery. We stumbled about amongst the hardened mud-holes, and our huge jack-boots soon blistered our feet so dreadfully, that by the second day we were almost disabled... By the road-side lay the dead bodies of horses and mules, some standing as they had died, still stuck fast in the deep, tenacious

Before and After

Prices of staples at Sailor's Bar, near Hope, in 1858:

Flour .... $1.00 per pound
Sugar .... $2.00 " "
Bacon .... $1.00 " "
Tea .... $4.00 " "
One miner's pick $6.00
A piece of rocker iron (for sluice box) $30.00

By 1862 prices had jumped:

Flour .... $2.00 per pound
Butter .... $5.00 " "
Matches .... $1.50 a box
Potatoes .... $115.00 per hundredweight
Nails .... $5.00 per pound

When the wagon road was finished, the prices changed again:

Flour .... $0.32–$0.35 per pound
Bacon .... $0.50–$0.75 " "
Butter .... $1.25 " "
Sugar .... $0.50–$0.60 " "
Tea .... $1.00–$1.50 " "

　　—Lily Chow

mud. We passed a score of them in one day in full view; and hundreds, which had turned aside to die, lay hidden in the forest which shut in the trail so closely.

This was the Cariboo Road as winter approached in 1863, enough to dampen the spirits of any bright-eyed gold seeker. The road reached Soda Creek toward the end of that year, was completed to Quesnel in 1864 and finally made it to Barkerville in 1865.

Death of a Barber

His name was Charles Morgan Blessing, and in the spring of 1866 he was travelling up the Cariboo Road. Like many before him, he hoped to find his fortune in the goldfields. Unlike most others who sought the mother lode, Charles never arrived at his destination. About halfway between Quesnel and Barkerville, he died.

Death was not an unexpected visitor during the gold rush. Mountain fever, typhus, pneumonia, starvation, infections and injuries all took their toll. Winters were vicious, sanitation primitive, vaccines and antibiotics unknown. Those who followed the lure of gold often died before their 40th birthday. Charles Blessing's death was unusual only because he was murdered. Of the more than 10,000 people who lived along Williams Creek, he was one of the very few to die at the hands of another human being.

When, six months later, his body was finally discovered, only one person could even guess at his identity: Moses Wellington, Barkerville's barber. Although Moses lived and worked in Barkerville during the spring and summer months, he left in the fall to escape the harsh Cariboo winters. Moses was returning to Barkerville in May 1866, when he and Charles met. For days they travelled together, until Moses broke his journey in Quesnel. But Charles, eager to begin his search for gold, went on alone.

According to the *Cariboo Sentinel*, Charles's body was "in a state of advanced decomposition," which is probably why it was buried right where it was found. Moses was only able to identify his friend when he recognized a few personal items marked with the initials CMB. But until months later, neither Moses nor anyone else was able to locate the oddly shaped gold nugget stickpin that Charles always wore.

Charles Blessing had been dead for a century before I ever learned his name. We are not related, yet we have a strong connection; for I wrote about him and his gold-nugget stickpin, about Moses the barber, and about Judge Matthew Baillie Begbie, who sketched the gold nugget at the trial. My book *Moses, Me and Murder! (A Story of the Cariboo Gold Rush)* was published in 1988 and has been read in hundreds of classes across British Columbia. Many of those classes have taken a field trip to reconstructed Barkerville, bouncing up the Cariboo Road in yellow school buses, sleeping in the Wells school gymnasium, buying the best jawbreakers in the world at Mason and Daly's general store, and staring entranced into Moses's barber shop. Sometimes those school buses stop about halfway between Quesnel and

Barkerville, and the students trek up a narrow trail to visit Charles Blessing's grave.

I believe that Charles is pleased when he has visitors. I also believe that he is listening when I tell yet another group of students—in Kelowna or Prince Rupert or Nelson or Surrey—about his untimely death. Charles had no children of his own; he has no great-great-grandchildren to remember his name and his life. My family had no part in this province's gold rush; I cannot proudly point to towns, roads or bridges named for my great-great-grand-parents.

Although Charles and I are not connected genetically, we do have a strong bond: Charles gave me his story to share with young readers and I, in return, have given him the gift of remembrance.

—Ann Walsh, Williams Lake

7

BOOMS AND BUSTS
The Other Gold Rushes

The scramble to the Fraser in 1858 and the push on to the Cariboo in the 1860s made headlines around the world. But while the newspapers in San Francisco and London talked up "Frazer's River" and William's Creek, smaller rushes were part of colonial life from 1850 right up to the Klondike in 1898. The Queen Charlottes, Rock Creek in the Boundary Country and Wild Horse Creek in the East Kootenay all had their day in the sun. They didn't have the drawing power or the staying power of the major gold strikes. But they were significant enough to compel Governor James Douglas to assert British control, impose licensing and, in some cases, build new trails and roads to insure control of commerce and sovereignty.

Queen Charlotte Islands

This was the original BC gold rush, a small affair by later standards. But it set the tone for future relations between American miners and First Nations. Gold was first discovered in about 1850 by the Haida, who took some nuggets to Victoria. Considering the time and the slow methods of communication, word spread quickly. Miners who had been part of the 1849 rush to California were primed for this kind of news, and by 1851, ships were stopping at Fort Victoria en route to the Charlottes. Governor Douglas wrote of one arrival in the fall of 1851: "The 'Exact', an American schooner, arrived here yesterday from Nesqually, bound to the Queen Charlotte's Islands with 32 passengers, all of whom are Americans, on board, being the second party of Americans who have gone this autumn to the gold mines. I could take no measures to prevent their going, neither does it appear to me advisable to do so at present, as they will be exploring the gold district and may be dismissed whenever Government may choose to eject them."

Word of gold in the Charlottes presented problems for the Hudson's Bay Company. It was not easy to find good workers, and Douglas wrote that the gold fever was making his employees restless: "I fear that many of them will in consequence leave their present employment to become gold hunters, a circumstance which will for a time retard the progress of settlement."

The American miners received a poor reception on the Queen Charlottes. One boat was looted and the miners were held hostage. Douglas, with authority from the Colonial Office, sent a Royal Navy vessel to the area. But the Haida were the best defence, and they made it clear that if there was any mining to do, they would do it.

The rush did not amount to much, but the events were instrumental in setting future policies in Fort Victoria. Governor Douglas was of the view that American intentions were "to colonize the island, and establish an independent government until, by force or fraud, they became annexed to the United States." It was a theme he would return to during the Fraser River rush. The Colonial Office took Douglas seriously on this occasion, giving him authority over the islands and the right to license miners. Any future mining would be allowed only under British regulation.

Opposite:
On the way to the mines, printed in *Canadian Illustrated News*, December 23, 1880

Magistrate Haynes

John C. Haynes was a "special constable" on the Fraser River and, I expect, saw some action with the Hill gang. He was rewarded with a customs and magistrate position at the Okanagan border, at Osoyoos. His career followed another gold rush eastward, strung along the "border country" starting at Rock Creek and ending at the Wild Horse Creek on the western flank of the Rockies, near Fort Steele on the Kootenay River. This was the terminus of the hastily built Dewdney Trail, starting from Fort Hope on the Fraser River at the coast.

Judge Haynes presided over a famous gunfight trial at "Fisherville" on the Wild Horse Creek, between American miners and Irishmen, possibly Fenians!

—*Stephen Pattison, Victoria*

Judge J.C. Haynes came to BC in 1858 and served as a gold commissioner and district court judge. He was responsible for an important customs post at Osoyoos, where his home still stands. *British Columbia Archives, B-04348*

Rock Creek

Today, Rock Creek is a quiet backwater on the Kettle River. But in 1860 it was the site of a stampede. It even sparked the interest of Donald Fraser, a correspondent of the London *Times*, who spread the word in England. At its peak, Rock Creek attracted about 5,000 miners, a considerable number for an area that was even more remote than the Fraser River in 1858.

There are two stories about how the rush started. One has it that a Canadian by the name of Adam Beame, who was headed for the Similkameen to pan for gold, decided to try his luck in Rock Creek near its confluence with the Kettle River. His luck was good. It was October 1859, and by next spring, news of Beame's discovery had caused a minor sensation.

In the other story, two American soldiers on patrol in 1858 made the first discovery when they wound up north of the border dodging hostile Natives. According to legend, they camped beside a creek and found a nugget of gold there. They stayed a few days, taking what gold they could from the surface. But soon they had to return to their base at Fort Colville. It was there, according to some old-timers, that Beame learned of their discovery and set out to stake the creek.

Peachland Gold to Golf

Our family farm in Peachland was the site of Camp Hewitt and the Gladstone mine, which were a result of the search for gold in BC after the Barkerville and Klondike rushes. My mother and father, George and Mary Smith, bought the 64-hectare farm in 1955. It was the site of Camp Hewitt, the buildings that had served as bunkhouse barn and cookhouse for the miners. As a young teenager I loved to explore the old buildings, looking for artifacts. My parents were only the third owners of the property. When they bought it, a sawmill was operating on the property, which had previously been logged with horses. Today it's the Ponderosa Golf Course.

Peachland was an important rest stop on one of the historic fur brigade trails, along which furs were transported from the BC Interior by horseback, via the Okanagan Valley, to the mouth of the Columbia River. In about 1895, a mining promoter, J.M. Robinson, found enough surface signs to establish a full-fledged underground gold mine in the hills half a mile above Peachland. This was the Gladstone mine. Ore cars were pushed along steel-topped wooden rails to an outside tip. A blacksmith shop was built on site, and there the steel hand drills were sharpened. For years, old rusty kerosene cans littered the nearby hillside. No large amount of gold was ever found in the two tunnels!

Robinson soon located another gold-bearing area 19 kilometres above the town near Glen Lake. There he laid out a townsite in about 1899 with the name Glen Robinson, in anticipation of a gold rush. It was a short-lived tent town for miners and soon became "the gold rush town that never was." The only gold Robinson finally found was the land where peaches grew, so he bought all the available land and sold building lots and acreages from his small real estate office, thus founding the town of Peachland. He was an ambitious promoter who went on to found Summerland and Naramata in the same way.

There is also the story of a lost gold mine across Lake Okanagan from Peachland. The rich gold outcropping was found by a Native man and an early pioneer, Leon McCall, in about 1905. They marked the area but were never able to locate it again. Needless to say, many others have tried to find the site since then. Shovels that had been left as markers were found many years later, and the area was even staked. To date, no gold.

Peachland's biggest mining story was the massive open-pit Brenda mine, 22 kilometres west, which opened in the late 1960s and operated for more than 20 years. That mine yielded copper, molybdenum, zinc, silver—and even *gold*.

—*Richard Smith, Peachland*

Most of the Rock Creek prospectors were Americans who came overland from mining areas in Washington and Oregon. They were followed by the Chinese, and it was a conflict between the two groups that sparked the so-called Rock Creek War.

The white miners were living by their own code and had drawn up some rather exclusive camp regulations. Lieutenant Charles Wilson, one of the Royal Engineers and secretary with the Boundary Survey working in the area, wrote about the vigilante rules: "The miners here have behaved very well, there has been no fighting since the place first started, which considering the style of men and that no English civil authority of any kind has been amongst them is rather surprising; they make their own rules at meetings en masse and generally stick to them; they will not allow any Chinaman to dig for gold, and resolutely refuse to pay any taxes until the colony gives them a regular set of officers."

Lieutenant Wilson also noted the miners' hostility to government men: "We were at first taken for customs house officers or gold collectors, who were supposed to be on their way from Fraser river, but after we had explained that we had no connection with the colony, we were most hospitably treated."

Wilson went on to describe the new metropolis on the Kettle River: "The town, or rather I beg its pardon, city has sprung up like a mushroom, there are about 350 inhabitants, miners, gamblers, sharpers, Jews, Pikes, Yankees, loafers & hoc genus omne. There are a good many substantial log buildings, stores, gambling houses, grog shops, butcher's shops etc and a good supply of everything, which of course has to be paid for pretty highly as they have to import everything from the Dalles and Fort Hope."

Slumach's Gold

The thought that buried loot and lost gold mines are still out there to be found remains tantalizing. The legend of the Lost Creek Mine stretches back 120 years, when word came that a Coast Salish man named Slumach had arrived in New Westminster carrying a bag of gold nuggets. He returned to town on more than one occasion, paying for drinks and women from an ample supply of nuggets. Some were said to be the size of walnuts.

Locals believed the gold came from a secret mine site somewhere in the mountains north of Pitt Lake (possibly in present-day Garibaldi Park). Prospectors tried to follow him into the mountains, but he always managed to give them the slip.

Slumach was convicted of murdering a Metis man named Louis Bee in 1890, and was hanged the following year at the BC provincial gaol. His secret apparently went to the grave with him, but rumours of a lost motherlode persisted. Ten years after Slumach's hanging, W. Jackson went looking; he's said to have left for California dragging a heavy sack and, before he died, to have given directions in a letter about where to find more buried gold.

Like any good legend, this one comes with a curse—and possibly a ghost. The story goes that 55 people died or disappeared searching for Slumach's gold. Over the years half a dozen books have been written about the legend, and at least one movie produced. Some believe the mine never existed; others think it was cleared out long ago.

The legend is just that: a legend. Rick and Brian Antonson and Mary Trainer, authors of *In Search of a Legend: Slumach's Gold,* point out that there is no mention in the newspapers of the time or in the judge's benchbook from Slumach's trial of any gold or wanton spending by Slumach in frontier New Westminster. Where the connection with Slumach came from is still unknown, despite decades of research. Still, there is considerable anecdotal evidence that people *have* taken gold from the high country northeast of Pitt Lake, and the enduring legend has the power to hold people 120 years later. So don't be surprised if you have a chance encounter with someone who has a theory about a particular lost gold mine just waiting to be found.

Like Ned McGowan's War in the Fraser Canyon, the Rock Creek War was more headline than hostility.

Apparently the gold commissioner sent to Rock Creek to collect licence fees and duties was run out of town. That drew the attention of Governor Douglas, who decided to intervene personally. He travelled to Rock Creek in September 1860 and, in a typical Douglas display of bravado, threatened the miners with a military intervention if they did not submit to British law. The licences must be paid and the Chinese must be allowed access to the diggings. As usual, the bluff worked.

Douglas needed the licence revenue to support another road project. He hoped a good trail along the border on the British side would again stem the tide of prospectors following an all-American route through the Washington Territory. Douglas had already hired a capable civil engineer, Edgar Dewdney, to construct "a good mule road from Hope to Similkameen." Dewdney was the lowest bidder and used a survey by the Royal Engineers to build the trail. But while his crews worked, the miners scrambled past them to get to Rock Creek.

The road would have to be extended from the Similkameen to the Boundary country. So Douglas contracted Dewdney to build the extension. Unfortunately, by the time the connection was completed in the fall of 1861, the boom was over and Rock Creek was all but deserted.

Fool's Gold

Terrence Keough reminds us that gold fever never dies. The evidence: "Two Men Who Moiled for Gold," a handwritten account by his father, John, recounting his search for gold at Goldstream River near Revelstoke in 1936.

Terrence writes that the area had seen "a substantial, if short-lived" gold rush in the 1860s, when the boomtown at French Creek mushroomed to 5,000 miners. "In the summer of 1935," Terrence writes, "John Keough travelled by bicycle the 55 miles from Revelstoke to Goldstream River on the old Big Bend Road... Keough's companion on the trip was a young man in his early twenties, Colin Laughlan, whose father was a CPR dispatcher in Revelstoke... Gold that year was worth $20 an ounce [about $300 in today's dollars]. A teacher earned no more than that in a week. The dream was compelling." It was also the Depression era.

The duo wanted to see a gold-mining operation at French Creek being run by a man named Remillard. "When Keough arrived at the camp, Remillard said he had seen everything now: he'd seen men show up on mules, horses, and on foot, but this was the first time someone had arrived on bicycle... Remillard told the story of his arrival in the region. Just before the First World War, he and a man named Olson had prospected Goldstream because of records he had seen regarding the gold rush of the 1860s. He said they found an abandoned sluice box full of gravel, worked it, and took out $1,400 worth of gold [more than $20,000 today] that had simply been left behind by the early prospectors."

Remillard also had a theory about locating the motherlode higher up the river at Caribou Creek. The two amateurs were intrigued and set off, quite poorly prepared: "By modern standards the two men were badly equipped for the bush. They carried no tent, no rain gear, no sleeping bags, no machetes, no insect repellent; and their packsacks, homemade from canvas and burlap, were low-slung and cumbersome." Food was basic: flour to make bannock, some bacon, dried navy beans, dried fruit and tea. "On the first night they lost a small bag of flour when playing mice knocked acid over it. But the loss was a minor hardship. They were bothered by mosquitoes, blackflies and sand flies (called no-see-ums because they are so small); they often couldn't sleep because of the cold."

As the days went on, tension between the two prospectors grew. They spent the entire summer in the woods "essentially going around in circles in a futile search for what can only in this context be called 'fool's gold.'"

—*Terrence Keough, Friends of the BC Archives*

Mission Creek

The Mission Creek discovery in the Okanagan Valley was really an offshoot of the Rock Creek rush. Adam Beame was again a player: In early 1861 he went to explore reports of gold near the present city of Kelowna. He reported to the gold commissioner:

We prospected nine streams, all tributaries of the lake and found gold in each averaging from three to ninety cents to the pan, the ground was much frozen and impeded our work. We are quite satisfied of the richness of these mines and shall as soon as feasible dispose of our claims on Rock Creek and leave for that section of the country, where a miner can grow his potatoes and other vegetables, besides keep his cow. We hand you some gold taken from William Peon's claim. He makes $4 per day with a rocker and as... old and practical miners [we] could realize more by sluicing and other methods.

In his book *The Guide to Gold Panning in British Columbia*, Bill Barlee says the Okanagan proved to be a disappointment, but mining carried on for another decade or so.

100 Years Above Boulder Creek

My grandfather, Pedro Cherbo, immigrated to BC from Italy in the 1880s and prospected around the Kootenay. One of the claims he staked was Osprey No. 1 and No. 2—I still have the documents today. He staked it as the Waverley Group, as written up in the "Report of the Minister of Mines," 1900. He and his partner hauled ore out by pack mule.

Then in the 1940s to 1950s, my father, Pedro St. Francis Cherbo, worked the claims with his two brothers. A tunnel was blasted in the mountain below the shaft, going in over 30 metres and locating the ore vein, which is about 45 centimetres wide. The ore is lead, zinc with gold and silver. My grandfather and father were trying to find a pocket of gold, but were unsuccessful. The claims were restaked as "The Silver Bell," but after a few years of low mineral prices, the claims were abandoned.

In 1967 my father and I hiked for more than five hours up the Jack Creek watershed, located the old workings of the claims above Boulder Creek, and restaked the two claims under my name. Over the years, with no road access, just enough work has been done to keep the claims active. In 1979, when mineral prices were higher, a consultant with a large company expressed interest in the claims. But before any deal could be negotiated, the stock market crashed in October, resulting in a huge drop in mineral prices.

Over the years a number of friends have assisted me in maintaining a trail and working the claims. It has been difficult to keep the claims active, but I have enjoyed the history, hiking and work involved with these century-old claims.

—*Robin Cherbo, Nelson*

Wild Horse Creek

The East Kootenay also had a rush in the mid-1860s. The scramble to the Wild Horse started after a discovery in 1863 and carried on for about five years. Miners returned in the 1880s, and the largest nugget taken from the area weighed about 1 kilogram. Bill Barlee thinks that about $7 million in gold was eventually taken out. But because the area was remote, and many of miners simply took their treasure across the border, we'll never know for sure. More important in the long-term development of the province, the strike was significant enough for the colonial government to extend the Dewdney Trail to the area. The route became today's Crowsnest Highway.

Other Rushes

Similkameen 1853

George McLelland found gold on the river near Vermilion Forks in the early 1850s. The town was later named Princeton by Governor Douglas on a visit to the area. Adam Beame said he was on the way to the Similkameen when he made the Rock Creek discovery. A bigger strike was made in the area in the 1880s, when Johnny Chance discovered Granite Creek.

Peace River 1862

The first reports of gold on the Peace River came in 1860, and in 1862, two miners named William Cust and Edward Carey claimed they had washed a thousand ounces of gold from the river. The "rush" was short—about two years.

Big Bend–Columbia 1864

In the mid-1860s, miners who had been working the Wild Horse Creek diggings headed

Robin Cherbo's nephew, Berne Driscoll, is shown at the entrance to the Osprey tunnel near Nelson. The Osprey claim was staked by Pedro Cherbo, Robin's grandfather, in 1900, and Robin still works the claim.
Courtesy Robin Cherbo

The Joe Dandy mine, near Fairview in the south Okanagan, is shown here in 1895. Gold was discovered in this area in 1890, long before the fruit industry took hold. The gold ran out in 1906, and Fairview faded as nearby Oliver became an important agricultural centre. *British Columbia Archives F-02865*

The Wright Nugget

My great-grandfather, Lt. Col. Joshua Wright, was a descendant of Philomen Wright, the first white settler in the Ottawa Valley. Joshua (1854–1907) took part in the Northwest Rebellion as commanding officer in the Duke of Cornwall's Own Rifles. After he returned he was at loose ends and had a large family to support, so the regiment invested in a gold mine somewhere near Fort St. James, and Joshua was sent out from Hull to supervise the mine. I have no idea how successful the venture was but I do have a nugget that he brought back for his daughter, my grandmother. It's a story my granny loved to tell. He ordered Christmas presents through the Eaton's catalogue, much to the chagrin of the family. They cut out the labels so no one would know.

—*Nancy Bain, Victoria*

up the Columbia River. By 1865 they thought they had a discovery to rival the Cariboo. The site drew hundreds of men—Americans, French-Canadians and Chinese. But by 1866 the rush was over. Miners returned in the 1880s to have another go, and tried again in the 1930s.

Leech River–Vancouver Island 1864

Lieutenant Peter John Leech, an astronomer with the Vancouver Island Exploring

This gold pan cabin at Leech River was a short-lived operation, like many gold-fuelled enterprises that got underway here after a former Royal Engineer discovered gold in 1864. The Leech River site was one of a very few gold finds on Vancouver Island, and it was abandoned by 1875. *British Columbia Archives D-07012*

Expedition, discovered gold here, and although the Island is not known for its gold deposits, "Leechtown" boomed for a few years.

Living off the Leech River Find

My grandfather, Charles Henry Jordan, was a ship's carpenter who left (jumped?) ship at Victoria. He took work as a ship's carpenter for the Hudson's Bay Company and later as "engineer" on HMS *Devastation*, which was involved in surveying the west coast of Vancouver Island. He arrived in 1862, volunteered for the Waddington expedition to "punish the Indians" and worked a find on the Leech River. According to some entries in the Gold Commissioner's Return in the BC Archives, he found some gold—enough to go to Australia, where his brother Edwin was ill with "consumption." He brought him back to Duncan, but

Edwin died, the first white man to be buried in the cemetery at St. Mary's in Somenos.

Charles was also able to buy/homestead just under 360 hectares between Lake Cowichan and Duncan at a place called Sahtlam. It consisted mostly of huge trees at that time. My mother (deceased 1959) told me that my grandfather still had enough gold nuggets and dust that when times were hard at the turn of the century, he would take some to the bank. I guess he thought it better than cash or investments.

My grandfather was born in 1839 in Gloucester; my mother, Pearl Jordan, at Sahtlam in 1892; and I, the youngest of five boys, in 1928 in New Westminster. Although my mother had a largish nugget on a clasp, which she wore on her blouse, naturally I have none!

—*Maurice A. Rhodes, Nelson (Balfour)*

Omineca 1869

When gold at William's Creek started to peter out, attention turned to the Omineca, where reports of gold surfaced in 1864. Miners took about $8,000 (about $106,000 today) in gold out of Vital Creek in about a month. Germansen Creek is probably the best-known producer. Manson Creek was another, and the boom lasted into the 1870s. Over a thousand miners worked the area at its peak, but they later moved on to better diggings in the Cassiar.

An Indescribable Scene of Human Endeavour

Following the influx of miners to the Cariboo, and before the Klondike strikes, the gold rush of the Omineca created plenty of excitement in the North Central Interior of British Columbia. As early as 1860, reports from the area drew Peace River miners south to try their luck on creeks in the region. Prospectors from the Cariboo goldfields, travelling the water routes of early explorers by way of the Fraser, Nechako, Stuart and Findlay Rivers, quickly followed. From the west came Chinese, Haida and others, hiking the old First Nations trails from Hazelton to Takla Lake and on to Vital Creek, site of the first major gold strike in the Omineca in 1869.

Travelling and freighting in newly charted areas was difficult. The work of building shelters to escape the horrendous mosquitoes and blackflies, constructing and setting up mining equipment, keeping themselves fed and working the claims until winter drove them out was, according to a report of the time, an "indescribable scene of human endeavour."

For most First Nations people, this was the first encounter with a substantial number of

This Marion steam shovel was brought into the Manson Creek area in 1936. It was rediscovered in a dry creek bed in the 1990s, then restored and put on display on the shore of Stuart Lake.
Courtesy Manson Creek Historical Society

154

other races. Their previous contact with outsiders had been limited to Hudson's Bay Company post personnel and Roman Catholic priests. Miners employed many First Nations people, who were familiar with the area, to work as guides and packers. The locals were no longer totally reliant on the fur trade and traditional salmon harvest.

By 1871, Gold Commissioner W.H. Fitzgerald reported 1,200 men working the creeks of the Omineca, and by year's end the recorded recovery from placer claims was 31,000 ounces (870 kilograms). How much gold actually came out of the Omineca goldfields is a matter of speculation, as an official report stated: "some white miners and most of the Chinese refuse to tell the Gold Commissioner how much gold they have recovered."

For the last 150 years, the creeks have produced a constant yield, continuing to lure miners and exploration crews to the vast region with the promise of gold still to be found in the old placer claims.

—*Joyce Helweg and Barbara Robin, Fort St. James, BC*

Cassiar 1873

The Cassiar rush produced the largest all-gold nugget ever found in BC: a beauty at 73 ounces (about 2 kilograms) found on McDame Creek in 1877. The creek was named for Henry McDame, a black prospector who came to the Cassiar in 1874. His creek was the richest in the area and produced $1.5 million in gold over 20 years.

Nellie Cashman, a prospector and businesswoman, is also remembered as the Miner's Angel. She saved the lives of many starving miners in the Cassiar during one particularly harsh winter, when she gathered food and supplies in Victoria and took them to the stranded men by dogsled—a journey that took 77 days.
British Columbia Archives D-01775

The Miner's Angel

She was known as the Miner's Angel in Nevada, in Arizona, California, in the Cassiar, the Yukon and in Alaska. These are the Sisters of St. Ann right beside her. They arrived early on and established a school here in Victoria, and they were nurses as well. Cashman donated money to help the sisters build hospitals.

Nellie Cashman herself never married, and was an independent woman. She came from County Cork, Ireland, to the east coast of the United States with her sister Fannie, and eventually they moved out to California. Her sister got married and started having kids. Nellie got interested in mining and prospecting, staked claims and became a businesswoman. Wherever she went, she would set up a boarding house or store. She's very well known in Arizona, in the Tucson and Tombstone areas. The US post office issued a stamp honouring her in the 1990s.

She got her name, "the miner's angel," in the Cassiar, when she went up during the gold rush and staked some claims. Like most prospectors, she came back to Victoria for the winter, and there she heard that some of the miners who had stayed there were starving and suffering from scurvy. So she organized a big shipment of food with six other miners and she mushed back into the

Cassiar in the middle of the winter. The caravan battled deep snow for 77 days before reaching the Cassiar, where Nellie helped nurse the 75 stranded miners back to health.

In 1898 she headed for the Klondike to open another restaurant and refuge for miners. Then it was off to Alaska, where she travelled by dogsled to Koyukuk River, north of the Arctic Circle. At age 60 she launched into another 20 years of prospecting. Cashman died in 1923 at St. Joseph's Hospital in Victoria, cared for by the Sisters of St. Ann in the hospital she helped them build.

—from a tour of Ross Bay Cemetery guided by Yvonne Van Ruskenveld, volunteer with the Old Cemeteries Society

The first strikes in the Cassiar were made in the early 1860s on the Stikine River. Angus McCulloch and Henry Thibert teamed up in 1870, and in 1872 they went up the Dease River to the Stikine. McCulloch froze to death in a snowstorm on the Stikine. Thibert returned to the area in 1873 and struck pay dirt on a stream leading into Dease Lake. He and his new partners made $125 per day each, not bad money in the 1870s—about $2,300.

More than 1,500 miners worked Thibert and Dease Creeks at their peak from 1874 to 1877.

Blind Channel Heroes

On BC's coast it was solitary men who searched for gold, rowing to their chosen spot with a two-year grubstake, tools, explosives and other supplies aboard. If you know where to look you can still find their crumbling tunnels—all collapsing and dangerous.

This inlet is no exception. Once it was densely populated by a Salish-speaking group called "the rich people," who were absorbed by another group in the early 1800s. Survivors, if there were any, fled and never returned. William Downie, a prospector who worked here in 1859–60, described the place this way in his book *Hunting for Gold* (1893): "During the summer months, the Indians from surrounding tribes come down here and fish, but none of them stay to winter in this locality... There are no settled tribes of Indians in this region, and when summer is at end, the whole country assumes an appearance of utter desolation and loneliness."

What fascinates me is how he coped. Having arrived by sea, whether in his own small boat or dropped off, it would have been tricky hauling everything ashore. And his neighbours—mice, mink, wolverine and bear—would have been eager to share his food and replacements a long way off. Did he bring dry wood to start a fire? Firewood should be felled, bucked and split a year in advance. Did he live in a floathouse or in a shack ashore? This region's westerly and outflow winds would do their best to tear anything from its moorings. Then each day he'd climb from sea level to his claim, lugging his gear uphill with horseflies, mosquitoes, rain, snow and/or ice as companions—struggling always upward, grabbing salal or branches as he went. Then slithering down at night, exhausted and wet through, to cold quarters and bleak

stores. And no one to ask him over for a hot meal, a drink or a chat. Poor guy! Let's hope he was lucky, but whatever happened, surely he and others like him were heroes!
—*Helen Piddington, Blind Channel*

Granite Creek–Similkameen 1885

Susan Allison, a Similkameen pioneer, wrote in her diary:

Johnny Chance... was too lazy to work... so he was sent out to get... a few grouse. He departed and strolled about till he found a nice cool creek which emptied itself into the [Tulameen] River. Here, he threw himself down till sunset with his feet paddling the cool water, when a ray of light fell on something yellow. He drew it towards him, picked it up and found it was a nugget of pure gold. He looked into the water again and there was another, and another. He pulled out his buckskin purse and slowly filled it. Then, picking up his gun, he strolled back to camp where he became [known as] the discoverer of Granite Creek.

Susan Allison and her family, shown here in the 1880s, lived and farmed in the Similkameen Valley. Allison's husband John joined the Fraser River gold rush in 1858, then moved on to the Similkameen in 1860 and reported that gold was plentiful. The Allison Pass is named after him. *British Columbia Archives D-08228*

Alex Ross was off to the Atlin gold rush when this photo of his wife Isabella and three of their children was taken in the early 1900s. He managed to support the family but was out prospecting for months or even years at a time.
Courtesy Alex Ross Raymond

Alex Ross and Jack McEwen worked as prospectors at Spruce Creek during the Atlin gold rush around the turn of the 20th century.
Courtesy Alex Ross Raymond

Eventually 700 miners moved into the area and established a boomtown with a dozen stores and its own Chinatown. Close to half a million dollars in gold was taken out ($10.8 million today), but by 1900 Granite Creek was a ghost town.

The Gold Rush that Got Away

My grandparents, David and Ethel Wishart lived at Esperanza about 1930, when two fellows asked to be taken to Zeballos. It took a day to row them in, and four days later Granddad went and retrieved them.

They plunked down quite a quantity of gold in various forms on the kitchen table and said they would include Granddad in the venture for giving them the ride. Granddad's words: "Never mind... you'll never get it out of the ground anyway," and declined the offer of being in on the ground floor of the Zeballos find.

Such is life.

—Dennis Wright, Cobble Hill

Bralorne 1896

The current owners claim Bralorne is the largest historic gold producer in the Canadian Cordillera. First staked in the late 1890s, the area is still being mined.

Atlin 1898

Alex Ross Raymond, a CBC listener in Saanichton, remembers sitting on his grandfather's knee, listening to tales of his adventures in the Atlin gold rush. "Although I was too young to remember the stories, I do remember that he could neither read nor write, and he signed his name with an *X!* He was a quiet man, and had no idea how much of his spirit of adventure he transferred to me. I spent 34 years as a hydrographic surveyor, surveying most of the BC coast and the Arctic, including the Northwest Passage. But—I've never been to Atlin! Maybe that's my next retirement project."

Alex Ross was lured by the gold rush from Moose Creek, Ontario, to Atlin, BC, at the turn of the century. On two occasions he left his family at their home in Moose Creek to go prospecting in northern BC. Each time he was gone between two and three years. He survived some severe challenges—for instance, in the winter of 1900 he was buried in a snow slide for the best part of a day, and he lived to tell the story. Amazingly he came home alive and well after both journeys. "My grandfather never struck it rich," Alex writes, "but somehow he made enough money to support his family back home while working at claims in Atlin."

8

AFTER THE RUSH
Carving Out a Colony

I f James Douglas was the man of the hour through the Fraser and Cariboo rushes, the next man at centre stage was one of his strongest critics. Amor de Cosmos, a prominent and feisty newspaperman, kept up a steady barrage of journalistic attacks on Douglas and his administration throughout the gold rush era. To de Cosmos, Douglas was anathema, a pompous tyrant working against the current of a rising democracy. Douglas might deserve the credit for saving Britain's Pacific colonies from sinking under an American tide, but de Cosmos had little admiration for his methods. The post-rush era belonged to the reformers, and de Cosmos would fundamentally reshape public opinion and the government, ending one-man rule and ushering in confederation with a new mother country, Canada.

De Cosmos was a disciple of Joseph Howe, the journalist-turned-politician who went on to dominate Nova Scotia politics for decades. Howe, through the pages of his newspaper, the *Novascotian*, kept up steady pressure until the Atlantic outpost became the first British colony to secure responsible government. It was an impressive achievement in 1848. Howe went on to become premier and a member of the Canadian parliament. De Cosmos and

Opposite: Government buildings in Victoria, seen in the *Canadian Illustrated News*, April 8, 1876

Amor de Cosmos (the former Bill Smith) was a newspaper publisher, reformer, politician and vocal opponent of Governor James Douglas. He was an early and relentless advocate of democratic reform and, later, confederation with Canada. He was elected premier of BC in 1872.
City of Vancouver Archives Port P1592 N896

followed in his footsteps, moving from crusading journalist to reforming politician and, ultimately, to premier and MP.

From the first issue of his newspaper, the *British Colonist*, published in Victoria in 1858, De Cosmos identified himself as an opponent of the status quo, a thorn in the side of the governor and his administration and an advocate of responsible government. His editorial policies were clearly laid out:

> In our local politics we shall be found the sure friend of reform. We shall aim at introducing such reforms as will tend to government according to the well understood wishes of the people. It will be the primary object with us to advocate such changes as will tend to establish self-government. The present Constitution we hold is radically defective, and unsuited to the advanced condition of this colony. We shall counsel the introduction of responsible government—a system long established in British America, by which the people will have the whole and sole control over local affairs of the colony. In short, we shall advocate a Constitution modelled after the British, and similar to that of Canada.

De Cosmos was preparing to fight Joseph Howe's battle all over again on Vancouver Island. He had grown up in Howe's Nova Scotia before moving to the California goldfields in the 1850s. In California, De Cosmos experienced a personal transformation. It started with a change of name, from the forgettable William Smith to a name meaning "lover of the universe." In his later years he claimed there were so many Smiths in the goldfields that he needed a more distinctive address to make sure he received his mail. But Smith also wanted a dramatic break with a past, a new identity appropriate to his reforming mission.

Potatoes, Logs and Gold

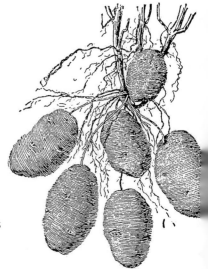

The story of my great-great-uncle William Pitcairn Mackie, born in Dundee, Scotland, in 1828, has been told by family members and recorded in the Vancouver Archives. As a young man he travelled around Cape Horn to the California goldfields in a sailing ship. In 1860 he jumped ship in Astoria, Oregon, and made his way north to Gastown (later Vancouver).

Bill Mackie pre-empted DL472—160 acres (64 hectares) in Fairview. There he planted potatoes before heading to the goldfields in the Cariboo and Cassiar regions to mine for gold. He was also a pioneer logger, cutting hand-hewn eight-panel spars in Fairview, Shaughnessy, North Vancouver and Ladysmith. He described some of his adventures to his nephew William Syme Mackie, and the stories were later recorded by Major J.S. Matthews, Vancouver's first archivist.

Mackie didn't make a fortune gold mining, but the wedding ring I wear was made from a gold nugget he found. He also lost his land claim when the Canadian Pacific Railway was given 5,000 acres (2,000 hectares) of land in Vancouver. From 1899 to his death in 1916, he lived with his nephew W.S. Mackie on a farm in Agassiz. He is buried there in the Kent Municipal Cemetery.

—*Barbara Kinahan, Richmond*

His critics in Victoria wrote De Cosmos off as just another California flake. To them, he was a traitor to Britain, a reckless muckraker out to defy the duly appointed colonial authorities. And to replace them with what, the anarchy of an American-style democracy? But in that first issue of the newspaper, he made it clear where his loyalties lay: "In our National politics we shall ever foster that loyalty which is due to the present government, and determinedly oppose every influence tending to undermine or subvert the existing connection between the colonies and the mother country."

De Cosmos thought direct representation for the new Pacific colonies in the British Parliament might fortify that link. But his first goal was representative government at home. He was an early advocate of uniting Vancouver Island and British Columbia, and proposed an overland wagon road, telegraph system and railway to connect Britain's North American possessions—an interesting echo of Douglas's aspirations, the first Trans-Canada highway!

Only two hundred issues of his first paper were printed. But De Cosmos had arrived with a bang, and Victorians took notice. It was the beginning of an assault on the Douglas administration that would not end until Douglas had left office. Others would raise their voices too, but De Cosmos led the charge.

Early Public Education in BC

In a roundabout way, the gold rush was the spark that ignited public education in BC. Education for the Colony of Vancouver Island was delivered by private and church schools in the 1850s. But as the population grew, so did residents' interest in establishing a non-sectarian public system.

As luck would have it, one of the Overlanders seeking gold in the Cariboo was a teacher, by the name of John Jessop. He had been inspired by Dr. Egerton Ryerson, an Ontario reformer, and had trained at Ryerson's new normal school in Upper Canada.

But after a brief teaching career in eastern Canada, Jessop caught the gold bug and headed west to seek his fortune. He made the trip the hard way, overland across the prairies, through mountain passes and along BC's river valleys. It was 1859, and the Cariboo was the new centre of the rush. But Jessop's dreams of riches were soon dashed—he was too late to strike it rich. After working for a while as a printer and newspaper publisher, he returned to teaching and opened a school in Victoria. At the time, Jessop was probably the best-trained teacher the colony had. But it was a struggle to enrol enough students in his first private school to keep it running.

He spent the early 1860s lobbying the colonial government to establish a public school system, hoping they would buy the school he had built in Victoria and use it as the centrepiece. But not until 1865 did the government finally establish a board of education and introduce a public school system.

Jessop was on the frontline from the start, but there were many ups and downs. In one economic downturn, Victoria was unable to pay his salary. So he and a colleague withdrew their services, taking part in what is believed to be the first teachers' strike in Canadian history. The schools in Victoria closed for two years.

After BC joined Canada as a province in 1871, the public school system was reorganized and Jessop became the first superintendent of education, at a salary of $2,000 a year (about $34,000 today). Jessop held the position until 1878, expanding public schools throughout the province. He travelled on horseback, canoe and any other conveyance available to inspect those early schools and became known as the founder of BC's school system.

During those years, he also helped establish a boarding school at Cache Creek for young scholars in the Interior. The co-ed school attracted controversy when it was reported that some older students were "fraternizing." But the reputation of the school was restored when another Overlander, Catherine Schubert, became matron.

Jessop's career as an educator was cut short by his political disagreements with the province, and he became "a ghost of history," largely forgotten by the public. He resigned in 1878 to protest government policies and never returned to the field. In 1883 he became an immigration agent, and an important chapter in the history of the province was closed.

—*Greg Dickson*

By the mid-1860s, the glory years were over and British Columbia and Vancouver Island were in decline—the boom had turned into a bust. The American newspapers, anxious to crow about the upstart colony's collapse, argued in print that British Columbia always had been a "humbug."

For the promoters and boosters, the next big thing was in American territory. New gold discoveries were made in Idaho, Montana and Colorado, and in the Nevada desert. British Columbia was yesterday.

Chase in the 1860s

In the early 1850s my great-great-grandfather Whitfield Chase crossed the Oregon Trail for the California gold rush. Horrified by the debauchery he witnessed in San Francisco, he headed north and spent some time in Victoria, then headed into "Fraser's Canyon" to try his luck. Eventually he gave up the dream of finding gold and settled as a farmer in the "Shuswap Prairie," as it was then called. This became the town of Chase, between Kamloops and Salmon Arm. His letters he exchanged with his family in New York were passed down through the generations. Years ago I transcribed and published them in a book, which can be found in the Chase Museum. And that's my Gold Rush connection.

—*Robin Reid, Vancouver*

But it was a brilliant yesterday all the same. BC's boom years were nothing to sneer at—more than $10 million in gold ($128 million today) had been exported between 1858 and 1863, and nobody knows how much wealth left the country through unofficial channels.

Gold Rush Forebears

Our family has three distinct branches associated with BC history, including the gold rushes of 1858 and the 1860s. The oldest branches of my mother's family are the Ogdens and Mansons, who are connected with the North West Company and then the Hudson's Bay Company. Both branches arrived west of the Rockies in the 1820s. My great-great-grandfather William Manson was taken across what would become western Canada by his father on the Hudson's Bay Company express and then to Scotland by HBC ship. In Scotland he was boarded with his aunt and sent to school, where he got a formal education to the level

of a bachelor's degree. On his return to New Caledonia he was given a junior administrative post at Kamloops, where he stayed from 1859 to 1863. From the point of view of the company's administrative hopefuls, the gold rush might be viewed in two general ways: on one hand the event was influential in bringing about the condensing of the fur-trade infrastructure and the accompanying loss of career opportunities; and on the other hand it opened a whole new world of possibilities associated with the gold rush and the settlement phase that closely followed. William Manson went on to establish a ranch and roadhouse at the 111 Mile House to service the gold rush trade. With his educational qualifications he soon found himself teaching his own children and then, as the house filled with the neighbours' offspring, accepting his lot as the local schoolteacher.

The other branch of my mother's family, the Martleys, arrived in the newly created gold colony of British Columbia in 1861–62, having travelled from England via Panama to Victoria and then New Westminster. Captain John Martley was one of a handful of semi-retired army officers offered land grants as an incentive to settle. He examined land in several parts of the Interior and eventually registered a claim on land being farmed by an American at Pavilion who had neglected to secure his claim. Martley and his wife Maria Josephine (Ballingal, previously widowed) moved to the site via the Harrison Trail. The Grange was established with the plan of farming and operating a roadhouse that would serve the gold rush traffic on the Cariboo Road, which connected the Harrison Trail at Lillooet with the route at Clinton. The Martleys were active socially with other established colonial families. John Martley was also involved in freighting, an activity his son continued for some decades. He also served as a justice of the peace in the district. The captain ran unsuccessfully for provincial office three times, but it is a measure of his status in colonial society that he was appointed ADC to the Marquis of Lorne during the governor general's visit to British Columbia in 1882.

My father's family arrived in British Columbia in 1859—although some believe they were present as early as 1852. My great-grandfather James Kennedy had in 1852–53 travelled from the east coast to Australia, South Africa and California, and was no stranger to the gold rush world. A diary of this journey still exists. He married Caroline Stone, then the couple came west via Panama to take up residence in the new capital, New Westminster. At first they lived in a tent on the banks of the Fraser River. Kennedy was trained as an architect and builder and it was in these pursuits that he chose to make his career. At times he also worked as a schoolteacher. Most of his buildings were later destroyed, in the great fire of 1898. The Kennedys were active in other settler enterprises, land acquisition, trail building and the colonial politics of the day.

None of these pioneer families chose to participate actively at the "sticky end" of the gold rush but instead settled with the intent of making a living in the infrastructure that had developed to serve it. A study of the gold rush years during the 19th century reveals considerable characteristics shared by all of them, the most noteworthy being that virtually none of the "rushers" panning and sluicing achieved any of the fabled riches that had drawn them across oceans to the goldfields around the Pacific.

My own active interest in researching the gold rushes of 1858 and the 1860s did not develop early, although I grew up in a gold rush town where the evidence—extensive ditch-lines and unavoidable tailings piles—was impossible to ignore. I came into early retirement in 2002 with a strong desire to write at least one credible academic paper in my field of geography and was fortunate to have the support and encouragement of Professor Cole Harris, recently retired and still active at the University of BC Department of Geography. Under his guidance I began examining and mapping a nearby set of long-defunct gold mines, but before long it became obvious, at least to Dr. Harris, that the real prize lay in the gold rush placer mining landscape of the adjacent Fraser River corridor. In the five years that followed, I have mapped in detail the evidence of early placer mining (ditchlines, tailings piles, wagon roads, tracks, etc.) through a 135-kilometre study section beginning at Lytton and running north. Research in the literature has followed to explore the nature of the technologies employed and their effect on the landscape. By delving further into the academic literature, I have gained a detailed understanding of the nature of gold rushes, and I have begun to create something of a picture of the identities of the early miners as they moved in time and space. I am hopeful that my initial paper will be published in time for the 2008 sesquicentennial.

—*Mike Kennedy, Lillooet*

The departure of masses of American miners after the gold ran out lowered the fears of annexation. The American historian Robert Ficken, in his book *Unsettled Boundaries: Fraser Gold and the British-American Northwest*, proposes that things might have ended differently. "Perhaps," he writes, "if the 1858 rush had lived up to its greater, outlandish expectations (and if level-headed, competent leaders had not prevailed), a mainland version of the San Juan crisis might have erupted, precipitating a border conflict between Britain and the United States."

But America's territorial ambitions were not completely extinguished. Once the Civil War was over, Washington was in an expansive mood again and purchased Alaska from the Russians in 1867. At the same time, the US government made some quiet moves to settle its differences with Great Britain. In 1863, London and Washington had signed a treaty to resolve the dispute over the Hudson's Bay Company's property south of the 49th parallel, and in 1869 compensation was finally paid. In 1872, the long-simmering San Juan Islands dispute was also settled, not in British Columbia's favour—under German arbitration, the islands went to the Americans. Douglas, by that time retired, mourned in his diary: "Well, there is no help for it now, we have lost the stakes, and must take it easy... The Island of San Juan is gone at last! I cannot trust myself to speak about it and will be silent."

Some Americans were still not satisfied. A few firebrands on Capitol Hill wanted Britain to hand over British Columbia to compensate for the empire's slights against the union during the Civil War. Those claims went nowhere. Then, in 1870, a group of disgruntled merchants in Victoria took the step of petitioning US President Ulysses S. Grant for annexation. Sixty-one people signed the petition, and the American Senate took notice. The new governor of the colony, Anthony Musgrave, was dismissive: "I do not believe that a single British subject signed the petition... The frequent notices of this matter in the American Papers have been a fruitful source of pleasantry in the Colony."

More pressing was the need to deal with colonial debts, and consensus was growing on the mainland of BC and in London that a united colony should be the first step. The citizens of Vancouver Island were less enthusiastic, suspecting that they might lose ground, financially and politically, in any amalgamation with a geographically larger territory.

A major political watershed was the departure of Governor James Douglas in 1864. Douglas had lost his lustre, the inevitable political scandals were getting a lot of ink, and his resistance to democratic reforms was becoming an embarrassment to London. The Douglas era was passing.

A Poke of Gold

My great-grandfather Albert Duck came out from England to work on his Uncle Isaac Duck's ranch on the Thompson River at Monte Creek. Isaac had bought this ranch in the late 1860s—from a Spanish man on the run from some legal problems—with a poke of gold he mined during the California gold rush. He probably supplied miners with beef. He sold the ranch to the Bostocks and retired to England in the late 1880s, so my great-grandfather bought land at Barhartvale, west of Duck's Range, Meadow and Hill (named after his Uncle Isaac).

—*Colin Gray, Vancouver*

What's a poke? Something to keep the parasites away. It is a small leather bag for carrying gold dust or nuggets, usually made of buckskin or moose hide. A miner wore the long, narrow poke on his belt, close to the body. Some miners wore two, to keep their balance.

His legacy was still an impressive one, though. As he prepared to leave the stage, the tributes started to flow:

During the period His Excellency has been in office, he has assiduously devoted his remarkable talents to the good of the country; ever unmindful of self, he has been accessible to all, and we firmly believe that no man could have had a higher appreciation of the sacred trust vested in him, and none could have more faithfully and nobly discharged it than he has. The great road system which Governor Douglas has introduced into the Colony is an imperishable monument to his judgement and foresight. It has already rendered his name dear to every miner, and future colonists will wonder how so much could have been accomplished with such small means. The colony already feels the benefit resulting from his unwavering policy in this respect, and year by year will the wisdom of that policy become more manifest.

Others were less generous. John Robson, editor of the *British Columbian,* wanted no tributes. "We are opposed," he wrote, "to any public demonstration being given to Governor Douglas."

London rewarded Douglas with a knighthood, but pushed him out before he could serve his full six-year term as governor of British Columbia. "I confess that I do not clearly perceive," he wrote in despair, "how my premature removal from office one year previous to the expiry of the term for which I was originally appointed can be managed without leaving an impression derogatory to the character of my administration."

The decision stood. Officials in London were tiring of the steady stream of complaints from the colonies, of Douglas's empire building and expensive road-building, of his sabre rattling at the Americans, of his obstruction of democratic institutions.

Even the governor's old friends confided that he was stern, pompous and too rigid for the new era. John Tod, one of Douglas's oldest compatriots, found it hard to be charitable. He wrote of a meeting, "I had a long chat the other day with our friend Douglas (now Sir James), ever stiff and formal as in times past, qualities which from long habit he could not now lay aside if he would, and probably ought not, if he could."

Ranching at Alkali Lake

My great-great-great-grandfather Herman Otto Bowe was born in Holstein, Germany, and he came to BC for the gold rush. Records show that in 1859 he was in the first group to find gold in the Cariboo, about 16 kilometres above Horsefly River. He worked Cardis Bar in 1859 adjacent to hundreds of acres of open grasslands. In 1860 he established a temporary trading post and saloon, and the year after that he pre-empted 144 hectares at the head

Herman Otto Bowe, shown here with his family at Alkali Lake, was one of the first people to find gold in 1859 after immigrating from Germany. Later he established a ranch at Alkali Lake.
Glenbow Archives NA-3483-16

The Bowe family ranch at Alkali Lake, photographed around 1890. *Glenbow Archives NA-3483-4*

of Alkali Lake. There he operated a roadhouse, and in 1862 he bought a herd of cattle. The animals were brought in from Oregon by L.W. Riske and Sam and Ed Withrow, who also ended up ranching in the area. The cattle were thin and exhausted from the long journey, but they recovered soon after they began grazing on the bunchgrass at Alkali Lake. My great-great-great-grandfather sold them for $100 (about $1,650) a head. That was the start of the Alkali Lake Ranch. Herman Otto Bowe married the daughter of the Great Chief of Alkali Lake Band, Caroline Belleau.

They were the parents of Henry Bowe, my great-grandfather, who was the father of my grandpa, Gilbert D. Bowe (his wife hasn't been identified yet). In 1925 Gilbert Bowe married Edith Pearl Pinchbeck, the granddaughter of William Pinchbeck, who in 1860 was sent over to the Cariboo as a policeman to maintain law and order as the gold rush gathered momentum. Pinchbeck occupied a prominent position in the Williams Lake Valley. My grandparents had eight children, starting with the oldest boy—my dad, Ivan Bowe, then my uncles Harvey, Stan, Gilbert and Henry Bowe. The girls were my aunties May, Gladys and Ivy Bowe. My dad told me that in the 1950s he worked for the Alkali Lake Ranch, started by my great-great-great-grandfather Herman Otto Bowe.

—*Sherry Bowe, Vancouver*

Williams Lake

This city took its name from Chief William, credited with keeping peace between local miners and First Nations during the gold rush. White people began to settle here in 1859, and in 2006 the federal Land Claims Commission ruled that Williams Lake had been stolen from Natives.

Tod went on to describe Douglas as "cold, crafty and selfish," an appraisal that seems a little harsh. Perhaps Douglas was all these things, but he had had much to overcome; humble beginnings and a struggle to succeed had made him more imperious than the imperialists. He was never strong on self-analysis, but in 1869 he wrote, in his own defence: "Self-reliance is a lesson that all must learn. Look at the man who is continually waiting to be pushed on by his friends, who is afraid to take a step that is not directed or steadied by another. Few men of that stamp ever make their mark in the world. It is the bold, resolute man, who fights his own way through every obstacle and wins the confidence and respect of his fellows."

McNeil Point

My grandfather, Benjamin McNeil, was 16 years old when he and his brother Lester arrived in Ashcroft from Ellensburg, Washington, in 1892, having been lured there by the goldfields. To augment their resources, they sold all but three of their horses and headed for Clearwater to trap marten. They built their cabin in a lakeside spot that early maps refer to as McNeil Point. The two of them nearly starved at one point during the winter, and they resorted to eating the bait from their traps. In the spring they traded what equipment they had left to Native trappers for furs and walked out. Grandpa became disenchanted with prospecting, invested in a 10-horse team and freighted on the Cariboo Road, supplying the miners with food and equipment. His home at his 105 Mile Ranch is now a tourist stop of historical interest. His change of plans may have saved his life—his oldest brother, Clarence, was killed in the Klondike slide of 1898.
—*Florence Joan McNeil Uhrig, Kamloops*

And so passed the era of Douglas. Two governors would fill his shoes: on Vancouver Island, Captain Arthur Edward Kennedy; and on the mainland, Frederick Seymour.

Seymour, who was leaving a post in the British Honduras, found the capital of New Westminster, a "melancholy... picture of disappointed hopes." He quickly set about trying to dress up the city with improvements to Government House: a new ballroom, supper rooms and beautified grounds. His hope was to turn New Westminster into a proper capital, and after years of taking second place to Victoria, mainlanders were thrilled with their new leader.

Soon Seymour faced his first major crisis: the Chilcotin War, an Indian uprising with a disturbing death toll. The incident had its roots in the rush for gold and had an added complexity—disease. Smallpox had wiped out nearly a third of the First Nations population during the gold rush era. And by the spring of 1864, Native people even in the most

Governor Frederick Seymour succeeded James Douglas as governor of the mainland colony and, after 1866, governor of the new united colony of British Columbia. Shortly after he took up his new position in 1864, he was faced with a major challenge: the crisis that became known as the Chilcotin War. He and Mrs. Seymour are shown here in 1865.
British Columbia Archives A-01751

remote parts of the colonies knew that the disease threatened the future of whole villages and groups.

The Chilcotin (Tsilhqot'in) people were a long way from the focal point of the epidemic, but that was about to change. A large number of newcomers had arrived in the BC Interior during the gold rush; not all of them had treated the land as First Nations' territory, and many of them had become permanent residents. In response to the growing population in the area, Alfred Waddington, a Victoria merchant, embarked on an audacious plan to build a road from the head of Bute Inlet to the Quesnel River—right through Chilcotin territory.

Bute Inlet, at the mouth of the Homathko River, was the location chosen by the entrepreneur Alfred Waddington to start building a road to the Cariboo goldfields in 1862. A confrontation between his road builders and a group of Tsilhqot'in men led to the "Chilcotin War." Eventually the project failed, and Waddington had to abandon it. *British Columbia Archives A-04140*

The Chilcotin War

Just a few years after its creation, the new colony of British Columbia was forced to deal with an issue that most colonial governments feared—violent Native resistance to the encroaching white tide of settlement. Gold was the principal catalyst behind the creation of the colony. By 1864 many fortunes had been made on the Fraser, and the Cariboo goldfields had proved just as alluring and profitable. A number of Victoria entrepreneurs (including Emily Carr's father, Richard) had prospered as part of the supply chain for the miners, but the Cariboo fields were difficult to reach, and the best available route in the early 1860s took trade through New Westminster, rather than its rival, Victoria.

To reclaim some of this trade, a private speculator, Alfred Waddington, lobbied for and received a charter to build a toll road to the Cariboo from the head of Bute Inlet on the north coast, through the mountains and on into the Interior plateau. This was the traditional territory of the Tsilhqot'in, a group of tribes known at the time as the Chilcotin. Waddington had selected his route based on reports from men who had used the Aboriginal trails along the Homathko River. Later, after the terrain had proved impassable, critics asserted that Waddington had "imagined" this route rather than discovered it. He did admit to having laid a ruler across a map while confined to bed with an attack of gout, and having decided—without any knowledge of the country between the inlet and the Interior—that the Bute Inlet route was the most direct. Nonetheless, Waddington had been successful in raising funds for the road-building project. By spring 1864 he had managed to spend $63,000 (over $800,000 in today's terms) to cut a rough trail through to the proposed pass through the Bute Inlet Mountains. Here the "road" ended at a great precipice overlooking the Homathko, a large and rapid river.

Waddington had hired men from the Takla tribe, who were nominally allied with the other Chilcotin people, to pack provisions and equipment for his forward road-building party, which was headed by a man called Brewster. On May 11, 1864, Victoria and Arthur Kennedy, governor of the Colony of Vancouver Island, received the devastating news that 14 men—most of the members of Brewster's crew—had been attacked and killed by the Takla on April 30. The incident raised the terrible spectre of a full-blown insurrection amongst the Natives, and grave danger for any white man in the area occupied by the Chilcotin.

Frederick Seymour, governor of the Colony of British Columbia, requested assistance from John Kingcome, vice-admiral of the British Navy unit in Esquimalt, in a letter dated June 1. "The Colony is passing through a crisis," he wrote, "the gravity of which we do not perhaps as yet fully appreciate... I need scarcely point out to you the difficulties and enormous expense which an Indian War in this vast territory would entail on the Imperial and Local Government, and the total ruin which would befall British Columbia were access to the Gold Mines of Cariboo rendered impracticable."

Inevitably, the necessity of working through proper channels of authority caused bureaucratic delays, and the first investigative party, led by Justice of the Peace Chartres Brew, didn't reach the scene of the massacre until May 20. A second mounted expedition, which was judged the most likely to capture the men responsible, was authorized by Seymour to approach the territory from the east, under the command of William Cox, one of the gold commissioners for the Cariboo. The distance they had to cover was such that they could not report for several weeks, and when they did, it was to report yet another death—that of Donald McLean, who had been second in command of the expedition and who was killed in a skirmish in the mountains.

While these search parties were being organized, the Takla men responsible for the attack on Brewster's party had fled back through the mountains, killing the only fixed settler in the region, William Manning, at his homestead. They also encountered another road-building party, whose members were unaware of the incipient uprising, and in this confrontation three more white men were killed. Finally, there was the death of McLean. As the reports of more deaths filtered back to Seymour, he became more and more concerned that this was indeed "an Indian Insurrection," and that it involved the whole Chilcotin nation, not just the Takla. Seymour was so alarmed about the situation that he took the highly unusual step of accompanying a third expedition, which approached the area via Bentinck Arm.

Once in the Chilcotin, the governor's party established contact with Alexis, the great chief of the Chilcotins, and a delicate political negotiation was undertaken between Seymour and Alexis. The chief stated that the Takla and their leader, Klatsassin, had renounced all connection with him and had a right to make war on the British without it being any concern of his. Seymour pressed him about why the hostilities had begun, but Alexis would only say that Klatsassin's men were "des mauvais sauvages, qui ne connaissant pas les bon Dieu." With little to show for this parlay, Cox's party was once again dispatched into the Bute Inlet Mountains to look for Klatsassin and the other men who were implicated in the deaths. Surprisingly, on August 15, Klatsassin and his men—eight men altogether—entered the camp of Cox voluntarily and surrendered. Much controversy about this "surrender" ensued: some said that Cox had offered inducements and that Klatsassin had no understanding of the consequences of his action. However, Matthew Baillie Begbie, the chief justice of the colony, interviewed Klatsassin before his trial and asked him, "Must you not have come in soon, on any terms?" and he had nodded "yes." He had been forced to surrender because of lack of food.

After a trial at Quesnelle Mouth, with Begbie presiding, five of the eight men were deemed to have committed murder and were hanged on October 26, 1864. Their names were Klatsassin, Telloot, Chessus, Piell and Tah-pit. These executions were followed by another later in New Westminster, when further testimony convicted Ahan of the murder of Mac-Donald, one of the white men.

The executions still reverberate in the region, where the Tsilhqot'in people firmly believe that the attacks on the road-building parties were acts of war, designed to keep the British out of Takla and Chilcotin territory, and that Klatsassin and his followers should not have been tried as criminals. Other contemporary evidence suggests that the men who turned on Brewster's party may have been treated badly, and that the tribe was on the verge of starvation. Smallpox had also ravaged the Chilcotin, and fear of reinfection may have driven them to try to keep the white men out. Even Governor Seymour could finally only comment: "All remains mere guess work respecting the motives which caused this melancholy incident."

Numerous documents survive to tell the story, including the governor's dispatches, correspondence with the Colonial office and court records. The spare text of a letter written by J. Boles Gaggin, who took custody of the Chilcotin men at Quesnelle Mouth, captures one moment of the sad sequence of events:

> Quesnelmouth 13 September 1864
> Sir,
> I have the honor to report for the information of His Excellency the Governor, that in conformity with a letter received by me from Mr. Commissioner Cox, I proceeded on the 9th inst. down the "Frazer" River to Alexandria, taking with me Constable Sullivan and on the following morning received from Mr. Cox at Alexandria seven (7) Chilacoaten Indians, charged with being participants in the Bute Inlet Massacre, their names as nearly as they can be made out, are
> Klatsassin
> Telloot
> Tappitt
> Kiddaki (George)
> Pierre
> Tansaki
> Tatchasla (old man)
> Immediately on receipt of the prisoners, I placed them on board the Steamer Enterprize, in charge of Constables Sullivan and Pine, and returned to this town, where I handed them over to the Chief Constable who lodged them safely in a building which I had previously rented, and had fitted up for their reception.
> They were properly washed and supplied each with one pair of new trowsers, one blue flannel shirt, and one good blanket, and are secure from any possibility of escape.
> I have the honor
> to remain Sir
> Your obedt. svt.
> J. Boles Gaggin

> —Ann ten Cate, Archivist and Outreach Coordinator, BC Archives

Some accounts from the time suggest that the "Chilcotin War" started over the theft of a bag of flour, and that one of Waddington's agents in the territory threatened local chiefs by saying, "All Chilcotins are going to die. We shall send sickness into the country, which will kill them all." The Chilcotins were already in rough shape. It had been a hard winter and many were starving. Whatever the causes, the attacks occurred, and the death toll rose to over twenty people, with casualties on both sides. The Native men considered themselves prisoners of war, not criminals. Even Begbie, "the hanging judge," was ambivalent about the outcome of the trial: "It seems horrible to hang five men at once—especially under the conditions of capitulation. Yet the blood of 21 whites calls for retribution."

The executions were a stain on Native–white relations for more than a century. Waddington's road was never completed, and in a strange twist of fate, Waddington himself died of smallpox. Over a hundred years later, in 1993 a justice inquiry recommended a pardon for the five accused men. In 1999, a plaque was erected in Quesnel, recognizing the Chilcotin chiefs not as murderers but as warriors.

The Chilcotin War was also a financial fiasco for Seymour's government. British Columbia spent $80,000 on the manhunt ($1 million today), and London refused to share in the expense. But instead of worrying, the colonial government spent more money. They rewarded the governor and his team with lavish gifts and cash.

Seymour was on a public relations roll. He set off on a tour of the Cariboo goldfields, where he was feted again. Then he embarked on an ambitious new program of road building. When gold was found on the Wild Horse Creek in the Kootenay, Seymour promptly ordered the extension of the Dewdney Trail to the new diggings. He announced the completion of the Cariboo Road from Quesnel to Barkerville, and he declared that there would be a new road from Hope to Yale.

The province still owed more than £50,000 on the original Cariboo Road, but Seymour's administration borrowed another £100,000 for more roads and public projects. He had other ambitious plans for his government as well. All this at a time when revenues from the goldfields were in steep decline.

The Lure of Cariboo Gold

My great-great-uncle, John Clapperton, sailed from Southhampton, England, on April 17, 1862, "to try our fortune as gold miners in Cariboo," and arrived in Victoria on June 2. He got to Antler Creek in the Cariboo on July 8, 1862, and over the next three summers tried his luck gold mining at Antler Creek and Barkerville. But he never struck it rich. In 1868 he moved to the Nicola Valley, where my great-grandfather, George Clapperton, joined him. They cleared land and farmed. In April 1872, John was appointed justice of the peace for the Nicola Valley. In this role he led a posse, including his brother George, that helped capture the McLean boys [four young outlaw cowboys active in the area during the 1870s] in December 1879. He served as government agent at Nicola Lake until 1900.

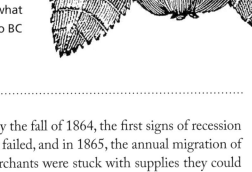

My great-grandparents, George and Maria (Woodward), later moved from Nicola to Kamloops and established a dairy farm and orchard in what is now Kamloops North. The lure of Cariboo gold brought our family to BC and we continue to reap the benefits of this great country.

—*Ruth Davis (Clapperton), Duncan*

The government raised custom duties, but by the fall of 1864, the first signs of recession were beginning to appear. A major colonial bank failed, and in 1865, the annual migration of miners from San Francisco did not happen. Merchants were stuck with supplies they could not sell, and even a minor rush at Big Bend on the Columbia River failed to turn around the government's fortunes.

On Vancouver Island the situation wasn't much better. The new governor, Arthur Kennedy, was far more charming than Douglas. But he also had a reputation for toughness, and Victoria had had enough of toughness. Kennedy quickly found himself on the wrong side of the House of Assembly, which challenged him at every turn. He had little experience with representative government, and Amor de Cosmos, now a member of the provincial assembly and a rival politician, was more than his match. With his colleagues John Helmcken and William Tolmie, de Cosmos set out to obstruct Kennedy in every way he could.

There were some economic bright spots during Kennedy's tenure. The coalfields at Nanaimo emerged as a major supply point, and Robert Dunsmuir began his rise to riches as a coal baron. Esquimalt became the North Pacific base of the Royal Navy in 1865. Minor gold rushes took place on the island, at Leechtown and Goldstream. And money was procured to build a road from Nanaimo to the Comox Valley, an emerging agricultural settlement.

But revenues were declining as they were on the mainland, and the government had to borrow heavily to keep the province afloat. In May 1865, the Bank of British Columbia cut the government off. Kennedy's complaints to London fell on deaf ears. Britain's Pacific colonies were in a serious bind.

Maine to Moodyville

Philander Wheeler Swett began a life of adventure in 1836 in Garland, Penobscot County, Maine, in the United States. He was the son of Noah Swett, a master mariner who died at sea in Hispaniola, West Indies, and Nancy Rice Wheeler, the daughter of a wealthy clothier. Several of his contemporaries began their journey to the Pacific Northwest when the lure of gold and a better life drew them to the west coast of America. Records show that he spent time in Santa Barbara, California; Moraga Valley, California, in 1858; then Portland, Oregon, in 1860. Soon after that, he landed on the shores of the Fraser River, in search of gold along with thousands of other men.

When gold did not pan out for him, he became a manager at the Moodyville sawmill. He never struck it rich with gold, but he did become part of the financial and social network that grew up around the gold rush. Philander W. Swett was a founding member of Mount Hermon Masonic Lodge number 491, SC, chartered on May 5, 1869. A memorial plaque still exists in Moodyville.

Like many men of that era, he took a "country wife"—a woman of Hawaiian and Native heritage. Cecile Marguerite Kanaka (Haile) and Philander were the parents of three children, Albert, Sarah Cecelia and Marie Agnes. Albert and his mother passed away about 1889. Philander placed Sarah and Agnes in St. Ann's, a school/orphanage in Cowichan, and left for Washington State. Cecile never gave up her Hawaiian name.

The South Bend Land Company was formed in Washington State by George U. Holcomb, Lewis N. Eklund, P.W. Swett and Charles H. Warner. By about 1890, the town of South Bend was flooded with speculators who assumed that this town would be the Boston of the West Coast. The railroad never came, and the harbour has never been much more than a successful oyster bed. The men became wealthy—not on gold, but on the peripheral endeavours that grew up around gold.

Philander Swett died from stomach cancer on Christmas Eve 1892, and a nine-year probate ensued that left his two surviving daughters penniless. Benjamin Springer found out about his death and forwarded his 1883 will from a safe in British Columbia to Pacific County, Washington. Swett's two daughters continued to reside in BC until they came of age. The worldwide crash of 1893, and the dishonesty of some prominent British Columbians and Washingtonians assured that these mixed-heritage children never received anything from his estate.

—*Roree M. Oehlman, great-great-granddaughter of Philander Swett, Big Island, Hawaii*

In January 1865, Amor de Cosmos introduced a motion in the provincial assembly calling for the immediate and unconditional union of the two colonies. On a trip to London, Governor Seymour found that the Colonial Office, the Foreign Office and the Treasury were all "very anxious for a union of the two colonies." Clearly, some officials in England wanted to be rid of the Pacific possessions altogether.

Sir James Douglas, now retired, worried about his treasured Vancouver Island falling under the control of the mainland. But in November 1866 the deal was done, and the union was proclaimed. Douglas wrote in his diary: "The Ships of war fired a salute on the occasion—A funeral procession, with minute guns would have been more appropriate to the sad melancholy event."

The union did not improve the economic climate. The glory days of the Cariboo were now definitely over, and the Big Bend gold rush was all but over too. An overland telegraph project that had raised expectations was abandoned. The Colony of British Columbia had debts of over $1 million, and Vancouver Island's debt was close to $300,000. New taxes and duties on American imports drove prices up and settlers out.

Victoria now looked little better than New Westminster. Two American officers travelling to the city reported that "Victoria presents the melancholy spectacle of premature decay and financial ruin."

Levi & Boas, Importers

Little did I know as a new bride and newly landed immigrant to Canada on February 17, 1967, that the storied great-grandfather of my California childhood had also been a pioneer New Westminster businessman and merchant in the Cariboo gold rush. The *Columbian* newspaper of February 13, 1861, carries a box advertisement for "Levi & Boas, corner of Liverpool and Columbia Streets, New Westminster, Importers, Wholesale and Retail dealers in groceries, provisions, dry goods, boots, shoes and hardware." This was my great-grandfather's BC base of operations. From here the company freighted goods by boat and overland to the Barkerville area. A *Colonist* report later, in 1892, describes Levi & Boas as "at one time... the chief business house in the province."

It was a cousin on my Canadian mother's side who discovered my great-grandfather's BC connection while doing research on pioneer San Franciscans about 20 years ago. Although Judah (aka John) Boas died 32 years before my birth in 1947 in San Francisco, I grew up hearing many stories from my father about his loving and very successful grandfather, who had died when my dad was only seven years old in 1915.

According to his San Francisco obituary, Judah Boas was born in 1837 in a small Prussian village, now part of Poland. At age 18 he travelled from Europe to New York City on a $14 steerage-class boat ticket, then immediately travelled on to San Francisco. There he rose from street pedlar, "private banker" and Chinese lottery hustler to become a respected businessman and a primary backer of the Crocker family, the founders of the Bank of America.

My dad was entirely unaware of his grandfather's sojourn to British Columbia's goldfields in 1859–1866 (family lore had it that his business success derived from the California gold rush), but it was here, according to his obituary, that he laid the foundation for his subsequent wealth. My dad loved to drive us around the streets of San Francisco and point with pride to the commercial and residential properties that had been built and owned by his grandfather and that survive to this day. He also fondly recalled the many weekend trips he made with his grandfather to the notorious San Quentin Prison, to deliver bags of gifts to "Granddad's" incarcerated cronies.

In July 1862 (according to the *Columbian* of September 19, 1863), a sensational murder occurred with which Judah was peripherally involved. Two prominent Jewish businessmen, Harris Lewin of Victoria and David Sokolowsky of New Westminster, and their Metis guide Charles Rouchier of Nanaimo, were murdered and robbed of $18,000 in gold (some $370,000 today) at Quesnelle Forks, north of Williams Lake. As no formal law-enforcement system was in place there at the time, several men from the community, including my great-grandfather, set out to find the trio when they went missing. The murderer(s) were never apprehended, and legend has it that the stolen cache of gold remains buried somewhere in the Quesnelle Forks area to this day.

On Februay 17, 2007, my husband Harold and I will mark 40 years in Canada. We have raised four children and are now grandparents to two little ones. We have enjoyed a wonderful life here, and I can only think that my great-grandfather would be nothing short of bedazzled if he could see the Victoria, Vancouver and New Westminster of today.

—Jessica Tichenor, Bowen Island

The mid-1860s were dark days for Victoria, but salvation would present itself. In 1867, word came that London was finalizing the confederation of Upper and Lower Canada, New Brunswick and Nova Scotia. De Cosmos and his fellow reformers grasped at the straw.

Once again Sir James Douglas watched from the sidelines. "Confederation with Canada is now one of the ruling manias," he wrote, "and my impression is that it will not long be delayed."

Search for Eldorado

My great-grandfather Hans Lars Helgesen was born to a shipbuilding family in Askar, a suburb of Oslo, in 1831. In search of adventure and economic betterment, he shipped aboard a trading schooner bound for the new world, working as first mate. Not bad at age 18. Upon arrival at San Francisco, the crew heard of the gold rush and deserted to a man. Helgesen and several crewmates formed a partnership and hit the trail for the goldfields. Somewhere along the way he met my great-grandmother, Lillian Colquhoun, born 1835 in County Donegal. She had come to New Brunswick with her shiny new teaching certificate to visit her uncles. Together they took ship down to Panama, walked the isthmus and took ship again to San Francisco. She worked there as a ladies' tailor. One of her uncles, Thomas Fulton, came to Fort Victoria and ran a clothing store with a partner. He persuaded Lillian to come up and keep house for him.

In 1858, when gold was discovered in the Cariboo, Hans visited Lillian in Victoria, and being the man he was, he found a couple of partners, built a skiff and set out. The skills he had learned in his boyhood ensured that their skiff made it to Hope—many others did not. He and his partners were in the party that named the Cariboo country—one James Kennedy having shot a caribou. In 1859, Hans Helgesen, Joseph Devlin, Frederick George Black, Duncan McMartin and Edward Campbell became the second party to move inland from the Fraser to the Horsefly area. That winter Hans stayed in Barkerville, to get an early start in the spring.

In 1862, Hans and Lillian were married in Victoria by the Reverend J. Hall, and Cariboo gold bought Section 5 in Metchosin from John MacGregor. Seven children were born to the couple, but only four survived to adulthood: my grandfather, Henry, Sara Jane, Thomas and Christian Alexander, an afterthought who was born when his father was 50 and his mother 46.

In the early years, after the farm was established, Hans continued to hunt for gold, leaving Lillian to run the farm, which she did successfully. He mined at Leechtown on Vancouver Island, and in Nevada, the Cassiar and the Yukon, being away from home for a year at a stretch. After the mining boom, he fished for cod and organized and ran a cannery at Rivers Inlet. His last great northern adventure was a sealing trip on the schooner *Juanita*, in which he had shares.

His last search for Eldorado had him in British Guiana, in search of emeralds! At the age of 78 he decided to revisit Norway, and take Sandy (Alexander) with him—he announced this on a Sunday night and said they would start in the morning. Uncle Sandy refused, and Hans gave him three days to get ready!

Hans represented both Esquimalt and the Cariboo in the provincial legislature for a total of 11 years, and also served his province as inspector of fisheries on the North Coast. He had a remarkable reputation for hardiness and honesty, to the point that partners were

partners, and if you hit it rich so did they, no matter where they were at the great moment. He always swore that he had seen the mother lode in the Cariboo one early winter, but on returning in the spring found that there had been a landslide and he never saw the rich gold again. Nobody who knew him—and when I was a child, quite a lot of people around Metchosin had—doubted that he had indeed seen a great vein of gold.

He died in Victoria in 1918, at age 87, and he is buried in the yard of St. Mary's church, beside Lillian. This is fitting, as he was the first people's warden of that church in 1873. The school in Metchosin is named for him, though the family still feels it should have been called the Lillian Helgesen school.

—Isabel Tipton, great-granddaughter of Hans Lars Helgesen, Victoria

The pro-confederation group, led by de Cosmos, set down their conditions for union:

1. Canada to become liable for the entire public debt of this Colony estimated at $1,500,000.

2. Canada to provide for federal officers and services.

3. To grant sufficient fixed subsidy, and per capita subsidy, to insure the support of the local Government, in addition to the powers of taxation reserved to Provincial Governments in British North America Act.

4. Representation in the Senate and Commons of Canada.

5. The construction of a trans-continental wagon-road, from Lake Superior to the head of navigation on the Lower Fraser within two years after the time of admission. This is regarded as an essential condition.

6. Popular representative institutions, including responsible control over Government.

The act of setting the conditions in type galvanized support and stirred up opposition. De Cosmos lost Helmcken as an ally but gained the backing of John Robson, editor of the *British Columbian,* and his New Westminster friends. In May the Confederation League was founded, and for a brief moment, Yale was back at the centre of things. A signpost erected by the province at Yale tells the story:

> By 1868, the gold rushes that had founded British Columbia were over, the public debt was soaring and many were dissatisfied with the colonial government. On September 14, 1868, 26 delegates from all over the colony met at Yale for a convention of the Confederation League. This convention did much to stimulate popular support for the idea of union with Canada as a solution to the colony's problems.

In 1871, the deal was done, and with the coming of the railway, the colonial days were over forever.

A French (Canadian) Connection

Joseph Poirier was born in 1829 in Quebec. After many adventures, his life came to its close at his home a continent away, in Sooke, in 1898. A century after his death, the legacy of his family is remembered in the name of a school built on land near Poirier's own pre-emption.

As a youth, Joseph Poirier, a francophone, set off with others from his Quebec village to join the fur traders heading west. The voyagers travelled the Canadian route to the settlement at Red River in what is now Manitoba. From there, they took a more southerly course to the Hudson's Bay Company's western headquarters, Fort Vancouver, on the Columbia River.

A French Canadian community, consisting of Hudson's Bay Company émigrés and their Native wives, had developed south of the fur-trading fort in the wide, fertile valley of the Willamette River. When the Oregon Treaty of 1846 declared this area part of the American republic, many of those of Quebec origin decided to move north into territory that remained in the British domain. The HBC posts at Fort Langley and Fort Victoria were natural destinations.

Joseph Poirier joined a wagon train travelling north. His group included Jean Baptiste Brule, also from Quebec, who had married Marguerite (originally from the T'Sou-ke First Nations people) in Fort Vancouver. Marguerite Brule's son from a previous marriage, Joseph Iroquois, and this man's wife, Mary Ann, of the Kalapooya nation in the Willamette Valley, also travelled in Poirier's group.

Jean Baptiste Brule and his family settled on the east bank of the Sooke River. Joseph Poirier learned of work in the area, falling timber for the sawmill of Sooke's first independent immigrant settler, the Scottish captain W.C. Grant. Poirier soon followed Brule's lead, taking up the land now known as Milne's Landing. During the Leechtown gold rush of 1864, Poirier and Brule rafted in sheep and cattle to their riverside base and sold mutton and beef to the miners en route to the goldfields.

Poirier married Ellen, a daughter of Joseph and Mary Ann Brule. The couple built a cabin on the river flats, then began raising their family. Fifteen children were born to them. By the mid-1880s, Joseph Poirier sold this riverside land to Edward Milne Sr., and moved his family to property on what is now known as Grant Road, near its junction with Otter Point Road.

Joseph and Ellen Poirier's firstborn was also named Joseph. When he grew up, Joseph Jr. worked in the sealing industry, then took up a section of land at today's West Coast Road and Kemp Lake Road, where he established a reputation as a farmer and steam engineer. He married Mary White, daughter of Aaron Denton White and Catherine (Owechemis) White, of Aboriginal origin, and they had four daughters and three sons. Besides "Poirier," their descendants, whose names are readily recognized in the area today, include the George Goudie family, the Walter and Claude Cook families and the Jessimans.

Joseph and Ellen's second son, Adolphus Poirier, went sealing with his brother, and the two were part of a consortium that purchased the first sleek East-Coast-built vessel *Agnes*

MacDonald for use in the sealing industry. A story was told, only half in jest, that Joseph Poirier Jr., a gregarious man with many attractive sisters, brought shipmates home each year to visit his family until all his sisters were married.

Best known of the families in Sooke, perhaps from this seal-hunting history, were Andrew and Isobel (Poirier) Davidson, and Thomas and Ellen (Poirier) Robinson. Son James Poirier married Alice White, daughter of Aaron Denton White and Catherine; well known among their descendants today is the Richard Poirier family of Jordan River.

Harry Dilley married into the Poirier family, and Dilley family descendants are also well known in Sooke. The Lidgates, O'Mearas and McMillans, too, are part of the Poirier family. The Poirier daughter who left the largest number of descendants was Sarah, who married Mandus Michelson, a seaman, and produced five sons: Mandus, Earland, Paul, Eric and Rolf. The couple's daughters have also left their mark—the eldest, Sarah, married William Vowles; Lily married Jimmy Goudie and then Alf Haywood; Agnes married John Bush, then Claude Dilley; Christine married Jack Blight; and Marie married Art Hay.

The extended Poirier family eventually provided what was probably the largest work-force in the district. Lily Haywood, now well into her eighties, reminisces today about Ellen Poirier: "I still remember Grandma Poirier. She was a little lady wearing black, very strict, who always spoke French."

The great-grandchildren of this family number in the hundreds. Among them are the 14 children of Sarah Michelsen and William Vowles.

The early generations of Poiriers gained an enormous local reputation for their skills as woodsmen, fishermen, hunters and farmers. Today they carry on these roles in addition to others—the fields of business, arts and culture and community leadership. Eric Michelsen, for example, a grandson of Joseph Poirier, works in the lumber business. He also developed Broome Hill Golf Course into a successful enterprise, and was serving as elected president of the Sooke Community Association when he passed away in 1973.

The impact and legacy of the Poirier family is immense—in citizenry of the area, in their many years of work in the various industries of the district, and in their contributions to the development of the region.

—Dennice Goudie, Nanaimo, with thanks to Elida Peers, Historian, Sooke Region Historical Society

9

LIVING HISTORY
The Gold Rush Today

The last people who remember the gold rushes of the 1850s and '60s passed away a few generations ago, but gold-rush culture lives on in the collective memory of all British Columbians—Aboriginals, others born here and newcomers. Many of us (and lots of others farther afield) have family connections to the miners, entrepreneurs, entertainers and original inhabitants of this land who laid the foundation for the diverse, challenging BC we know today. Here are some stories of those connections, from listeners and friends of *BC Almanac*. Their shared memories are testimony to the fact that as the years pass we learn more and more, and we understand our history in new ways.

Opposite: The Motherlode Café in historic Hedley. *Courtesy Michael Kluckner, originally published in* Vanishing British Columbia

Descended from Douglas

I was born in San Fernando, Chile, on November 18, 1939, and lived in Chile for the first 10 years of my life. My dad was John Sinclair Bushby. His mother, Violet Bushby (born in England), the widow of George Bushby, visited Chile shortly after I was born and stayed with us until we all moved back to British Columbia in the summer of 1950. My grandfather, George Bushby, was the son of Arthur Bushby and Agnes Douglas, daughter of Sir James Douglas.

Grandmother Bushby lived in the past. She told me the most exciting stories about her life in Victoria, her travels to South Africa and England to see her daughter Audrey and five grandchildren. The parties, what people wore—everything was explained to me in great detail. She told me many things about their life in Canada, and it was better than any storybook. But if she did mention Sir James Douglas during that time I can't honestly remember.

I believe I first heard about him after we arrived in Victoria. Of course, being in Victoria

The famous packer Jean Caux, known as Cataline, greets travellers in the Hazeltons. *Mark Forsythe Photo*

**Sir James Douglas, governor of the
colony of BC, and Lady Douglas.**
*British Columbia Archives A-02834
and A-01229*

it was hard not to see his name everywhere you went. My father took my mother and me to visit his Aunt Rose and Aunt Dot for tea. My mother did not speak English and therefore did not notice how they snubbed her; but I had gone to English private schools and could understand them quite well and found them to be nothing but snobs. I guess Dad did too, because shortly after, we all packed up and moved to Vancouver. My mom, dad and grandmother lived there until they died.

The first school that I attended in BC was Sir James Douglas Elementary School, on Victoria Drive in Vancouver. It is pretty interesting that Douglas happened to be our neighbourhood school, considering how many schools there are in Vancouver. Unbeknownst to me, my father had in his possession the Sir James Douglas Bible. He allowed the school to display it in a glass case near the entrance. I attended the school for one year before going to John Oliver High School. When my family returned to Chile, the school returned the bible and my father left it with me. The bible now resides in the City of Vancouver Archives, where it was taken in by Major J.S. Matthews. It was then that I started to realize the importance of my great-great-grandfather.

Cynthia Fleming, the great-granddaughter of Governor James Douglas, seen here (right) with her sister Gloria Bushby at Fort Langley in 2006, didn't know she was a descendant of "Old Square Toes" until she was ten years old. *Mark Forsythe photo*

In 1971, Mom and Dad gave me a large stepping stone, which says *1971 British Columbia Centenary of Confederation with Canada*. I still have the stone, and it travels with me every time we move and is displayed in a prominent place outside my front door. During a trip to Bali I met a fellow who worked for the BC government, and it was from him that I learned that Sir James was of mixed blood. Until that time no one I knew had mentioned this. Since then I have learned many things and become very interested in all that Sir James did, and I am proud that I am related to him.

From the time we landed in Victoria in 1950, my father updated our family tree at the Victoria city hall, and since he passed away in 1983, I have updated the information. The archivist, a volunteer who served for many years, was a relation of ours named Aimsley Helmcken. He too has passed away.

As a retirement present, I received a copy of the fascinating book *Old Square Toes and His Lady*. It is the life story of James and Amelia Douglas. I was completely floored to read in this book that early in their life my father had moved to South America and his sister to South Africa, and that there are no descendants with the name Bushby left in British Columbia. I quickly got hold of the author, John Adams, and informed him about our side of the family, complete with an updated family tree. He said that I would be totally surprised at the number of cousins that I have. They haven't surfaced yet...

I have a file of photocopied documents pertaining to Douglas and I have also verbally passed on information to my children and my five grandchildren. I do not know whether this will one day become important to them as it has to me. One thing is for sure: we might not be living in this beautiful Canadian province if it wasn't for the sacrifices made by my Great-Great-Grandfather and Grandmother Douglas.

—*Cynthia Katharine Fleming (nee Cynthia Katharine Bushby Diaz), Nanaimo*

2008: A Celebration of Wisdom

British Columbia has a mixed track record in marking historic anniversaries. Too often, milestones are remembered from a Eurocentric point of view. In one version of the story of Captain Cook's voyage, for instance, the great European explorer brings civilization to this savage wilderness. The First Nations reject this limited vision, conflict ensues and we are left with an incomplete picture of how modern BC was founded.

As 2008 approaches, we have an opportunity to tell the story differently. Instead of marking the 200th anniversary of the great explorer Simon Fraser conquering the river that bears his name, we can celebrate the bicentennial of the First Nations of BC guiding Fraser and his expedition down the river that pulses like an artery through the heart of their traditional territories. Rather than feting Governor James Douglas (although he deserves to be feted) for taking bold action during the gold rush of 1858 and stopping mainland BC from falling into the hands of the Americans, we can honour the sesquicentennial of the immense courage of First Nations leaders like Chief Spintlum of the Nlaka'pamux, who prevented a bloody war between Aboriginal people and miners.

Prior to European contact, the centre of the Nlaka'pamux world was Kumsheen (present-day Lytton), where the Thompson River joins the Fraser. This complex society was built on the

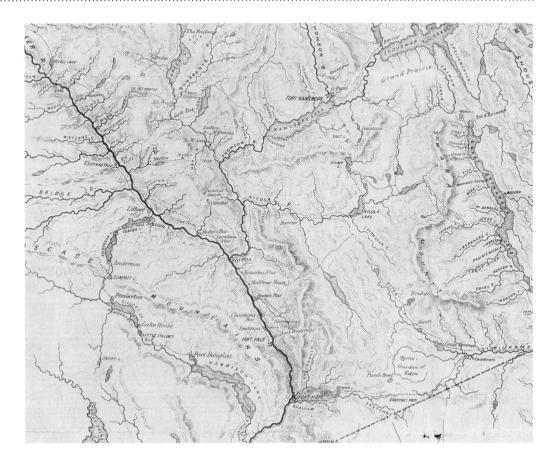

Long before miners from around the world claimed territory on the banks of BC rivers, the confluence of the Fraser and the Thompson was a site of great importance to the Nlaka'pamux nation. *British Columbia Archives CMA-127-1862*

rich salmon resources of the two rivers, and the language and culture were intimately linked to the land. For the previous 50 years (starting with Fraser's journey), the primary contact with European civilization had been through a symbiotic trading relationship with the Hudson's Bay Company. Native people were equal partners who received highly prized trade goods in exchange for the furs that were in demand in Europe's fashion markets.

The rush of 1858 turned this world upside down. Tens of thousands of miners ascended the river, disturbing fishing spots, hunting grounds and burial sites in search of the elusive golden mineral. The impact of two cultures colliding reverberated throughout the mainland. Not yet colonized, the territory was governed by the First Nations with a few small HBC outposts, which operated under company rules, not British law. In the absence of Euro-American laws and courts with jurisdiction (or any means to enforce them), atrocities were committed on both sides.

The conflict escalated into the Canyon War in July–August 1858. Heavily armed miner militias roamed the canyon, killing and destroying. It took enormous effort and bravery for Spintlum to negotiate a treaty with the peace-making faction of the miners, led by Captain Henry Snyder. Were it not for Spintlum, an all-out war on the non-Native miners could have blazed from Kumsheen to the mouth of the Columbia River, embroiling the embryonic Crown colony in an international incident that might well have led to annexation by the United States. We can also peel off the thin veneer of whitewash slapped over our history, which would have us believe that a few thousand white gold seekers laid the foundations of our modern province—mostly British subjects who remade BC in the image of their empire. In fact, the gold rush of 1858 was a multicultural event in which miners from China, Hawaii, Mexico and other countries came to this place. A large black community from San Francisco became the influential business class. It is they who helped lay the foundations of modern BC, along with Chief Spintlum, and their descendants still live, work and play in this province.

The people of Lytton and the Fraser Canyon are preparing to celebrate in 2008, recognizing the wisdom of Chief Spintlum as one of the Fathers of British Columbia, as well as the contributions of the ethnically diverse miners who came seeking gold and who stayed because of their connection to the land. We invite you to join us.

—*Chris O'Connor, Mayor, Village of Lytton, and Don Hauka*

....

Likely

This small centre was named after "Plato John" Likely, who lectured miners on Plato and Socrates in the area at Quesnel Lake. They in turn would tell him where to look for gold.

....

Gold Trail Ghost Town at Quesnel Forks

As the gold seekers pressed north along the Fraser River, the precious metal was detected at the mouth of the Quesnel River, now known as the town of Quesnel. A few men chose to travel along the south bank of the river. Upon their arrival at the confluence of the Cariboo and Quesnel Rivers (known then as the north and south forks of the Quesnel River) in summer 1859, they realized that they should cross to the north bank to locate gold. With determination, a couple of men filled a boat with rocks, dropped them into the Quesnel River at a particular spot, then repeated the process at several locations until they had built multiple protrusions of rocks as pylons to support narrow planks. The result was the first bridge to the site now known as Quesnel Forks.

Gold was abundant at first—it was found to be lying on the surface just under the water at many sites. News travelled quickly and attracted a stampede of prospectors, so a town of tents and rustic cabins grew at "The Forks," as it was called. The cornerstones of a community grew: food and supply depots, a law authority, a post office and a mining claim office were established at Quesnel Forks. For several years the town anchored itself as the end of the wagon road. Anyone who went on from there, continued on foot, sometimes with the assistance of a horse or mule if the miner was well funded or lucky.

Eventually the surface gold was depleted, and news of even richer strikes came from more northerly sites such as Antler Creek, Lightning Creek, Stanley and Cameron Town, or Cameronton, in what is now the Barkerville area. Quesnel Forks still played a vital role supplying goods and services not yet available farther north, and was even considered a prime candidate for the capital of BC, because all other locales were too far away from the goldfields.

The exodus of gold seekers left behind a well-established town that soon filled with miners of Chinese origin. Unlike the previous stampeders, these miners were not looking for fast riches to retire on; they were more resigned to eking out a living day by day from the gold beneath the surface, which was still plentiful. Chinese newcomers quickly outnumbered the white miners and merchants.

Today Quesnel Forks offers the travelling historian a true gold trail ghost town with abandoned buildings nestled in the tall grass. The site includes the oldest Tong House (Chinese fraternity) in Canada and the second oldest in North America, adorned with Chinese writings among a peppering of paint ball splatters. A picturesque cemetery is beautifully maintained by the Likely Cemetery Society and boasts grave markers dating to 1862.

Fortunately, much restoration work on the remaining structures has been done through the Quesnel Forks Restoration Project under the guidance of the Likely and District Chamber of Commerce. It's a volunteer effort, with occasional funding from the provincial government. Unfortunately, this area steeped in rich history is threatened daily with the many grave robbers and bottle diggers that the revitalization project attracts. The decay is arrested but the vandals are not, and no protection of this heritage site is offered by the province. The goal of the Quesnel Forks Restoration Project has now shifted from "Protection of the public from the collapsing buildings" to that of "Protection of the remaining buildings from the public."

To experience a remarkable slice of BC history, visit the town of Likely, BC (one hour

east of 150 Mile House). A treasury of knowledge of yesteryear can be had at the Cedar City Museum and the outdoor mining displays at the Cedar Point Provincial Park. You may want to drive the 13-kilometre goat trail from Likely to the gold trail ghost town of Quesnel Forks. If you come armed with metal detectors, shovels and paintball guns, prepare to be thrown in the river—Likely folk are losing patience with those who would damage this historic site.

—*Jim Smith, Foreman, Quesnel Forks Restoration Project, Likely, BC*

Charles Donaldson's pack train along the banks of the Quesnel River in 1868. *British Columbia Archives A-04036*

193

Theatre as Historical Research

Music gleaned and reclaimed from the tailings of history offers today's listener or reader a way of understanding a people and a time, a way of seeing another layer of a society, of hearing voices of our past.

The troupe of entertainers who perform at Barkerville Theatre's Gold Rush Music Hall Revue, seen here in 2007, keeps gold-rush era song and dance alive at Barkerville and through tours around the province.
Mark Forsythe photo

In the case of the British Columbia gold rush, a series of events that led to the founding of a new colony, we can find not only the music that miners brought with them, but the songs written in and about the goldfields. A song such as "Far from Home," found on a cabin door in Yale, clearly evokes a miner's melancholy mood. Through music we can eavesdrop in a gold rush-era saloon and hear the hurdies dancing, then hear the Scots poet James Anderson and his songs about the "Dancing Girls of Cariboo." We can gather around an Overlander's evening campfire and hear the tunes and lyrics that moved them, such as "The Yellow Rose of Texas," found carefully copied into the back pages of Robert McMicking's 1862 journal. Even today we can sit on a bench in the Theatre Royal in Barkerville, and laugh or reminisce with an audience generations past.

If we take a cursory glance at the rough life of miners in the Cariboo goldfields, we might overlook the day-to-day lives and emotions of miners and dancing girls. But in music we are reminded that men and women in this hard, harsh land still fell in love, hence "Lover's Lament"; missed their family, as in "Do They Miss Me at Home"; bore children; had political dreams, as in "The Song of the Dominion"; and harboured visions beyond the wealth that might lay in the creeks' cold gravel, as Anderson so eloquently wrote in his popular song, "Rough But Honest Miner."

Through songs and poetry we can hear prejudices, fears and political voices. We hear the hopes, dreams and the laughter of the day when we listen to the work of Anderson, Rebecca Gibbs, Tal o'Efion or the black miner and ex-slave J. Lawrence. In a poem we can hear the sorrow of a town ravaged by fire, a miner reduced to one torn shirt, the love of the Cariboo country or the hardships in "Know Ye the Land."

Music has always given us another voice, allowing us to express emotions not normally part of everyday conversation. History through music takes us beyond the cold facts of vital statistics records to a layer of emotional understanding. If we listen, we will hear the human voices of a time past.

There is another side to the reclamation of history's music. At Theatre Royal, musical and dramatic shows are presented each year by Newman and Wright Theatre Company. The shows are based on solid musical and historical research. As one might expect, the shows are therefore accurate and representative of the 1860s and '70s, when the Cariboo gold rush was at its peak. What is more unexpected are the solid, tangible links to history that emerge from the shows themselves, beyond any new research.

In the summer of 2004, the Newman and Wright made a radical departure from the usual Theatre Royal shows and presented the "Campfire Tales of Captain Jack Crawford." Crawford, known as "the poet/scout," was a US army scout, a sometime partner of Buffalo

The poet Jack Crawford, called "the poet/scout," had his own Wild West show. It toured Barkerville and Victoria in the early 1870s. *British Columbia Archives C-08669*

Bill Cody and Wild Bill Hickok. Cody and Crawford performed shows together for years, but the partnership ended with a bang and bottle when Cody appeared drunk on stage and accidentally shot Crawford. Crawford put his own "Wild West" show together and took it to Victoria and Barkerville in his show wagon. He presented many of his Campfires and Trails shows at the Theatre Royal in 1871, while he investigated and invested in mining claims. By some accounts he fell in love there.

Word of the 2004 Theatre Royal Captain Jack Crawford show reached the Kootenay and prompted three generations of a family there to travel to Barkerville, where they presented to the stage character Captain Jack a photo of their grandfather with Crawford, taken in the 1870s. Crawford was pictured as a wild man with long, unruly hair, armed to the teeth, returning from a raid on Natives in which many men were lost. The photo, which no one else had known about, was presented onstage. A historic moment.

In 2006 the Theatre presented Amy Newman's one-woman show, the "Dancing Girls of Cariboo." During the show one of the Williams Creek hurdy dancers, Miss Georgiana Henrietta Wilhemina Nactingall, told her story and explained about the hurdies. As part of the show, she asked a member of the theatre audience to dance with her. Impresario Richard Wright chose a man, who was "Miss Georgie's" great-great-grandson in real life. So the 1870 character of Miss Georgie danced with a grandson who would not be born for close to 100 years. That year a stage manager brought forward information on her family and a man who might be Billy Barker's brother.

The highly popular weekend British Music Hall shows have uncovered more music during research work in England. This research led to the historically correct music for "Dancing Girls of Cariboo" and "Young Man From Canada," both sung to the tune of "I'm a Young Chap from the Countree," an early music hall song.

So the discovery and reclamation continue. Research leads to a musical or dramatic show, and the show itself uncovers more stories in the shallow tailings of gold rush history.

For more information, see theatreroyal.ca, "Barkerville" or "Castles in the Air" by Richard Thomas Wright.

—*Richard Wright*

Hands-on History

Werner Kaschel, a Surrey elementary schoolteacher, has a passion for teaching BC gold rush history. "To start, I read to them about the Fraser River gold rush to introduce them to the social, economical, political and multicultural world in New Caledonia in 1858–59. I then hand out copies of primary sources (maps, newspapers, journal articles, receipts), which they read and use for their projects. The goal is to have students write a historical narrative, in a journal or diary format, from the perspective of a miner or a historical character, utilizing both historical facts and empathy (a key component to historical understanding). I bring my resources and some of my collectibles into the class to create a more intriguing and enriched program."

His grade seven students are equal to the challenge, and some have won Canadian Heritage Fair contests. In 2004, Emily Yamniuck earned a trip to Montreal to share her project, and in 2006 Adam Schmidke won a week in Halifax.

40 Questions

A few years ago, when I attended Sullivan Elementary School in Surrey, our class was assigned a project that changed the way that I look at education in Canada.

It all started when my grade seven teacher, Mr. Kaschel, assigned the class a project on the Cariboo gold rush. He told us that the best two projects would be entered in the Historica Heritage Fair and those two students would have a chance to go to Montreal to attend the National Heritage Fair. He had been teaching us the subject for quite some time via reading from the text, giving short lectures and, what I remember most vividly, huge tests. When he assigned the project, he took us to our school's computer lab and allowed us to do research on the Internet. Mr. Kaschel sent us to a few websites on the subject of the gold rush and highly recommended the BC government Cariboo gold rush website since it had many primary sources.

The summer before, I had taken a trip up the gold rush trail to Barkerville with my family, and I thought, why not narrow down the subject to the famous town and its founder, Billy Barker? Mr. Kaschel agreed. I then created 40 questions that I would need to answer in my project, based on Mr. Kaschel's suggestions. I researched for weeks, finding the government website very useful, trying to answer all the questions and finding out interesting facts about Billy Barker and Barkerville.

I wanted to present my project in a distinct way. I have always been strong in public speaking and drama, so I decided to play up those aspects. I decided, instead of being a dirty, imprudent miner, to create a vibrant, charismatic, interesting character with a unique background and story. I created Flora Nachnamen, a hurdy gurdy girl who was taken from her home in Germany at a young age to become a dancer in Barkerville. I had the character tell the story of Billy Barker and what Barkerville was like in those days from her own perspective.

I'll make this long story short: I presented the project in front of my class, then at the regional Heritage Fair run by Historica, and again at the National Fair in Montreal, since I had been chosen as the regional fair winner. It was an amazing experience. About twenty youths from each territory and province came and presented their projects at the National Fair. We also had a week to sightsee, learn about that area of Canada, attend workshops and make fast friends. I still keep in touch with people from the fair over the Internet. I thought it was amazing that the Canadian government was providing such an opportunity and program to encourage education. I still volunteer with the Heritage Fair in Richmond every year and hope to go on another trip with Historica as an alumni member.

—*Emily Yamniuk*

Being Governor Douglas

The character that I imitated was the first governor of the colony of British Columbia, James Douglas. I chose to dress up and talk about his life and the hardships that he endured while governing this colony during the gold rush. I had collected many notes about him, and that made it easier to write a detailed and descriptive presentation/project.

What I enjoyed the most about creating this project was making the rocker box (a tool used to mine gold). I am fairly good at woodwork so it made my job a little bit easier.

Some of the facts that I found about the whole gold rush were amazing, especially the many skirmishes with Natives, American and British miners. BC could have ended up smaller or belonging to the Americans if gold hadn't been discovered and if the British hadn't responded so quickly with Douglas's leadership. If we didn't have this very wonderful event, the gold rush, BC would be different today, and it might not be a flourishing province with the rich diversity of cultures that we currently have in our beautiful province of British Columbia.

—*Adam Schmidke*

Mr. Barkerville

High in the mountains, in the upper tributaries of the Fraser River, nestles old, historic Barkerville, centre of the Cariboo gold rush. In the 1930s, when Fred W. Ludditt settled in the area to placer mine for gold, the voice of Barkerville's romantic past was practically silent. While searching old mining reports looking for leads to placer sites and hearing the old-timers recount their memories, Fred got a sense of the grandeur of the area's past and knew instinctively that this priceless capsule of our history had to be preserved.

Fred Ludditt was a gold miner, historian and author, and the original member of the Barkerville Historical Society. More than anyone else, Ludditt led and sustained the campaign to stop the loss and destruction of local historical relics to souvenir hunters and salvagers. He worked hard to persuade the provincial government to preserve this moment in time as a heritage site.

Thanks to Fred's many years of tireless work and attention to countless details, this story is not just another dying echo lost in the silent mountains, but can be read in his book *Barkerville Days* and relived by the hundreds of thousands of people who visit old Barkerville each season. Those privileged to know this colourful gentleman appropriately referred to him as "Mr. Barkerville."

—*Betty Baldry, Campbell River*

Mining for Mercury

When I was growing up, I used to hear so much about the gold rush from my father and grandfather. They owned the Emory Lodge at Emory Creek, which was a big-time place in the heyday of the gold rush. Occasionally we would find artifacts from those days. I remember digging up little Chinese opium bottles in our garden one day.

About 45 years ago I went to school in Hope, and rode the bus there each day. One day our science teacher told us that one item on her agenda was to teach us about mercury and the properties of it, but she sadly informed us that whoever supplied the mercury couldn't deliver any. I told my dad at suppertime that night and he said, No problem! We grabbed a gold pan and shovel and sauntered down to the Fraser River. He spent only a few minutes digging into a rocky backwash area, getting down to the rocks with a bit of sand. He panned it out and came up with a good-sized lump of mercury. A few more pans and we had enough to fill a vial about half full, which was plenty for the school board's science experiments.

Imagine how much mercury the miners would lose in the sluice box gold-mining process! It's still out there in the back eddies of the Fraser River, settled into the areas where the gold used to be.

—*Noel Wotten, Tlell, Haida Gwaii*

Ghosts and Memories of Atlin

The bell rings in the bar and we all know a big nugget has come in from one of the creeks. Was it Boulder? Spruce? Pine Creek? Or maybe it was out by Ruby Creek. A round for the house, as the nugget is passed from hand to hand, seeming to feel warm to the touch. Memories rush forward of the miners who worked so hard, so long ago, for a nugget like this.

Did Miller and MacLaren (the men who discovered gold on Pine Creek and touched off the Atlin rush) celebrate in this way back in 1898, when Atlin held the lives of as many as 10,000 people in goldfields, homes and stores? Was the frenzy less exciting—as it was for many of us who looked for gold when the town was only 500 strong?

Many of the buildings and mine sites had long since been reclaimed by nature, but still we could feel the ghosts of long ago. An old outhouse built on the side of a creek: whatever transpired there went back into the creek, and the multi-hole facilities made you wonder about the morning constitutional conversations.

An old garbage dump gave up a few treasures, like old bottles that may have held medicine, rusted-out cooking pots, bottles that once held good, strong liquor. Shovels without handles and a pickaxe or two—how long did a man toil before the tool ended up in the dump?

For a time I lived close to Noland Mines, which came into its own in the early 1900s, and it intrigued me with its deep mine shaft and little mining cars that brought gold to the surface when the men were lucky. Old buildings where the miners lived, loved and cooked. Porcupine inhabit the buildings now as a present-day miner scrapes at the gravel, hoping to find some fine gold or maybe a nugget to take to the bar, where the bell will be rung to establish bragging rights.

My husband Al and I lived in Atlin in the 1980s, nearly 100 years after the big rush, but even then it wasn't hard to feel the spirit of the gold rush era, when you would encounter a grizzled-out prospector sitting outside by the MV *Tarahne*, where it rests in its restored state on the shores of Atlin Lake.

—*Brenda Mallory*

Soda Creek Memories

My link to the gold rush has to do with growing up at Soda Creek, on a ranch that includes Lots 1 and 2 in the Cariboo region, originally deeded to a Peter Dunlevy, who recognized the opportunities to be had in supplying produce to the miners in the goldfields. The ranch is still a jewel—Dunlevy had a great eye for productive agricultural land, as did my grandfather, who also sought opportunities in agriculture in the 1950s and '60s.

Soda Creek was an important link along the Gold Trail: paddlewheelers were able to navigate the Fraser River from there to Quesnel. The cemetery at Soda Creek still has graves from that era. I recall as a child the quiet, solemn gravesites with the wooden picket fences similar to those at Barkerville and other locations in the Cariboo. The large log barn on the ranch where I grew up is one of the impressive structures from those days, still standing and fully functional, having had some foundation and roof improvements recently. I marvel at the ingenuity of our forefathers and foremothers, who accomplished so much completely without the technology and equipment that we take for granted. Here I am, warm and comfortable at my computer, remembering how I chopped firewood and cared for my 4-H steers in a barn that had sheltered livestock and adventurers all those years ago.

—*Kathy Kaufman, Williams Lake*

Soda Creek

This spot, where the Cariboo Road rejoined the Fraser River north of Williams Lake, was named for the white alkali powder that dries on the rocks.

Historic Hedley

We passed through Hedley on our way to the Okanagan, as many people do through the summer. This community was founded on two gold mines, and now it hosts tours of the restored building precariously perched on the cliffs above town. Hedley has restored many of its historic buildings, and its citizens are proud of their community. We enjoyed the hospitable people of this small town—Susan at the B&B who took us in even though she hadn't vacuumed, and the elderly gentleman who invited us into his shop, which was closed, so we could use the telephone, and the lady at the jewellery shop, and the very knowledgeable women at the museum, who told wonderful stories about the mine and the community back then. If you visit Hedley, be sure to stop in and ask about the poor man who hung onto his tiny claim in the face of pressure from huge mining companies. Thank you, Hedley!

—*Kathleen O'Malley, Victoria*

Gold into Jewellery

It may be hard to come up with a closer connection to the Fraser River gold rush than this: recently, in the course of my regular business as a jeweller, I took in trade a half-ounce of Fraser River gold dust—a very rare item today. This was payment for a larger gold nugget from the Atlin goldfields, which I had incorporated into a finished piece of jewellery.

From the time I was nine years old, I took an interest in BC's gold rush history, and in hands-on mining and prospecting. I had some initial training from the veteran Cariboo miner Fred Ludditt in Barkerville, and I was hooked on the pursuit of gold. In the late 1960s, while on a rock-hunting trip at Hope on the Fraser, I met an elderly gentleman miner by the name of Carl Hesse. A graduate of the Berlin Fine Arts Academy, Carl had been all over the world in search of gold and had ended up on his claim on the Fraser River, mining by hand. Thanks to the site's close proximity to Vancouver, the art of recovering Fraser gold became my

main pastime during my high school years.

Upon my graduation from Lord Byng secondary school, H.C. Weber, a neighbour of mine who was a lawyer with mining clientele, enlisted my services to restake a group of gold claims in the Yukon. On August 17, 1973, the 75th anniversary of the Klondike gold rush, a couple of other cheechakos and I dug enough gold on the Discovery claim on Bonanza Creek to cover our restaurant, bar and dance hall bill in Dawson City that night.

In need of a grubstake, I spent that winter in the Yukon hard-rock mining for United Keno Hill mines. By the following summer my bills exceeded the value of the gold I had accumulated, so to get a higher price I converted the raw nuggets to fine jewellery and souvenirs for gold rush tourism venues. In 1977, Canadian Placer Gold Ltd. was formally established and began serving clients worldwide.

The sternwheeler *Enterprise* took miners upriver from Soda Creek, where they left the Cariboo Wagon Road and embarked on vessels to take them to Quesnel. *British Columbia Archives A-03908*

201

A key historic property came up for sale in 2005: the original Barnard's BX Express on Front Street in Yale. I had realized its importance for many years and purchased it immediately. The property, which at present holds just a miner's shack, will be my current (and, I hope, permanent) connection to the gold rush legacy. With a restored BX office already in Barkerville and close extended family in Wells and Barkerville, I will revive and extend (on a limited basis) the business of the BX well into this century. The plan for the site includes a Fraser/BC gold museum and a reconstructed BX Express building, plus a museum store. A Barkerville information service will also be provided.

We also hope to include the original discovery claim on Hill's Bar across the river and downstream. The claim owner, Mel Zieler, and I have been discussing its fate off and on for around 30 years. Considering the important role the First Nations played during the gold rush, a joint venture with local groups will be pursued.

My professional and personal connections to the gold rush are part of my daily life, and I look forward to the coming years of focused activity. Visit me at placergolddesign.com.

—*Mark Castagnoli, President, Placer Gold Design, Vancouver*

Gold Miner's Wife

Among the occupations I have had during my sixty years of married life, first as a rancher's wife, then mother to two children and, at the same time, a sawmill cook for 20 men, I have also been a gold miner's wife. As I look back on those first 20-odd years, I think they were some of the hardest but happiest years. My husband Wilf and I left the Horsefly country in 1960 and settled in Quesnel, where the children could attend school and Wilf could pursue his interest in gold mining. He also had academic qualifications, and to keep the wolf from the door, he took a position as a counsellor with Canada Manpower (now Human Resources Canada). But every evening and every weekend was spent prospecting and mining gold on the river bars around Quesnel. We mined with old machinery—at first with a TD 15 cat. When the tracks came off or some other part failed, Wilf, who had grown up fixing machinery on a cattle ranch, would soon get the machine running again.

Before long we had staked claims on outlying creeks, the Swift, Cottonwood, Sovereign and Lightning. On weekends we loaded up a small house trailer and, with the children, spent the time mining and enjoying the countryside. Most of the time I was in charge of operating a washing plant. As a swift, steady flow of water was pumped into the box, I sent the large rocks over the grizzly and regulated the dirt falling down onto the screens below. I climbed up and down a short ladder many times in a day, and it was not long before I was as slim as an arrow.

After the children had left home, we mined on the lower Cottonwood with a Lorraine crane, a very inexpensive method of mining.

One fall our son and his family came down from Prince George to spend Thanksgiving with us, down where we were mining, and we watched a mother bear, her twin cubs and two others as they sat swaying around in the wind, up a big cottonwood tree. We also observed white trumpeter swans resting on the river bar during their long migratory flights, and even sandhill cranes.

My husband Wilf, now 85 years old, is still mining. The summer of 2006 was long and dry, and the creeks and rivers—including the Fraser—were as low as we have ever seen them. The low water exposes streaks of gold not usually seen, and in the fall, while the weather held, Wilf and our son were out catching the fine gold on the Fraser.

—*Branwen C. Patenaude, Quesnel*

Watching the Gold

My gold rush connection is in the Cassiar mountains on McDame Creek—just a couple of kilometres upstream from where BC's biggest nugget (72 ounces—about 2 kilograms) was found in the 1870s. We've combined our search for placer gold with modern technology and have come up with our "Adventure" website—www.hollowaybar.com. We've installed a satellite Internet link and four webcams around the property. Oh—and we also found some gold.

—*Al Sande, Terrace*

The Ne'er Do Well mine at Grouse Creek, near Barkerville, was operating when the Grouse Creek war erupted in 1867. Governor Frederick Seymour stepped in to mediate the dispute, which was essentially an attempt by a group of promoters to jump an existing claim. *British Columbia Archives A-00351*

Restoring the 1861 Gold Rush Pack Trail

In 1860, four men—Keithley, Rose, McDonald and Weaver—left Keithley Creek in search of gold and found rich diggings on Antler Creek. Further discoveries were made at Grouse, Williams and Lightning Creeks, and trails were needed to bring in miners and supplies. A number of trails were developed, and these were the first pack trails into the goldfields.

My husband Gary and I have enjoyed hiking over the years. Since the early 1970s we've spent a lot of our time looking around the Barkerville area because of its rich history, and we've hiked many of the creeks, existing trails, townsites and mining camps. The local history is fascinating and the scenery is spectacular.

In the fall of 1991, Gord Lester of the Friends of Barkerville asked us if we would be interested in finding the old pack trail. Our first thought was, does it still exist? Well, indeed it does! Most of it is quite well preserved, due to the heavy use it once had. We gathered and studied old maps, such as the Amos Bowman maps of 1881–85, Lieutenant Henry Palmer's map published in 1863, and aerial photos from 1950. I had gathered bits of information from old newspapers about the rush to the Cariboo. The *British Columbian* of September 12, 1863, says: "The journey from Keithley's to Antler (25 miles) is somewhat tedious. The trail first ascends a mountain 5 miles in length, then descends the same, and next plunges through a swamp. Then there is the Bald Mountain whose heights, once gained, command a magnificent view of mountain scenery." This inspired our imagination.

In our first season out, in 1992, we familiarized ourselves with the country and terrain, to get a better sense of where the trail might be. By 1993 we were ready to locate and mark the trail. Over the next five seasons, we managed to connect the bits into one 32-kilometre trail.

We started near the old Richfield courthouse and crossed Williams Creek because according to the old maps, the trail was on the other side. In fact we were starting our search at the end of the gold rush trail. By the time fall arrived we had managed to find pieces of the trail from Richfield up to the Bald Mountain plateau, and with perseverance we stayed out till the first skiff of snow fell. Wouldn't you know it, that's when we found a continuation of the trail at the base of Chumley Summit, which headed uphill. We were very excited with this find and sad that we had to quit now and only think about it over the winter.

As we gradually found other parts of the trail, we hung ribbon and blazed trees, making it easier to see, and we spent many hours on our hands and knees, snipping away overhanging brush. After that, the trail became quite visible and the ground still had the beaten look to it. Switchbacks were very well defined. Hardly anything grew on the trail itself, as it had been packed down very tightly.

It's hard to explain the feeling that overcame us in retracing the steps of both men and animals, and how they must have felt after their long trudges uphill with heavy loads, having struggled through some very wet, swampy ground. Our packs were light, to say the least, compared to what they carried. Their stamina was amazing. They had to venture through terrible conditions—blowdown everywhere, swamps, bugs, cold rainy days and sometimes snow.

As of fall 2006, the gentle uphill grade from Richfield to Bald Mountain, which reaches an elevation of 1,860 metres, passes by old mining sites, quartz outcrop workings along

Mount Proserpine, and an old cabin site with a fallen-down rock chimney at the top of Bald Mountain, possibly a rest stop. The trail then plunges down a steep descent to Maloney's Road House of 1861 and Racetrack Flats, where horseraces were held. You can still see the straight four-furlong track with rocks piled along the sides. It is also the site of two old graves. When they left Maloney's Road House and headed to Barkerville, the pack trains had a very steep climb to the summit of Bald Mountain, weighed down with a load of gear and supplies. I remarked to a group of people who had hiked this way, many of whom had paused to rest a few times, "Imagine what it must have felt like for the men and poor pack animals."

In the spring of 1994 we were back on the trail from Sawmill Flats to Chumley Summit. To make things difficult, Palmer's map showed the trail on the west side of Victorian Creek. We spent many hours hiking all over the area, searching for the trail. Finally we had to give up, but it is not in our nature to give up easily, and we decided to try the opposite side. Luck was with us—there it was on the east side!

Before the long trudge uphill, the trail is basically level, but it gets lots of spring runoffs, which makes it very wet and boggy. This must have been one of the worst parts of the trail for the animals. We worked hard cleaning up this section—it was very brushy with lots of blow-down, and the drainage was slowly washing away the trail so it had to be diverted in places. I could picture the miners fighting their way through the deep black muck.

Another summer went by on this section alone, and then we went on to the summit of Chumley. As you near the crest, the timber changes to small, scrubby balsam, and open

From the Richfield Courthouse, Judge Matthew Baillie Begbie and other magistrates dispensed justice in the Cariboo during the gold rush years. The courthouse is the last remaining building in Richfield, a short wagon ride from historic Barkerville. *British Columbia Archives C-04439*

meadows begin to appear. At the summit of about 1,800 metres, the terrain opens up to large, grassy alpine meadows with patches of subalpine fir scattered around. It truly is a magnificent site, and you feel like you're on top of the world! To the east you can see the beautiful high, jagged mountain peaks of the Cariboo Range in the distance. In the near distance is Roundtop Mountain, a familiar landmark that must have caught the eye of the early gold seekers. I am sure they were mesmerized by the beauty surrounding them, as we are.

It is here that the trail passed by upper Leon's stopping house. You can still see the outline of its walls and tumbledown rock chimney. It would have been a welcome sight for the miners in the loaded pack trains on the way to Barkerville. They would need to rest after the steady climb from Weaver Creek. Water would have been available here—below the cabin we found a spring that still bubbles up out of the ground. One could also imagine Judge Matthew Baillie Begbie resting here on his way to court trials. In his book *The Man for a New Country*, David R. Williams says that Begbie preferred this route if he was on horseback, because of the easy riding country, even though at journey's end there lay a climb over the mountains. Also he had observed that there was more feed for the horses.

When approaching wet meadows in the alpine, it would sometimes be difficult to keep track of the trail. The packers avoided this and skirted alongside the timber edge, where it was drier. In many places along the trail, the ground appears wavy as you walk; this was caused by the animal's gait, the results of which are still well embedded.

After leaving Leon's roadhouse, the trail meanders through the timber and then runs along Horseshoe Nail Ridge. Just before this, along the side slope of First Peak, there is a gulch above the trail that we know as Harris Gulch, named after the late R.C. "Bob" Harris. He was a historical writer and mapmaker for *BC Outdoors* magazine. He spent many summers on Snowshoe Plateau looking for the trail, and he generously gave us a copy of Palmer's 1863 map. He was delighted when we told him we had found the trail.

In another scenic view to the west, the Swift River valley lies below and Breakneck Ridge looms in the distance. Once you cross the Snowshoe Plateau, which is an easy walk of about 6 kilometres across the alpine and drops slightly in elevation, you first cross a wide valley, then make another short climb to Base Mountain. You cross and descend into another narrow valley before reaching French Snowshoe Mountain, elevation 1,860 metres. The trail continues along a wide ridge to the last summit, which we call Falconer Summit after Dave Falconer, sadly now deceased. He was a schoolteacher in the town of Likely who taught his students the history of the gold rush. He was very generous in sharing with us his knowledge of this part of the trail, from Keithley Creek to Snowshoe Plateau.

Near the end of our search for the trail, Robin Grady joined us and became as obsessed as we were. He spent countless hours in preparation for trail signs, markers, getting the trail GPS'ed, making a map and getting campsites ready with tables and bear caches, to name a few of his efforts. We chose to end the trail at Weaver Creek, as logging activity has now engulfed many parts of the original route to Keithley Creek.

The 1861 Gold Rush Pack Trail can be hiked. We had our inaugural three-day hike in 1999 with 37 people attending. Many were enchanted with its beauty while in the alpine, and eager to get through the swampy bogs in the valleys. Unfortunately it rained for most of the

Starting in 1991, Lana and Gary Fox helped locate and reopen the original 1861 gold rush pack trail from Weaver Creek to Barkerville.
Courtesy Lana Fox

hike, but it gave people an understanding and appreciation for what the miners and packers had to go through all those years ago. The 1861 Gold Rush Pack Trail is also now part of the National Hiking Trail of Canada.

I had hoped to find a horseshoe somewhere along the way. I never did, but one of the brushers later hired to do some cleaning of the trail found a mule shoe. What I did find in the alpine beside the trail was an old piece of leather harness sticking out of the ground. To my delight, I also found a very old three-piece mould bottle, in perfect condition. It was lying in a thicket of trees beside the trail and had been preserved for over 140 years.

Gary and I recently went for a short day hike over part of the trail, and as we walked, all the memories came back—the gear we had to pack in and out for each trip, the power saw, gas, snippers, food, water, bug dope (the bugs were ferocious at times), and the walk back out with our sore, aching muscles at the end of a long day. But it was all worth it! The men and even a few women who used the trail are now memories of the past, but the trail survives as a tribute to their existence.

—*Lana and Gary Fox, Quesnel*

Hydraulic

A massive "bullion pit" was scoured out of the landscape near this town by pressurized water jets.

Still Living the Gold Rush at Hydraulic

I live at Hydraulic, BC, in the old roadhouse about eight kilometres from the bullion pit, one of the biggest man-made pits in the world, and about 16 kilometres from Quesnel Forks. That's where my gold lease is, on the south fork of the Quesnel River. I have two claims and a lease. We have a small family operation—my wife, me and three grown-up children—and we drag the granddaughter (five years old) along with us. She thinks we live in a museum and loves to play in Grampa's big sandbox. Our operation is small compared to any hard-rock operation; we have a backhoe, an excavator, a loader, two dumptrucks and a de-rocker wash plant. The approximate value is 150,000 bucks.

Our ground is historic gold ground. There's a ditch dug by the Chinese and many holes they dug, with 120-year-old trees growing in them—all dug by hand. The ditch is several kilometres long, and we now have a 10-centimetre pipe 1.4 metres from a water source. It's magical to walk around down there. You never know what you are going to see—grizzlies and black bears, river otters, birds of every shape and size, moose, deer and the occasional pack of wolves. You must take a gun when out prospecting, because you can't trust a wolf when his eyes are open.

My hobby is collecting old iron. I have everything from miniature blacksmith tools to a 63-tonne Northwest #6 shovel that was in the Philippines during World War II before finishing its life on Yanks Peak Mining. I have two complete blacksmith shops, one from Soda Creek and one from the house I live in. Also a giant #6 Monitor and a #4, used for hydraulic mining, and a Philadelphia piecrust table that came to Horsefly 125 years ago by horse and buggy. My parents had an antique store in Williams Lake in the 1960s, and that's when I started collecting treasures.

This house was the last stagecoach stop on the way down to the Forks. There were two beds in every room, there was a post office here and Proir was a butcher. Cattle were driven here from the 150 Mile Ranch. He had a slaughterhouse here, and fresh eggs and dairy items like butter and milk. He also sold the basics like bacon, beans, flour, coffee, sugar, tobacco and salt, and he supplied the miners.

We've been restoring the big dining room to turn it into a kitchen, and we have found that the walls and ceiling are lined with newspapers from 1914 and 1915—from Victoria, Vancouver and Calgary. The old roadhouse has entered the 21st century—now it has 200-amp service with electric heat in all rooms, both satellite TV and satellite computer linkup with satellite phone. The water comes from a spring in the ground and is the best you have ever tasted. It is ice cold, and gravity-fed to the house. We need two large wood heaters to keep this water warm when the weather gets down—about 15 full cords of firewood per year. We hope to have the house finished for 2008, the 150th anniversary of the gold rush.

—*Jim (and Wendy) Gibson, Hydraulic, BC*

Last of the Fraser River Gold Miners

The first time we encountered Walter and Pat's place, it was like walking into a wrinkle in time. We were not prepared to see a couple of gnarly miners working their claim along the banks of the Fraser River. Granted, we were a similarly strange sight for them as we floated past their claim on large river rafts on our first reconnaissance of the Fraser River between Churn Creek and Yale. Using Simon Fraser's journal of 1808 and a 1:50,000 topographical map to track our position, we knew where we were relative to the Gang Ranch bridge, but the vision of miners standing in the river shovelling gravel was a surprise.

Behind their bent silhouettes, and spread over the surrounding hectares, was a tangled collection of old trucks, trailers and derelict heavy earth-moving equipment. I assumed this place was a remnant from the 1960s and that a still or a grow-op must be in proximity. However, the site was magnetic, and the temptation to stop and explore was irresistible. When the raft pontoons bumped the shore, the kids immediately jumped out onto the fine fluvial sands and started to somersault, cartwheel and play tag. Their frolicking was soon stopped by the sound of a shrill voice yelling, "Bear, Bear, come back here!" The kids scampered back onto the raft and we all stared up the trail to see what would happen next.

It was showtime on the Fraser. First down the trail came Bear, the largest St. Bernard–German shepherd cross north of Spuzzum. Right behind Bear came Pat, shouting commands, and then Walter, who extended his hand and shouted "Welcome to WalPat Mining!" After introductions, Walter explained that he and Pat are the most recent in a long tradition of placer miners that have worked this claim. They showed us their operation, enthusiastically pointing out a sequence of historic mining gear that must date back over a hundred years. The newest machine, currently in use, is a moderate-sized power slosh box; the oldest ones are windrows of river boulders commonly associated with the Chinese placer mine operations of the 1880s.

Walter and Pat, partners in WalPat Mining.
Rick Blacklaws photo

We all tramped along behind Pat as she explained that placer miners look for gold that has settled into the river gravel. It is free-standing gold that is simply waiting to be washed and separated from the gravel. Placer miners use water to wash gold from the sand and gravel. They hose water onto the land and wash the gravel, sand and clay down a trough and over some screens where the gold settles out. In theory it is that simple. In practice it is hard work that requires moving tonnes of earth. Over the past hundred years, placer mining has lowered the surface at the WalPat claim by at least three metres.

With a tilt of his head and a squint in his eye Walt asked if we would like to see some gold. We nodded in unison and off he went to the trailer. He brought back a few vials of water with gold dust settled on the bottom, and a few gold-mining pans. He said that he and Pat placer enough gold each year to supplement their savings, and they have being working this claim for about 20 years.

His gold pan and enthusiasm transformed him from a weathered man of the northern reaches to a kid, all in the twinkle of an eye. Wading knee-deep into the cool, silted water of the Fraser, he showed us the art of gold panning. With a shovel he loaded his pan with river gravel, then slowly swirled the pan, dipping it back into the Fraser occasionally. It didn't take us long to realize that panning is not as simple as it looks. As the summer sun scorched our heads, Pat added that panning is used to evaluate the gold potential of a gravel bar. If the pan shows good signs, she said, they bring in the slosh box and work the area. If the signs are poor, they keep looking. They have been looking for 20 years. We were mesmerized by their demonstration and their repartee, which was peppered with stories.

We left Walter to seek his fortune and the kids to pay for university, and made our way into the shade by an old picnic table. Still describing the fabric of the place, Pat retrieved her photo album and, with the aid of her poetry, took us on a visual journey of their time at the WalPat claim. She showed us 20 years' worth of hunters with their game, fishers with their salmon, and travellers in trucks, quads and now rafts.

That first visit to WalPat took place 15 years ago, and not a year has gone by that we don't stop in or wish we had. Pat has shared her poetry, love and laughter in telling stories of the rugged life. Walter challenged us not only in horseshoes and target shooting, but also in the essence and excitement of what it takes to be a miner. Although they have never hit the motherlode, they have experienced the seasons and lived their dream by enjoying their land and working their claim.

The Fraser River is a river of gold, salmon and culture. Unfortunately, a part of the river's culture was recently lost a few years ago, when Walter died. Pat still goes back to the Fraser in the summer but does not mine very much. After nearly 150 years, it is anyone's guess what the future holds for the WalPat stake and the last of the Fraser River miners.

—*Rick Blacklaws*

History Beneath Our Feet

"What can you say about gold that hasn't already been said? Heavy (with a density of 19.3), malleable, slow to tarnish and rare, gold has been the cause of more human disruption, effort, valour and failure than all the other minerals combined."

—Rick Hudson, *A Field Guide to Gold, Gemstone & Mineral Sites of British Columbia*

In 2006, Mark Forsythe and Greg Dickson joined Fraser River Raft Expeditions of Yale for a unique view of the historic Fraser Canyon, remnants of the Cariboo Wagon Road and Aboriginal fishing sites.
Mark Forsythe photo

Sometimes the obvious is beneath our feet, or a few paces from the front door. As Greg and I finish this project to rediscover the Gold Rush colony and immerse ourselves in 1858, I find myself running along the trail near my Fort Langley home. It links today's Fort Langley with Derby, where the Hudson's Bay Company first drove palisades into the ground in 1827.

I pause to catch my breath where James McMillan and his band of 20 men built the first fort. Here the HBC traded with local First Nations and farmed to feed the workers at their North Pacific operations. A stone obelisk marks the spot just a few metres from where the first gold miners passed in canoes and riverboats loaded down with hundreds of pounds of gear. People from so many countries, carrying hopes and dreams, far from families back home. So many of them didn't find their personal Eldorado and were driven back home by harsh reality. I often touch this obelisk for my own good luck. Just in case.

Back in 1858 it was rumoured that Derby would become the capital of the newly minted mainland colony of British Columbia. Land speculators went crazy. A town was laid out and the lots were sold in a frenzy at auction. But the political masters had other plans: the mainland's capital was to be built on higher ground, across the river at New Westminster, where the Kwantlen people had traditional winter camping grounds. From here, attackers from the south could be seen before they crossed the river. Governor James Douglas offered land at New Westminster to those who'd been caught up in the speculation, as he now had a colony to build and settle, and Derby became an instant ghost town.

My run finishes at Parks Canada's Fort Langley historic site, with a life-sized bronze of Governor Douglas standing guard in front of the fort. It was here, during the dedication of the statue, that I wondered aloud whether any descendants of Sir James happened to be about. A woman standing beside me said softly, "He was my great-great-grandfather." Cynthia Fleming had come from her home in Nanaimo to honour the man who so dramatically shaped modern British Columbia, a man that she and her sister Gloria had not known about but were coming to understand (see pages 187-89).

Herbert Allsopp was there too. He reminded me that James Douglas was born in Demerara, British Guiana (now known as Guyana). A "Scotch West Indian," Douglas was the son of a Scottish merchant and a "free coloured woman." Herbert comes from Guyana himself and figures Douglas should be a national hero there. He's doing what he can to raise awareness with officials about the Douglas legacy. Stay tuned.

Greg and I enjoyed a whole new perspective on the Fraser River when we hooked up with Fraser River Raft Expeditions in Yale. Our journey began near some old placer tailings just west of Boston Bar; our young guide Dan Pereda had a keen interest in gold rush history and loves to haul out gold pans so kids can search for golden flakes. They usually find some. He expertly threaded the needle at Hells Gate where the river narrows and roars through the throat of the canyon. "You want to hold on with a couple of hands going through here," he said, as yawning whirlpools attempted to suck our raft to the bottom.

Dan pointed out short stretches of the original Cariboo Wagon Road that hug the canyon walls. "It's hard to imagine the Old Cariboo Road wrapping around the cliffs and the wooden trestles they had supporting it," he remarked. "Coming around this cliff in a stagecoach, maybe in the middle of the night, or whenever you could afford to come through, it's just amazing. It was another world back then, that we can so easily forget about now. A couple more of these walls fall down and some construction on the highway, and it's like none of it ever happened. It's nice to remind everyone of what went down here and how many people lost their lives building these old roads and making this country accessible."

The river is always changing its personality, and as it became a gently flowing giant, we slid overboard for a dip in the Fraser—much warmer and greener than I had imagined. We floated on our backs, drifting through time. Then Alexandra Bridge slipped into view. This old suspension bridge may be derelict, but its simple elegance still captures you. The original crossing was built here in 1863 by Joseph Trutch to help miners move farther north to the Cariboo. We then shot through standing waves at Sailor Bar rapids, drenched and laughing, and the raft returned for a few more runs. The old wagon road reappeared near Yale, where the Sto:lo have fashioned fish camps on the stony bed, and where red salmon was being wind-dried on wooden racks that day. I pledged to never drive through the Fraser Canyon without pausing to absorb more of its remarkable human history, beauty and wildness. I resolved to dip a gold pan into the river at Hope, soon.

When *BC Almanac* panned for memories from our listeners, we asked for personal connections to the gold rush and earliest days of the colony; many are included in this book. There were others—a woman called with delight to describe the Barkerville Theatre show she'd seen; another told us her family owns Alexandra Lodge, one of the original roadhouses in the Fraser Canyon—today's building may include bits and pieces of the original. Then there were the stories of ancestors who came for the gold and stayed to become farmers and build communities: Ashcroft, Chilliwack, Quesnel and many more. Communities along the gold rush trail don't want us to forget, either. They've come together to create the New Pathways to Gold Society with the hope that British Columbians will reflect on this amazing history—and pay a visit during the Sesquicentennial.

We located a CBC Radio documentary broadcast in 1967, narrated by the late actor Robert Clothier. Listening to the voices and memories of gold prospectors and their descendants brings the history to life even more vividly. For instance, a descendant of Chief Spintlum at Lytton recounts how he helped defuse the Canyon War. The history of the gold rush colony continues to fascinate us. The BC-born writer Claire Mulligan recently published a novel, *The Reckoning of Boston Jim*, set in Victoria in 1863. Her characters venture into the Cariboo goldfields and through some intriguing personal terrain: here is BC history made relevant for another generation.

The gold rush truly was a shifting of tectonic plates beneath the story of BC. So much changed, and aftershocks continue. Although James Douglas undertook to make treaties with First Nations people, we have a lot of catching up to do now, 150 years later, to forge meaningful relationships on which all British Columbians can build a future together. There is still something of the gold rush in the air in British Columbia. People from across Canada and around the world want to live here, or visit for a while. It remains a place to hope and dream, to sift the possibilities.

—*Mark Forsythe*

Memories, Dreams and Gold

As Mark and I looked back in history during the making of this book, we were both surprised by how profoundly the gold rush changed this place. During the 1860s, the pace of democratic reform quickened, and the people, sensing that their lives could improve, joined community leaders in supporting it. Not everybody wanted the united province that emerged, but it has survived and prospered. Before the gold rush, transportation was difficult on Vancouver Island and worse on the mainland. The times demanded sturdy wagon roads through hardscrabble terrain. As Mark and I travelled the gold rush trail we could see that modern highway builders couldn't improve much on the routes chosen by the Royal Engineers. That's why it's hard to find traces of the original gold rush trail—much of it now lies beneath rails or blacktop.

Those things are part of the legacy of the gold rush era. But what if you want to reach out and touch the artifacts, or walk the streets of a gold rush town? For that, you have to look a little deeper, to the wonderful museums and archives around BC and to a few special heritage sites.

The story of Fort Langley has become part of Mark's life. For me, a trip to Barkerville in 2005 rekindled my interest in the gold rush and fulfilled a childhood dream.

As a kid growing up in the Okanagan, I loved the books written by two legends of popular BC history: Bruce Ramsey and Bill Barlee. Ramsey wrote a memorable guide to Barkerville and one of the first bestsellers on BC ghost towns. Bill Barlee, who later served as MLA, was the publisher of *Canada West* magazine and a series of guides to ghost towns and gold mining sites. I still have a dog-eared copy of his first magazine from the spring of 1969.

This painting of the 137 Mile House roadhouse is one of many created by Michael Kluckner, who travelled throughout BC sketching and painting historic buildings.
Courtesy Michael Kluckner, originally published in Vanishing British Columbia.

Back then, I dreamed of seeing Barkerville. Nearly 40 years later, my wish came true.

My wife and I stayed at the St. George Hotel on Barkerville's main street and experienced an incredibly peaceful night in the heart of the old town. A night at the peak of the gold rush must have been quite different—a lot smellier, for one thing, with pigs and cattle and horses in the muddy streets, a thousand wood fires burning in little hovels on the hillsides, the coal smoke from blacksmiths' shops and of course the unwashed masses of humanity. Fuelled by alcohol, the streets must have been a lot noisier too.

You can still feel the spirit of the place, in the creak of horse-drawn wagons in the streets and the clatter of boots on boardwalks. We sat in St. Saviour's Anglican Church and looked out through the beautiful old windows to the green hillsides around the town. Religion was probably not the first thing on the minds of those first prospectors when they arrived in town. But after a few months of hard labour, bad food, poor results in the diggings and the company of equally desperate men, maybe there were a few converts.

The hillsides of Barkerville are green these days, and sweet with the smell of wildflowers. But in the 1860s there weren't any environmentalists. The miners clearcut the mountains right to the summits in the endless search for firewood and building materials. Williams Creek was a scoured-out boulder field. The town's main street was either flooded or thick with mud. Barkerville was an eyesore on the frontier, one of the biggest cities in BC and one of the ugliest.

In 2005, I had the good company of my wife, and the streets were full of families taking in the sights. But in 1862, Barkerville was a town of many men and few women. Men paid for their dances or danced with other men.

Those are the things that come to mind as you fall asleep in a Barkerville hotel today. You remember those miners who came from around the world to this place in the middle of nowhere, full of dreams that, for most, were soon dashed.

Yale is another town that I came to appreciate more as we worked on this book. For me Yale had been just a place to pass through in the rush to get to Vancouver or Calgary, pretty insignificant jammed in between a busy highway and the Canadian Pacific Railway. I didn't understand how important Yale was to BC history. The raft trip that Mark and I took from Yale was an eye-opener—after experiencing gold rush country from the river, you never look at it the same way again. Yale stops being a gas station and becomes a living, breathing town with deep roots in BC history. There's a beautiful little graveyard at Yale with gravestones that still speak of that haunted past. I spent an afternoon wandering through it and reading the inscriptions. The gold rush legend Edward "Ned" Stout is buried there. Ned started prospecting near Yale, struck it rich in the Cariboo and returned to die on the Fraser. "Edward Stout of Stout's Gulch Barkerville," his tombstone reads. "Born 1824 – Died 1924. Grandfather." There's "Gertrude" who left this memorial: "I know that my Darling is waiting for me." The grave of a child named Daisy bears the message: "She faltered by the wayside and the Angels took her." Another gravestone cries out, "But oh for the touch of a vanished hand and the sound of a voice that is stilled." The voices of old Yale speak to you in that cemetery.

Not far away you can see modern prospectors panning for gold at the river's edge, and the local museum will show you how to use a pan if you want to try it yourself. The river is quieter today, but it's still a dangerous place, particularly during high water—"forever mad, ravenous and lonely," as Bruce Hutchison wrote in the late 1940s.

My British Columbia includes other gold rush towns too. One of them is Rock Creek, in the Boundary country, where a popular fall fair draws enough people to remind you of what it must have been like in 1860, when thousands of men built a boomtown near the Kettle River. I think it was the first place I dipped a gold pan as a kid, but I never had the patience for that kind of work. Osoyoos, my hometown, started its modern life as a customs house to collect fees from miners and cattle drovers headed for the Cariboo. Once known only for its mosquitoes, Osoyoos Lake is now a tourist centre renowned for fresh fruit and an impressive Native Heritage Centre. The new gold rush is real estate.

That brings me back to the people who were here before the gold rush. Some First Nations took a hand in the prospecting, but most watched as the rush for riches marginalized their way of life, brought illness that they could not fight off, and swallowed up lands without discussion or treaty.

We were reminded, as we wrote, that reconciliation is still a work in progress. Modern day treaties are being negotiated on Vancouver Island and the Mainland. Murals at the BC legislature that depist colonialism and conquest during the gold rush era are coming down. History is being rewritten.

As we get ready to mark this sesquicentennial, we remember that BC's gold rush anniversary is a good opportunity to think about the things that were done here so many years ago, good and bad. They made us what we are today.

—*Greg Dickson*

Acknowledgements

Mark and Greg would like to thank Iona Campagnolo and Jean Barman for encouraging them to write this book. Greg would like to thank his parents, Doug and Elaine Dickson, for a childhood of roadtrips to B.C. ghost towns where the gold rush was still alive, and his wife Sheryl for encouraging him to take on another book project. Mark would like to thank his B.C. Almanac listeners for their contributions, and the B.C. Almanac team (led by producer Theresa Duvall) for letting him pursue another project. His wife Catherine puts up with it too.

We acknowledge the work of historians and writers who have gone before us, in particular, Margaret Ormsby, Terry Reksten, Bill Barlee, Bruce Ramsey, Jean Barman (who tracked down contributors and wrote a lot for us herself), Bruce Hutchison and our publisher Howard White. Thanks to Dan Francis for looking over the manuscript. Thanks also to some of the other professional writers and historians who took the time to write pieces for us: Chris O'Connor and Don Hauka in Lytton, Richard Wright and Lily Chow in Barkerville, Mike Kennedy and Mike Cleven in Lillooet, Branwen Patenaude in Quesnel, Rick Blacklaws in Vancouver, Brenda Mallory in Telkwa, Ann ten Cate and Frederike Verspoor at the Archives in Victoria, Helen Piddington in Blind Channel, Dan Marshall at the University of Victoria, Charles Perkins in Langley, Lynn Stonier-Newman for the excerpt from her new book before it is even published, Patricia Roy of the British Columbia Historical Federation, colleague Bernice Chan, Sonny McHalsie in Sto:lo Territory, Ann Walsh in Williams Lake, and our many Friends of the BC Archives, in particular Marie Elliot and Terrence Keough. We appreciate the remarkable work of the late Phil Thomas, who collected and sang folk music in B.C. for more than 50 years. Thanks also to artist and author Michael Kluckner for contributing two of his fine watercolour images and Doug Tuck at Vancouver Opera for producing the excellent Opera Speaks forums.

Thanks to Yvonne Van Ruskenveld who gave Mark an enlightening tour of the Ross Bay Cemetery, Mike Starr at Fort Langley, our friends at Fraser River Raft Expeditions for a wonderful day on the river, and of course, our faithful editor Mary Schendlinger and the design team at Harbour who found some gold in sand and gravel we sent them. Special thanks are always in order for the Harbour promotion crew who help us spread the word.

Net proceeds from this book will be directed to the British Columbia Historical Federation.

Selected Bibliography

Adams, John. *Old Square Toes and His Lady: The Life of James and Amelia Douglas.* Victoria BC: Horsdal and Schubart, 2001.

Akrigg, G.P.V. and Helen B. *British Columbia Place Names.* Victoria: Sono Nis Press, 1986.

Anderson, James. "The German Lasses," in Yvonne Mearns Klan, *The Old Red Shirt: Pioneer Poets of British Columbia.* Vancouver: New Star Books, 2004.

Anonymous. *Cariboo, The Newly Discovered Gold Fields of British Columbia.* Fairfield WA: Ye Galleon Press, 1975 (orig. 1862).

Antonson, Rick, Mary Trainer and Brian Antonson. *In Search of a Legend: Slumach's Gold.* New Westminster: Nunaga Publishing, 1972.

Barlee, N.L. *The Guide to Gold Panning in British Columbia.* Summerland BC: Canada West Publications, 1972.

Barman, Jean. *Maria Mahoi of the Islands.* Vancouver: New Star, 2004.

Barman, Jean. *The West Beyond the West: A History of British Columbia.* Toronto: University of Toronto Press, 1991.

Benjamin, J.J. *Three Years in America, 1859–1862,* vol. 2. Philadelphia: Jewish Publication Society of America, 1956.

British Columbia Official Centennial Record 1858–1958: A Century to Celebrate. Vancouver: Evergreen Press, 1957.

Carlson, Keith Thor, ed. *A Sto:lo Coast Salish Historical Atlas.* Vancouver: Douglas & McIntyre, 2001.

Champness, W. *To Cariboo and Back in 1862.* Fairfield WA: Ye Galleon Press, 1972.

Downie, William. *Hunting for Gold.* San Francisco: California Publishing Co., 1893.

Cheadle, Walter B. *Cheadle's Journal of Trip across Canada 1862–1863.* Edmonton: Hurtig, 1971.

Dickinson, Christine Frances, and Diane Solie Smith. *Atlin: The Story of British Columbia's Last Gold Rush.* Atlin BC: Atlin Historical Society, 1995.

Ficken, Robert E. *Unsettled Boundaries: Fraser Gold and the British-American Northwest.* Pullman WA: Washington State University Press, 2003.

Francis, Daniel, ed. *The Encyclopedia of British Columbia.* Madeira Park BC: Harbour Publishing, 2000.

Harrison, Eunice M.L. *The Judge's Wife: Memoirs of a British Columbia Pioneer.* Vancouver: Ronsdale Press, 2002.

Hauka, Donald J. *McGowan's War: The Birth of Modern British Columbia on the Fraser River Gold Fields.* Vancouver: New Star Books, 2003.

Hayes, Derek. *Historical Atlas of British Columbia and the Pacific Northwest.* Delta BC: Cavendish Books, 1999.

Hill, Beth. *Sappers: The Royal Engineers in British Columbia.* Ganges BC: Horsdal and Schubart, 1987.

Hutchison, Bruce. *The Fraser.* Toronto: Clarke, Irwin, 1950.

Johnson, F. Henry. *John Jessop: Gold Seeker and Educator.* Vancouver: Mitchell Press, 1971.

Johnson, Peter. *Voyages of Hope: The Saga of the Bride Ships.* Victoria: Touchwood Editions, 2002.

Johnson, R. Byron Johnson. *Very Far West Indeed: A Few Rough Experiences on the North-West Pacific Coast.* London: Sampson Low, Marston, Low, & Searle, 1872.

Johnson, William Weber. *The Old West: The Forty Niners.* New York: Time Life Books, 1974.

Langston, Laura. *Pay Dirt! The Search for Gold in British Columbia.* Victoria: Orca Book Publishers, 1995.

Luxton, Donald, ed. *Building the West: The Early Architects of British Columbia.* Vancouver: Talonbooks, 2003.

Lyons, C.P. *Fraser & Thompson River Canyons.* Surrey BC: Heritage House, 1986.

Lyons, C.P. *Milestones on the Mighty Fraser.* Vancouver: Evergreen Press, 1958.

Marshall, Daniel Patrick. "Claiming the Land: Indians, Goldseekers, and the Rush to British Columbia." Thesis, University of Victoria, 2000.

Mather, Ken. *Buckaroos and Mud Pups: The Early Days of Ranching in British Columbia.* Surrey BC: Heritage House, 2006.

McKelvie, B.A. *Fort Langley: Birthplace of British Columbia.* Victoria BC: Porcepic Books, 1991.

McNaughton, Margaret. *Overland to the Cariboo.* Vancouver: J.J. Douglas, 1973.

Murphy, Claire Rudolph, and Jane G. Haigh. *Gold Rush Women.* Anchorage AK: Alaska Northwest Books, 1997.

Ormsby, Margaret A. *British Columbia: A History.* Vancouver: Macmillan, 1958.

Patenaude, Branwen C. *Gold Below the Canyon: The Life and Times of William Barker.* Victoria BC: Trafford Publishing, 2005.

Patenaude, Branwen C. *Golden Nuggets: Roadhouse Portraits along the Cariboo's Gold Rush Trail.* Surrey BC: Heritage House, 1998.

Paterson, T.W. *British Columbia Ghost Town Series: Fraser Canyon.* Langley BC: Sunfire Publications, 1985.

Pethick, Derek. *James Douglas: Servant of Two Empires.* Vancouver: Mitchell Press, 1969.

Ramsey, Bruce. *Barkerville: A Guide to the Fabulous Cariboo Gold Camp.* Vancouver: Mitchell Press 1961.

Ramsey, Bruce. *Mining in Focus.* Vancouver: Briden, Anfield & Co., 1968.

Reksten, Terry. *The Illustrated History of British Columbia.* Vancouver: Douglas & McIntyre, 2001.

Roy, Patricia E., and John Herd Thompson. *British Columbia: Land of Promises.* Don Mills ON: Oxford University Press, 2005.

Sheller, Roscoe. *Ben Snipes: Northwest Cattle King.* Portland OR: Binford and Mort, 1957.

Swindle, Lewis J. *The Fraser River Gold Rush of 1858: As Reported by the California Newspapers of 1858.* Victoria BC: Trafford Publishing, 2001.

Waddington, Alfred Pendrell. *The Fraser Mines Vindicated, or the History of Four Months.* Victoria: P. De Garro, 1858.

Watters, Reginald, ed. *British Columbia: A Centennial Anthology.* Toronto: McClelland & Stewart, 1958.

Williams, David R. *The Man For a New Country: Sir Matthew Baillie Begbie.* Sidney BC: Gray's Publishing, 1977.

Woodcock, George. *Amor de Cosmos: Journalist and Reformer.* Toronto: Oxford University Press, 1975.

Worrall, Brandy Lien, ed. *Finding Memories, Tracing Routes: Chinese Canadian Family Stories.* Vancouver: Chinese Canadian Historical Society of BC, 2006.

Wright, Richard Thomas. *Barkerville, Williams Creek, Cariboo.* Surrey BC: Heritage House, 1998.

Yee, Paul. *Saltwater City: An Illustrated History of the Chinese in Vancouver.* Vancouver: Douglas & McIntyre, 2006.

Index

Harbour Publishing Co. Ltd.
P.O. Box 219
Madeira Park, BC
V0N 2H0
www.harbourpublishing.com

Printed and bound in Canada
Text design by Roger Handling, maps by Yvonne Maximchuk
Cover: British Columbia Archives A-00351, design by Anna Comfort

Harbour Publishing acknowledges financial support from the Government of Canada through the Book Publishing Industry Development Program and the Canada Council for the Arts, and from the Province of British Columbia through the British Columbia Arts Council and the Book Publisher's Tax Credit through the Ministry of Provincial Revenue.

THE CANADA COUNCIL FOR THE ARTS SINCE 1957 | LE CONSEIL DES ARTS DU CANADA DEPUIS 1957

BRITISH COLUMBIA ARTS COUNCIL
Supported by the Province of British Columbia

Library and Archives Canada Cataloguing in Publication

Forsythe, Mark
    The trail of 1858 : British Columbia's gold rush past / Mark Forsythe and Greg Dickson.

Includes index.
ISBN 978-1-55017-424-3

    1. British Columbia—Gold discoveries. 2. British Columbia—History— 1849-1871. I. Dickson, Greg, 1956- II. Title.
FC3822.4.F67 2007   971.1'02   C2007-904198-1

Also Available from Harbour Publishing:

The BC Almanac *Book of Greatest British Columbians*
Mark Forsythe and Greg Dickson

"The result is [a] picture-rich look at some of BC's noted players, big and small, split into fascinating categories—conservationists, adventurers, writers, rogues, sports figures—presented in bite-sized chunks."
—John Threlfall, *Monday* Magazine

"This is popular history based on human interest, well illustrated and unencumbered by encyclopedic detail. And it breathes of the dynamic personality of this place called British Columbia."
—Mike Youds, Kamloops *Daily News*

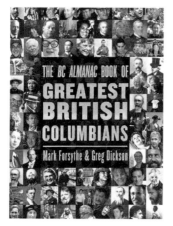

CBC Radio's *BC Almanac*, not to be outdone by the parent corporation's nationwide search for the 100 Greatest Canadians of all time, called upon its listeners to nominate the 100 Greatest British Columbians of all time. This cornucopia of West Coast characters, collected and bound by *BC Almanac's* host Mark Forsythe and director Greg Dickson, is the edifying and entertaining result. Divided into such categories as Crusaders and Reformers, Scientists and Innovators and Rogues and Rascals, the book throws new light on such well-established names as David Suzuki, Emily Carr and Terry Fox. Equally intriguing are the "wildcard candidates," including such little-known gems as the indomitable overlander Catherine Schubert and Fightin' Joe Martin, one of BC's shortest-lived premiers. Other highlights include Percy Williams, unlikely hero of the 1928 Olympics and pretender to the title of BC's greatest athlete; gold rush jack-of-all-trades C.D. Hoy, who overcame racism to leave a photographic legacy; Joseph Leopold Coyle of Aldermere, inventor of the egg carton; and Lucille Johnstone, the secretary who rose to CEO in the testosterone-laden towboat industry.

Full of historical sidebars, anecdotes, illustrations and archival photographs, *The* BC Almanac *Book of Greatest British Columbians* is a spirited celebration of the people who built the province.

ISBN 978-1-55017-368-0
8½ x 11, 158 pages, cloth
200 b&w photos